USING EDU-TAINMENT FOR DISTANCE EDUCATION
IN COMMUNITY WORK

USING EDU-TAINMENT FOR DISTANCE EDUCATION IN COMMUNITY WORK

Communication for Behavior Change, Volume 3

Esta de Fossard
With contributions from Michael Bailey

SAGE Los Angeles • London • New Delhi • Singapore
www.sagepublications.com

First published in 2008 by

 SAGE Publications India Pvt Ltd
B1/I-1 Mohan Cooperative Industrial Area
Mathura Road
New Delhi 110044, India
www.sagepub.in

SAGE Publications Inc
2455 Teller Road
Thousand Oaks, California 91320, USA

SAGE Publications Ltd
1 Oliver's Yard, 55 City Road
London EC1Y 1SP, United Kingdom

SAGE Publications Asia-Pacific Pte Ltd
33 Pekin Street
#02-01 Far East Square
Singapore 048763

Published by Vivek Mehra for SAGE Publications India Pvt Ltd, typeset in 10.5/12.5pt BruseOldStyle BT by Star Compugraphics Private Limited, Delhi and printed at Chaman Enterprises, New Delhi.

Library of Congress Cataloging-in-Publication Data

De Fossard, Esta.
   Using edu-tainment for distance education in community work/Esta de Fossard with contributions from Michael Bailey.
      p. cm. — (Communication for behavior change; v. 3)
   Includes bibliographical references and index.
   1. Community development personnel—Training of. 2. Mass media in community development. 3. Distance education. I. Bailey, Michael. II. Title.

HN49.C6D43	361.2071'5—dc22	2008	2007048866

ISBN: 978-0-7619-3642-8 (Pb)   978-81-7829-807-8 (India-Pb)

The SAGE Team: Ashok R. Chandran, Anushree Tiwari, Girish K. Sharma
Cover design by Kamal P. Jammual

CONTENTS

Part 2
For the Writer

Part 3
Auxiliary and Support Materials

Part 4
The Internet and Distance Education by Michael Bailey

Contents

APPENDIX

PREFACE

This book—a specialized tool for behavior change initiatives—is designed specifically as a guide for the creation of Distance Education programs for community workers who are responsible for providing on-the-ground support to Behavior Change Communication programs in developing countries. The book aims to fill a specific gap in the available guidance on distance education. It does not, therefore, offer guidance on familiar, standard forms of distance education.

The book contains specific guidelines for the creation of **Edu-tainment** media-based programs that provide motivating distance education for learners whose training access is severely restricted, because of low literacy levels, lack of access to a classroom or even a teacher, or because of the remoteness of the area in which the learners live.

Whereas the program format known widely as Entertainment–Education (which is presented in the two previous books in this series*) puts the primary emphasis on entertainment to engage and hold the attention of the general public, **Edu-tainment** turns the process around and puts the primary and undisguised emphasis on **teaching**. In order to hold the attention of learners who have no access to a teacher, however, these programs are given some—usually minor—entertainment basis or content that will help to attract and hold the attention of the learners.

There is a growing realization of the importance of educating community personnel, such as volunteer health workers and HIV counselors who can provide on-the-ground support and information to encourage the general public to adopt and—more importantly—to maintain recommended behavior change. For this support audience, **Edu-tainment** is increasingly being recognized as a truly effective approach.

While providing guidelines for Program Managers on how to set up the Edu-tainment project, this book also provides writers with a 6P Process of teaching which can be a useful template for media-based teaching. It also includes samples of a variety of appropriate program formats that have proved successful in reaching and educating the invaluable community support audience.

---

* *Communication for Behavior Change, Vol 1: Writing and Producing Radio Dramas*, de Fossard, Esta; *Communication for Behavior Change, Vol 2: Writing and Producing for Television and Film*, de Fossard, Esta and John Riber.

ACKNOWLEDGMENTS

This book is dedicated to the wonderful young people with whom I have worked in many countries of the world. Their eagerness to learn about and practice Behavior Change Communication has been an inspiration to me over the years. Special recognition goes to: Manishita Gosh and Giasuddin Selim in Bangladesh, Ganesh Singh and Kuber Gartaula in Nepal, Almaz Beyene in Ethiopia, Mansir Nasir Imam in Nigeria, and to Sara Chitambo in Namibia.

The book is also dedicated to the memory of two talented young writers who lost their lives far too soon: El Sagir Abubaker in Nigeria and Damien LeClerq in Namibia.

Special thanks to my husband Harvey Nelson for supplying the photographs for the book and for being a constant support and help with all the work I have been doing.

PART 1

Project Development and Management

1

PROVIDING DISTANCE EDUCATION THROUGH EDU-TAINMENT

Distance Education provides Community Workers with knowledge and skills to support behavior change in the general population.

DEFINING DISTANCE EDUCATION

The term 'Distance Education' is typically used to identify an educational process that takes place when the teacher and students are physically separated from one another, but usually maintain some means of contact. This contact, which can include discussion, might be by mail, telephone, or—increasingly in 'developed countries'—through the Internet. Over the years, many different names have been used for this out-of-the-classroom learning: correspondence course; home study; independent study; open learning; distance teaching, and so on. All these terms describe to some degree the typical understanding of distance education that acknowledges 'it is important that the student in a distance system can profit from dialogue with the institution that provides the learning materials; the student should be able to initiate this dialogue and not just be a recipient of it.'*

Distance Education and the Teacher

Ever since education became the right of all social classes and is no longer a privilege of the wealthy and aristocratic alone, there have been people eager to obtain educational qualifications, but unable to attend an educational institution for a number of reasons. It was for these people that distance education was first introduced. In its early days—over 100 years ago—it was delivered primarily by mail. Those who wanted to take a particular course would be sent a printed entrance-test, which they would complete and return to the school, together with details of their previous academic standing and success.

---

*Keegan, Desmond: Foundations of Distance Education.

Students accepted into the distance education class would receive text books and assignments by mail, together with a calendar showing the dates on which various assignments were to be completed and mailed back to the teacher. In response, the teacher would send the students regularly a package containing their corrected assignments with comments, guidelines for improvement, and directions for the next round of readings and exercises. If all assignments were completed on time and up to the standard, the student would be granted a certificate or diploma. Obviously, such courses demanded that the students be literate, that there was a teacher to answer questions and grade assignments, and that mail services were available and affordable.

THE CHANGING NEEDS OF DISTANCE EDUCATION IN THE MODERN WORLD

The original distance education delivery systems were, therefore, originally intended as modified versions of standard classroom teaching. Students had to prove their eligibility for the class before being accepted into it. The lessons taught were for academic purposes and based on traditional classroom methods of instruction. Today, the term 'distance education' can apply to several other and different educational approaches. It is now also used to describe learning environments where students have little or no previous formal training and—more importantly—have no contact of any kind with an actual teacher. It is for situations like these that Edu-tainment is being increasingly used.

DEFINITION OF 'EDU-TAINMENT'

Edu-tainment is a form of distance education that enhances the possibility of reaching, engaging and educating students who are denied any contact with a teacher and where it might not be possible to measure the previous or ongoing educational levels of the students.

BOX 1.1

DEFINITION OF EDU-TAINMENT

Education (Latin) = 'To lead out of'

Entertainment (Latin) = 'To hold the attention of'

The word 'Edu-tainment' is a combination of 'education' and 'entertainment', and an understanding of the actual etymology of these two words can help explain its meaning.

The English word **education** derives from the Latin verb *educare* meaning 'to lead out of'. Interestingly, the Latin word originally meant 'to assist at the birth of a child'; so, in modern terms, the word more accurately means 'to lead a person out of ignorance into a re-birth of knowledge' or 'to encourage an individual's growth and development'.

The word **entertainment** also comes from Latin: e*nter* = among, and *tenere* = to hold. With an original meaning of 'to keep up' or 'to maintain', in today's world it means to 'attract and hold the attention of an audience'.

People's attention is most easily attracted and held through engagement of their emotions. Not all entertainment is fun. Tragedies and horror stories can also engage the emotional attention of the audience and qualify, therefore, as entertainment.

Edu-tainment: When the two words 'education' and 'entertainment' are put together, the meaning becomes 'encouraging individual growth and development in a learning environment that commands and holds the emotional attention of the learners.'

The Difference between Edu-tainment and Entertainment–Education

It should be noted that in the past, some behavior change communicators have used the term Edu-tainment interchangeably with 'Entertainment–Education', but the difference between the two formats is now being more widely acknowledged and used throughout the communication world.

Entertainment–Education programs are created to appeal to a general audience. The primary emphasis of these programs—as the name implies—is on entertainment: attracting and holding the attention (emotions) of the audience. This is done most frequently in the form of a powerful serial drama, where audience members can empathize with various characters and gain from them a sense of self-efficacy, which is vital to their ability to adapt to new behavior. Into this engaging emotional experience, the essential behavior change messages are woven and modeled gradually, naturally, and subtly. The entertainment is the primary focus, and once the audience's attention is engaged through the entertaining story and characters, the important behavior change models and messages can be introduced and demonstrated in a life-like and believable manner. The ongoing story can reveal characters considering and taking the steps of behavior change naturally, so that audience members have time to think about how adopting these changes might positively affect their own lives. In the Entertainment–Education model, it is the entertainment, as much as or even more so than the educational message, which encourages the adoption of new behaviors by a general audience.

With **Edu-tainment**, the emphasis is turned around. The primary purpose—as this term implies—is **education** and the fact that the program is intended as a teaching tool is made clear from the start. **Edu-tainment**, however, represents an approach to education that is less formal than usual. In a typical classroom, it is the teacher who engages the students' attention throughout all lessons. Where students have no access to a teacher—either in person or through a communication channel—it is necessary to provide some other 'hook' to engage and hold their attention. In Edu-tainment, this 'hook' is provided through an entertaining background story, or through entertaining characters who can attract and hold student interest. The programs, therefore, are designed to engage the emotional attention of (to entertain) the learners so that they will want to pay attention to all the lessons and make use of all the instruction that is provided for them, even if there is no teacher available to check on their progress. Rather than using a direct education-only presentation, the Edu-tainment format encases the instruction in real-life (if fictional) situations and is therefore more engaging and more likely to promote self-efficacy than traditional distance teaching might be for certain audiences.

The E Structure

Both Entertainment–Education and Edu-tainment rely on what might be called the **E Structure** to engage and motivate their audiences. Both formats rely on:

E ngagement of the audience, through

E motional involvement, which inspires

E mpathy for certain characters, who then provide

E xamples that demonstrate to the audience how they can accomplish the desired behavior and also provide a sense of

E fficacy or self-efficacy for audience members who make the desired changes or acquire the desired knowledge and gain a degree of

E go-enhancement (personal growth).

Fable and Fact

Even though both Entertainment–Education and Edu-tainment motivate similar responses in their audiences, there are differences in the approaches. The essential difference between Entertainment–Education and Edu-tainment can be quickly understood by comparing one of Aesop's fables with a structured lesson.

Sample A: Entertainment–Education: Fable	Sample B: Edu-tainment: Lesson
The Wind and the Sun The wind and the sun once had an argument as to which was the more powerful. Each was sure he had the greatest strength, but they could see no	**Persuasion versus Force** In today's lesson in our series 'Positive Self-Growth,' we're going to talk about 'getting your way'. The world is full of people who want to make their presence

(Contd.)

Sample A: Entertainment–Education: Fable	Sample B: Edu-tainment: Lesson
way of settling the dispute until suddenly a traveler came into view along a road down below.	felt or 'get their way'. We have all been in situations where we are quite sure we are right and we want to make others agree with us. How do we do that? By persuading them or by forcing them?
'Here's our chance,' said the sun. 'Now we'll see who's right. Let us agree that whichever of us forces this man to remove his coat is the stronger. You go first to see what you can do.'	What is force? What is persuasion? Force is defined as 'strength or power; violence'.
While the sun hid behind a cloud, the wind blew an icy blast with all his might, but the traveler did not remove his coat. The more strongly the wind blew, the more closely he kept it wrapped around him. At last, the wind had to admit he was beaten.	Persuasion means 'urging, luring, or enticing'. Imagine yourself in a situation where you and three other people are locked in a car at night. You cannot open the doors and you cannot make the lights work. Not one of you has a cell phone. One of the other people wants to attract attention by setting fire to a piece of paper with a cigarette lighter. You realize this would be extremely dangerous. To prevent this action, you could attack that person physically, but that would probably start a general fight in the car. It would be wiser to explain to everyone, gently and logically, that it would be safer to bang loudly on the car windows.
The sun now came from behind the cloud and started to shine down upon the traveler. Gradually, the man began to feel warm with the gentle heat of the sun's rays. As the sun gradually added more heat, the man loosened his coat, and then he took it off altogether, and even sat down under the shade of a tree to cool himself.	
Moral: Persuasion is stronger than force.	So—to end our lesson today, please tell me, right now:
	What is the definition of persuasion?
	What is the definition of force?
	And remember this week, to practice PERSUADING rather than FORCING.

Aesop's presentation (Sample A) puts the emphasis on the story—the entertainment. There is certainly a lesson to be learned from the story in Sample A, but it is presented much more subtly than it is in Sample B in which it is obvious from the start that a lesson is being taught. Nevertheless, the second example does provide an 'entertainment' platform for the teaching, by inviting the learners to put themselves in an imaginary situation.

Substituting for the Teacher through Edu-tainment

One of the world leaders in Distance Education, Professor Bõrje Holmberg, devised in 1985, a theory of distance education which he called 'guided didactic conversation' in which he related 'the effectiveness of education to the impact of feelings of belonging and cooperation as well as to the actual exchange of questions, answers, and arguments in mediated conversation'. Although Professor Holmberg added considerably to his theory 10 years later, his original ideas still relate very cogently to Edu-tainment. His theory outlined seven important points, which he stated as the essential basics of distance education. These seven 'background assumptions' were described by Professor Holmberg as follows:

Holmberg Principles of Learning

1. Provide students opportunities for interaction with teacher and/or with learning materials.
2. Provide subject matter and teaching methods that appeal to the students.
3. Ensure that students enjoy what they are learning.
4. Involve students in decisions about what should be learned.
5. Motivation encourages learning.
6. Teaching should be interactive, not didactic.
7. Good teaching is reflected in good learning.

1. The core of teaching is interaction between the teaching and learning parties; it is assumed that simulated interaction through subject matter presentation in pre-produced courses can take over part of the interaction by causing students to consider different views, approaches, and solutions, and generally interact with a course.
2. Emotional involvement in the study and feelings of personal relation between the teaching and learning parties are likely to contribute to learning pleasure.
3. Learning pleasure supports student motivation.
4. Participation in decision-making concerning the study is favorable to student motivation.
5. Strong student motivation facilitates learning.
6. A friendly, personal tone and easy access to the subject matter contribute to learning pleasure, support student motivation, and thus facilitate learning from the presentation of pre-produced courses (that is, from teaching in the form of one-way traffic stimulating interaction, as well as from didactic communication in the form of two-way traffic between the teaching and learning parties).'

7. The effectiveness of teaching is demonstrated by students' learning of what has been taught.*

Professor Holmberg puts a necessary emphasis on 'emotional involvement in the study' and this is where much of the emphasis of Edu-tainment lies—in engaging the emotional attention of the audience, and providing them with a 'friendly, personal tone and easy access to the subject matter'.

The real challenge of any distance education arises when the students have no contact with the teacher—neither personal nor by 'mail'. In these circumstances it is often difficult to maintain the interest and attention of the students, and it is in these circumstances, that Edu-tainment can be especially valuable.

In order to replace the physical presence and personality of a distant teacher who can explain details and guide the students (as happens in the classroom or through assignments), Edu-tainment lessons can be led by 'hosts' or 'fictional teachers' who are representative of the people known to and trusted by the learners. Against an entertaining backdrop, the programs allow for a believable **demonstration** of the value of what is being taught. Edu-tainment programs also provide periods of Interactive Questioning that encourage students to check what they have learned from the program by giving immediate oral answers to questions. Questions of this nature were used in Sample B on page 21. If this lesson was being delivered by radio, the teacher (or reader) could pause after each question to allow the learners to provide an answer. Further guidelines for the use of Interactive Questioning are provided on page 99 of this book.

Interestingly, the term **Edu-tainment** is being increasingly used by toy manufacturers to describe products that are primarily designed for educational purposes, but offered in the form of a game or toy in order to attract and hold children's interest. Children's television programs such as *Sesame Street* employ this same format, in acknowledgment of the fact that their young learners have no opportunity to physically interact with their television 'teachers'. Similarly, as this book will demonstrate, the Edu-tainment format can be used successfully for teaching and motivating community support workers to bring about behavior change in their local population.

THE IMPORTANCE OF DISTANCE EDUCATION IN BEHAVIOR CHANGE PROJECTS

Many projects in today's developing world are designed to encourage positive behavior change in the local population. Currently, the majority of these changes are related to personal and family health, but there is an increasing interest in matters such as global

---

*Simonson, M., S. Smaldino, M. Albright and S. Zvacek. 2006. *Teaching and Learning at a Distance*, p. 46. Merrill Prentice Hall.

warming, democracy and governance, and environmental protection. The desired end-product of Behavior Change projects, no matter what the recommended change, is the establishment of permanent social norms that will lead to improved standards of living for all people, and the maintenance of a stronger, healthier world.

Community-Based Support for Behavior Change

Behavior Change specialists are increasingly aware of the absolute necessity of community-based support for members of the general public, to help ensure that people not only adopt but—more importantly—fully understand and maintain these essential behavior changes. A great deal of effort, time, and money is being spent worldwide to provide these workers with knowledge and Interpersonal Communication skills, so that they can provide this necessary support and encouragement in an appropriate and accurate manner.

Many of these essential helpers, such as community health workers are unpaid volunteers who have neither the time nor the opportunity to attend formal training courses. It is not practical to expect them to acquire a passing grade in a classroom or to earn a university degree or college certificate in order to qualify for their jobs. It is, however, vitally important for them to be equipped with the skills and knowledge necessary to be able to understand and support the behavior changes being encouraged in the lives of their community members.

The Role of the Community Support Worker

The importance of the community-helper in a social or Behavior Change project cannot be overstressed and can be compared to the importance of a coach to an aspiring athlete. Consider the situation of a young man who decides that he does not want to spend the rest of his life chasing wayward cattle; he wants to become an Olympic champion. To some degree he can train himself, but it is clear that his chances of success are heightened if he is given ongoing assistance and encouragement by a professional coach. Similarly, Behavior Change communication programs motivate people to make the personal effort to improve their own lives based on the knowledge they have been given. And, just like the athlete who needs the help of the coach, people can be greatly helped and encouraged to maintain the behavior changes by having a 'coach' in the form of community-helper who is educated in the necessary knowledge and Interpersonal Communication skills.

ADVANTAGES OF DISTANCE EDUCATION

It is perhaps natural to think that classroom instruction, where the student and teacher can interact, is the ideal environment for learning. Carefully structured and attractively presented distance education, however, has advantages that are not necessarily found in every classroom. Whether the lessons are based on an existing curriculum, or created especially for a small group of non-professional learners, all students in distance education classes, no matter where they are, receive the same high level of instruction that has been carefully crafted to meet their specific needs. The lessons are taught in ways that have been researched and proved to be appropriate and effective for both the learners and the medium being used. All distance education learners, therefore:

- receive instruction based on careful research that has determined exactly what is needed for this particular group of learners
- receive the same amount of instruction
- receive the instruction at the same time
- receive instruction in their homes or at their workplace without the need to travel long distances to reach a classroom
- usually do not have to pay fees for their instruction.

BARRIERS AND CHALLENGES TO DISTANCE EDUCATION FOR BEHAVIOR CHANGE SUPPORT

Despite these advantages, there are serious challenges, even barriers, in some communities to the provision of effective distance education. These barriers include the cost of classroom-based training programs and the difficulty of reaching ALL community-helpers, especially those in remote or impoverished areas of the world. The need to overcome these barriers has led to a growing interest in the development of media-delivered (radio, TV, Internet*) distance education programs that can provide the necessary community-helper training.

Yet, the challenge remains: how to provide instruction and motivation to those community workers who are not only beyond the reach of typical and regular classroom or workshop instruction, but also beyond the reach of any form of interaction with a teacher. It is here that Edu-tainment can play a vitally important role.

Edu-tainment puts the primary focus on education, with the lesson presented against an entertaining background, in order to achieve four important learning goals:

1. to attract and hold the attention of the learners
2. to provide interactivity that will allow the learners an opportunity to check what they have learned during the program
3. to demonstrate the relevance of the lesson to the learners
4. to provide the sense of a teacher's presence

---

*Although use of the Internet for education of community-helpers in remote areas of the world is still greatly affected by digital exclusion, Chapters 12–15 of this book provide some introductory guidelines to the use of the Internet, for the benefit of those who are hoping or planning to make use of it in the future.

All educational programs, no matter who the intended students are, and no matter if they are taught in the classroom or through a distance medium, require very careful preparation. However, while regular classroom teaching allows the teacher to adjust the lessons in accordance with student response, distance educators must try, without personal interaction with their students, to anticipate and meet the likely challenges and difficulties they might face. While assignments that teachers can receive from the students will help in determining if the teaching is appropriate, nothing is ever quite as effective as immediate student–teacher interaction.

Distance education programs designed to support Behavior Change offer perhaps the greatest challenge when they are unable to allow even written contact between the teacher and students. Such contact can be virtually impossible in remote or inaccessible areas where most of these learners live. Moreover, the cost of any form of interaction between these students and their teacher(s) can be prohibitive. Many of the students receive very little or no salary at all and cannot afford to pay for assignment needs, such as paper or mailing costs.

Likewise, the community governing body or even the national government cannot always afford to provide formal education or educational materials for them, even when educating them is considered necessary. A further drawback to student–teacher contact in such situations can be lack of literacy or limited literacy. In cases where little or no student–teacher contact is possible, it is doubly important that the distance education program format is one that will truly attract and hold the attention of these important distance learners.

Obviously, there can be no set or even standard curriculum or typical lesson plan for education of this type because the needs of the learners differ from country to country, and sometimes even from region to region within the same country. The major preparations needed for this type of distance education are:

- To determine the most appropriate medium (radio, TV, print, Internet) for lesson delivery
- To determine the most effective and culturally appropriate ways of presenting the lessons
- To determine the details of the curriculum and the amount of knowledge that should be provided
- To try to provide some methods of interaction—however slight—between teachers and learners

And most importantly:

- To create a program format which will ensure that the lessons attract and hold the attention of those who need the knowledge and skills, even when they are not initially willing to devote the necessary time and concentration to attain them.

Using Edu-tainment

As noted earlier, most, if not all typical distance education classes (whether traditional or open) tend to follow a standard curriculum and a somewhat formal approach to teaching. The instruction is provided by a qualified teacher. Students are given exercises or assignments that will allow them to learn and apply new knowledge. Encouragement to undertake and complete such courses is provided by one of several motives: acquisition of basic skills such as literacy; promise of promotion or extra pay; and recognition with a certificate or diploma. However, distance education programs designed to instruct and support community behavior change workers are not typical, perhaps because of low literacy levels, or because learners feel threatened by or unable to cope with traditional teaching, or because of the limited amount of time they can devote to learning. It is for learners like these that the **Edu-tainment** format can be appropriate and effective.

REQUIREMENTS FOR CREATING EDU-TAINMENT PROGRAMS

Edu-tainment is still a relatively new approach to distance education; so it is necessary for those planning to use it, to give careful thought to all the needs of the project before committing to it. Before the program format or even the curriculum is developed, there are some important management and project development steps to be undertaken. These steps are discussed in Chapter 2.

SCRIPT SAMPLES: STANDARD TEACHING AND EDU-TAINMENT

The following brief script samples demonstrate the basic difference between what might be called 'direct teaching' (Example A) and Edu-tainment (Example B). The topic being taught is Interpersonal Communication, and both programs were designed to be delivered through the medium of radio.

Example A: Standard Teaching Approach

1. Teacher A: Good evening students. Today, I am going to teach you some of the rules of good Interpersonal Communication. Interpersonal Communication means communicating with other people and there is more to it than just talking. Interpersonal Communication involves attitude and body language as well as words.

2. Teacher B: In fact, there are five components of good Interpersonal Communication:

   (a) Tone of voice
   (b) Attitude
   (c) Words and sentences
   (d) Questioning
   (e) Body language

   Let's look at these, one at a time.

3. Teacher A: First rule: Tone of voice. When you speak to your clients or patients, your voice will have an effect on them. If you speak too loudly and you sound demanding or as if you are giving orders, you will make them afraid to speak to you. So your tone of voice must be gentle, friendly, and encouraging.

4. Teacher B: Second rule: Attitude. Attitude means the way you feel. And this includes how you feel about yourself, how you feel about your job, how you feel about your client, and how you show that feeling. And no matter how you feel about all these, the important thing is what attitude the client sees in you. No matter how you personally feel on any given day, your attitude towards your client must be friendly, non-critical, and encouraging.

And so the lesson continues, giving clear definitions of each of the rules of Interpersonal Communication.

Example B: Edu-tainment

1. YASMIN: Hello, health-worker friends. I am Yasmin, your friend and teacher, and I am so happy to be with you all, again today. Last week, you remember, we went with Tania to visit a young husband and wife who wanted to learn more about the best foods for their six-month old twins, and we noticed the clear and simple information that Tania gave them. Clear and simple. That is a sensible guideline for all of us to remember when talking with our clients. Today, Tania will be meeting a young couple who want to know more about family planning methods. We will join her as she talks with them. So, this is a good opportunity for us to revise the components of good Interpersonal Communication. Those five components are:

2. **SFX: GONG**

3. YASMIN: (a) Tone of voice
                (b) Attitude
                (c) Words and sentences
                (d) Questioning
                (e) Body language

          Now, let us find out how Tania makes use of these five components. I can see that she is just about ready to start her day's work.

          But, Oh … my goodness, she does not look very happy today. I hope everything is all right. Let us join Tania and her husband Shamim to see if we can find out why she is unhappy.

4. **MUSIC … SCENE CHANGE MUSIC**

5. SFX: **BACKGROUND OF TANIA'S HOME … BIRDS CHIRPING.**

6. SHAMIM: Dear wife, I do not like to see you unhappy. But we must be patient. The doctor told us that it could be a few days before we know whether your mother will recover or not.

7. TANIA: I know, but sometimes it seems so unfair. Here I am helping people who cannot stop having children, and I am my mother's only child. There is no one to look after her but me.

8. SHAMIM: I am here, dear wife … I promise I shall come in from the fields every hour and check to be sure she is all right. Please cheer up. What can I do to improve your attitude before you leave home?

9. TANIA: (SMILING AS SHE SPEAKS): Ah! Shamim, you are right. Attitude. I must improve my attitude right now so that I can interact properly with my clients.

10. **MUSIC (BRIEF)**

11. YASMIN: Interact properly with her clients … Yes, Tania is right about that. In spite of her own feelings, she must remember the importance of good Interpersonal Communication with her clients. So, let us go with Tania now and see if—despite her personal concerns—she can recall those five important points:

                (a) Tone of voice
                (b) Attitude
                (c) Words and sentences
                (d) Questioning
                (e) Body language

Listen carefully for all five points, and I'll have some questions for us later.

The program then moves to the scene where Tania meets the young couple and discusses several family planning methods with them. Despite her own sadness, she demonstrates appropriate use of all five points. The program concludes with some Interactive Questions provided by Yasmin, and some suggestions as to how the audience—during the coming week—can make use of what they have learned about Interpersonal Communication.

The important difference between these two samples is that the first one concentrates only on the education, whereas the second makes the education more personal by presenting it through a believable, but fictional 'teacher' and within the context of a realistic story. This approach indicates an empathy on behalf of the program creators, for the real-life difficulties faced by many of the students. It creates some emotional suspense as listeners wonder whether Tania's mother (whom they have met in several previous programs) will survive the accident she recently experienced.

The creation of Edu-tainment programs for distance education presents many challenges that do not exist with standard distance education. Proper management of the Edu-tainment program can help alleviate many of these challenges.

2

MANAGING THE
EDU-TAINMENT PROJECT

Effective Management requires the skills and cooperation of a team of professionals.

MANAGERIAL RESPONSIBILITIES FOR THE EDU-TAINMENT PROJECT

All Distance Education projects require careful and sustained management, because 'to be effective, programs need to be sensitively adapted to local contexts and culture and do more than just deliver (health) messages. They must avoid promoting behaviors which people cannot adopt, even if they want to, and must build essential life skills, such as self-confidence, communication skills, and the ability to resist peer-group pressure. Programs also need to do more than just deliver successful learning gains. They must take account of the structural, managerial, financial, and political factors which influence sustainability.'*

The project should be headed by a Program Manager who is an experienced person. It is certainly advantageous if he has knowledge of and experience with distance education. However, since this is not always possible, a good manager can carry out the necessary responsibilities by studying and understanding what is needed for a project that can effectively reach and train community workers in distant areas of developing countries. It is the Program Manager's task to ensure that these requirements are met and sustained. Fundamentally, this means ensuring that everyone connected with the project believes in its importance and is committed to doing everything possible to ensure its success and sustainability.

There are some basic guidelines that can assist the manager in developing a successful project:

---

*Pridmore, P. and S. Nduba. 'The Power of Open and Distance Learning in Basic Education for Health and the Environment' in Chapter 11 of *Basic Education at a Distance, World Review of Distance Education and Open Learning*, Vol. 2, p. 192. Routledge Farmer.

Staff and Personnel Needs for a Distance Education Project

As with all educational undertakings, the success of any distance education or Edu-tainment project rests primarily with good, experienced management, beginning with a staff of appropriate personnel, which will include:

- Project Manager (Executive Producer)
- Curriculum advisors
- Evaluator(s)
- Program/Lesson Writer(s)
- Clerical staff
- Production team (depending on the chosen medium) including actors/presenters
- Support material writers(s), for situations where it is practical to consider support materials
- Research and Evaluation Specialist or Team

Some of these people might be required part-time or on a consultant basis only, depending on the size, scope, and budget of the project. Some might be recruited in response to the Request for Proposal (RFP), as described on page 38.

PRELIMINARY GUIDELINES FOR PROJECT MANAGEMENT

Box 2.1

ESSENTIAL STEPS FOR EDU-TAINMENT PROGRAM DEVELOPMENT

Ensure:

1. Knowledge of the culture of the audience
2. Knowledge of the learning style
3. Ongoing Behavior Change campaign
4. Adequate research and evaluation
5. Government support
6. Performance objectives and timelines
7. Review team
8. Lesson monitor
9. Pilot testing or Pre-testing
10. Archives and lessons learned

Know the Culture of the Audience

The need to be acquainted with the culture cannot be stressed too often. In the case of distance education programs that are designed to train community workers to assist and encourage successful community adoption of a major behavior change, it is essential for everyone working on the project to be aware of two cultures: (1) the culture of the community-helpers for whom the lessons are being designed and (2) the culture of those members of the general public who will benefit from the work of the community-helpers.

The Program Manager should ensure that writers, producers, directors, and even the actors spend time with both these groups. All those engaged in the project need to be very clear about the relationship between the two groups so that this relationship can be accurately portrayed in the lesson programs. It is very often the case that community members are not immediately willing to accept people from their own community (even if they are clearly identified as semi-professionals) to be their guides and mentors. Often, especially in small communities, there is a feeling that local people cannot possibly be smart enough to give other members of the same community instruction in new methods of living. If this feeling exists, the programs have to help overcome it, perhaps by stressing that the community-helpers' most sincere wish is to help, not to show off or claim to be superior in any way!

Know the Learning Style/s of the Audience

Knowing the culture also means knowing and analyzing the learning style(s) to which the distance education students have previously been exposed. If the learning style has been mostly didactic, the programs might have to move slowly from beginning with a somewhat formal teaching approach in the direction of more interactive learning.

Ensure that there is Ongoing Activity with the Behavior Change Campaign which the Distance Education Project Plans to Support

For example: There is little point in setting up a distance education project to train school teachers to educate their students and parents on the importance of attending Vitamin A days, if these special days are no longer occurring regularly.

Ensure Adequate Research and Evaluation

Every distance education project designed for community workers in developing countries should have a competent researcher or research team on board to carry out vital research and evaluation. It is essential to ensure that adequate baseline research has been done on the real learning needs of the intended audience. It is not enough to take an existing curriculum from another country or even from a local college and put it into a distance education mode. A competent research team should thoroughly examine the current knowledge and attitudes of the learners, together with their willingness to learn more and practice new behaviors themselves. The findings of this research will provide the foundation for program development. Once the programs are underway, there should be some method of ongoing evaluation to ensure that the program continues to appeal to and meet the needs of the learners. At the end of the project, an experienced researcher or research team should carry out **summative evaluation** to determine to what extent the original objectives of the project have been accomplished.

Ensure Government Support for the Distance Education Venture

Close association with the relevant government ministry is vital. Often, this also means ensuring that the local government recognizes that the project is strengthening their current work, rather than seeming to criticize or oppose it.

Establish Clear Performance Objectives

The overall performance objectives will be based on the results of preliminary research carried out to determine the instructional needs of the audience. Once these objectives are determined, it is time to determine details of the instructional strategy and individual lesson content. These objectives can be precisely shaped during the Curriculum Design Workshop (see Chapter 4).

Timelines

One of the other important primary needs of the project is the establishment of **strict, but reasonable, timelines** for the various steps in project development: research; the Curriculum Guide development; contracting with writers, producers and others, support material creation; program writing; pilot testing of all materials; evaluation, and other activities that might be needed. Establishing timelines begins with an overall understanding of the length of the life of the project—which usually depends on available funding. It is important to work with all those involved in the project development to come up with realistic timelines and with rescue plans in case any part of the timeline slips behind. Other performance objectives include setting and maintaining quality program creation (writing and production) and regular evaluation. To maintain these objectives, it is essential to have trained writers and producers and a professional research/evaluation team on board.

Review Team

A review team should be set up to carefully review all materials that will be distributed by the project—whether they are scripts for the broadcasts, support booklets, discussion group guides, or flipcharts for community-helper use. It is always valuable to have one Review Editor who oversees the production and review of all materials by the review team, and is therefore able to ensure consistency among all the materials. When scripts are written on an ongoing basis (1 or 2 scripts a week), as they almost always are, it is especially important for the review team or editor to be given and to agree upon a timeline, so that all scripts are completed and delivered to the producer on time. Indeed, delay in any one component of the overall project can slow down or even ruin the project impact.

Appoint Review Team Members and Arrange Script Review Meetings

It is essential that Edu-tainment programs be carefully reviewed to ensure that all lesson information is accurate, correctly presented in a manner suited to the audience, and contained in an 'engaging environment'. Information on choosing review team members and how review can be done in a time-saving manner are included in the chapter on Curriculum Development (Chapter 4).

Lesson Monitor

In order to avoid possible misrepresentation of the lesson during audio recording or filming, it is useful for the Program Manager to appoint a 'lesson monitor' who can attend all recording sessions to ensure that no mistakes or omissions are made. All those working on production must agree to abide by the lesson monitor's decisions.

Pilot Testing

Pilot Testing. Pilot testing (also called pre-testing) of the programs can be difficult in communities where:

- the learners are spread out over a wide area
- much of the area is difficult to access
- the numbers of learners using the programs is limited.

Nevertheless, every effort should be made to pilot test the Edu-tainment programs before they go on air, and it is advisable to test them not only with representatives of the community-helper learning audience, but also with members of the general public who will be the ultimate beneficiaries of the knowledge gained by the community-helpers. It is really valuable to test whether the interaction of community-helpers and general public as presented in the lesson programs truly reflects what is happening in the community or what could happen as a result of appropriate training.

Pilot Testing of TV Programs

Pilot testing of TV lessons can be expensive because of the production and editing costs involved. However, television scripts can be tested adequately by transferring them into audio productions or by having then 'acted out' live in front of the audience.

Maintaining Archives of Programs and Lessons Learned

All distance education projects should maintain archival records of what they have broadcast during the project. This means that all scripts, even if they are stored in a computer or on a CD, should also be filed in paper copies. These archived paper scripts should be the ones that were used during actual production and should have clearly marked on them any changes that were made (with the agreement of the lesson monitor) during production.

Lessons Learned

It is valuable for every behavior change project—whether it is for the general public or for distance education purposes—to keep notes on what has been learned by those working on the project so that strengths can be utilized in other projects and weaknesses can be avoided.

CONTRACTING WITH ORGANIZATIONS AND INDIVIDUALS

The Program Manager will be responsible for the negotiation of contracts with various people or organizations contributing to the project. This could include contracts with:

- a local research agency
- writer(s)
- media production house or individual director/producer—radio or TV—or with an Internet program-writing organization or individual
- actors (artists) if these are not included in the production house contract
- publicity and promotions agent
- support material writer/s

A common method of locating all appropriate personnel for the production side of the project is to issue a Request for Proposal (RFP) to which various production houses and agencies can respond. The RFP should make clear certain conditions that are necessary for successful Edu-tainment production. Those responding to the RFP should be required to show evidence of:

- **previous production experience** in the chosen medium and format, including a full listing and recorded samples of their work. (In cases where the Edu-tainment format is being used for the first time, bidders should be required to present examples of previous dramas or instructional programs they have produced.)
- **availability of appropriate production needs.** In the case of radio, this will mean an adequate drama-recording studio, an ample sound-effects library, and up-to-date editing equipment. In the case of TV or video, this will mean avail-ability of all necessary filming and editing equipment. (If this is not owned by the production house, they should indicate from where they can rent it and whether or not it is necessary to reserve this equipment in advance.)
- **availability of actors (artists).** In the proposal, the production house should give evidence of their knowledge of where and how they can find the most suit-able actors for the project. They should be willing also to present an audition tape of possible actors once the initial scripts are written. This audition tape allows the project leaders to ensure that the actors chosen sound or look like the cultural group for whom the programs are being created.
- **willingness to agree to abide by the script.** As with Entertainment–Education production, it is essential that directors and producers of Edu-tainment programs understand and agree from the outset that the nature of these programs requires that no changes are made in the script during production without the full agreement of the Program Manager or an appointed lesson monitor.
- **willingness and ability to abide by the timelines of the project.** While it is almost always necessary to allow some flexibility in the production timelines, the response to the RFP should indicate clearly that the production house will be able to meet the required timelines of the project.
- **local talent.** In order to encourage local **capacity-building**, some funding organizations like to ensure that all those working on the project are citizens of the country where the project is being developed.

SELECTING THE WRITER

If the production house wishes to be responsible for the script-writing activities of the project, as well as for production, it is imperative that they supply the names and CVs of at least three writers, together with samples of their work, and that the final choice is left to the project management. Sometimes several writers can be invited to attend the Curriculum Guide Workshop and submit an Audition Package at the end of it, or soon after. Attendance at the Curriculum Guide Workshop allows the writers to decide whether they really want to do this type of writing, and allows the project leaders to gauge the writers' interest in and ability for the job.

Writer's Audition Package

Writers who are not able to attend the Curriculum Guide Workshop, but are being recommended by the production house in their response to the RFP, should be given a copy of the completed Curriculum Guide and also asked to prepare an Audition Package.

The Audition Package should contain:

- a clear explanation of the format chosen by the writer and the reasons for selecting this format
- if a serial format is chosen, the Audition Package should contain a brief outline of the complete story of the serial
- if a series format is chosen, the writer must outline the main location in which most programs of the series will take place, and list the names of the main characters who will appear in all programs
- if a magazine format is chosen, the audition package should include an explanation of the various segments of the magazine that will be used each week and the reason for selecting these segments
- if a case study format is chosen, it should be accompanied by a clear explanation of why this choice was made
- a detailed character profile of the main Host or Teacher
- character profiles of other characters who will appear regularly in the programs or dramas
- a sample script showing where the 6Ts of the Teaching Process will come into the lessons (The 6T Process of Teaching is detailed on page 96.)

PROMOTION AND ADVERTISING

It is possible to find agencies that are capable of being responsible for the production of the programs as well as for all promotional and advertising activities. Generally, however, it is better to appoint separate organizations: one for the production; one for promotion and advertising. Working this way also saves money, because if an advertising agency is contracted to be responsible for the production, the project can end up with higher costs as the advertising agency usually will put a bonus for itself on top of the actual cost of the production house.

TRAINING NEEDS

If experienced personnel are not available, it is necessary to determine if likely candidates can be recruited locally, and whether there is someone readily available to train them. The main areas for which training is needed in the creation of distance education programs, especially Edu-tainment programs, are writing and production. Creating programs of this nature to support behavior change and maintenance is still a new and very small business worldwide, and in many developing countries there are few, if any, people trained for writing Edu-tainment programs. Before commencing the project, therefore, it is necessary to consider if training will be needed for writers and producers. It might also be necessary to provide training for ancillary staff such as Discussion Group leaders.

Arranging for and providing adequate training can take time, so it is vital to consider these needs and allow appropriate training time before lesson design and program writing gets underway. The role of the writer is of paramount importance and later chapters in this book are intended to provide writers who are new to this work with some suggestions and guidelines for program creation in various formats (see Chapters 6–10).

CHOOSING THE MEDIUM OR MEDIA TO BE USED

The decision of which medium or media to use for program delivery depends largely on:

- accessibility
- range
- cost
- current educational standard of the intended audience
- existing local professional experience with the medium
- the nature of the topic being taught (some topics, for example, require visual demonstrations rather than words alone)
- the availability of writers who are trained and competent in the chosen medium and who are willing to work closely with the curriculum specialists to devise educational and entertaining programs.

The choice of medium can also be influenced by the topic(s) to be taught and the major purpose of the programs. For example, a program designed to give specific instruction to a limited audience—such as midwives—and not released to the general public might be more effective on video than on radio. Some guidelines on the strengths and weaknesses of the various media and formats are given in Chapters 6–10.

The obvious first and strongest influence on medium choice, however, is availability of facility.

Determining Facility Availability

Media facility availability can be examined with the following questions. Even where a production house will be contracted to carry out all aspects of production, it is advisable for the Program Manager to request answers to these questions:

1. Are local production facilities for the chosen medium adequate. For example: studios, recording/filming equipment, actors?
2. Is a broadcast outlet available that will reach the whole geographic area where learners reside?
3. Is infrastructure in place for learners to receive and use broadcast—radios, TVs (or video vans), meetings rooms or classrooms if group learning is planned? Computers, if Internet is being used?
4. Is electricity or other power available for radios, TVs, Internet?

While the decision of which medium or media will be used for the project is largely determined by what is available and affordable, it is also important to know the medium to which the audience is most accustomed. For example, if the project leaders decide to make use of video programs, delivered by video van, it would be helpful for them to know if video is a new experience for their audience or if it is something to which they are accustomed. If it is something totally new to them, it might be necessary to create two or three introductory programs that contain little actual teaching, but are designed to accustom the learners to the medium and how it will be used for instructional purposes. Similarly, when the Internet is to be used, it is wise to begin with a few programs that contain little instruction in the topic, but considerable guidance on how to use the computer and the Internet.

THE MAJOR CHECKLIST

A project of the size and complexity of a distance education Edu-tainment project can present many challenges. One of the Program Manager's most necessary tasks is to determine and use methods of *problem control.* Initially, this requires the development of a major checklist showing the essential tasks to be accomplished. This checklist should be displayed prominently and all those involved with the project should become acquainted with those parts of the list that are their responsibility. The sample **major checklist** that follows is a suggestion only; the list will differ to some degree for each project. The Program Manager and staff must determine all the details essential for the completion of their own project.

In the following example, the **DONE** column can be used for entering the date at which once-only activities have been completed (such as the conducting and analyzing of the pilot tests). The **FOLLOW-UP** column is used to record steps still to be undertaken to complete the activity. It can also be used for comments on how to bring a particular activity up to date if it has temporarily slipped off track.

Major Checklist

All necessary Formative Evaluation completed.	FOLLOW-UP	DONE
Preparation		
On air start-up date and overall project duration established.		
Choice of broadcast outlet (radio/TV station) made.		
All necessary staff hired.		
Budget established.		
Production houses researched for adequate resources.		
Availability of local writing and acting talent explored.		
Possible frequency of broadcast and duration of each lesson researched with broadcast outlet.		
Preliminary agreement reached with broadcast outlet, with regard to availability of time and estimates of cost.		
Resources needed by learners (e.g., support booklets, flip charts) determined and preparations begun for their creation.		
Curriculum Design		
Date set for Curriculum Design Workshop.		
Curriculum Design Workshop site chosen and reserved.		
Design Team members selected and invited to workshop.		
Preparations for Curriculum Design Workshop completed.		
Design Workshop held.		
Writer auditions completed; writer/s chosen.		

(Contd.)

	FOLLOW-UP	DONE
Review panel selected. Initial review panel meeting held to outline responsibilities and review methods.		
Curriculum Design document completed and shared with writer and producer.		
Training needs established and training for writer(s) organized if needed.		

Pilot (Pre)Testing

Pilot-test sites selected and arranged.		
Pilot-test dates established and pilot audiences invited for those dates.		
Program design and shape (including character profiles) completed by writer, and reviewed and approved by review panel.		
Pilot-test programs written.		
Pilot-test programs and support materials (where necessary) reviewed.		
Pilot-test programs recorded.		
Pilot-test questions prepared and reviewed.		
Pilot-tests carried out (with writer/s present).		
Pilot-test results compiled immediately after pilot-tests.		
Pilot-test results reviewed by Program Manager, writer, and review team.		
Decisions made with regard to changes to be incorporated in future lessons and support materials.		
Timeline completed, agreed upon and shared with all who must abide by it.		

Contracts

Production houses invited to submit proposals.		
Proposals examined and selection made.		
Production house contract prepared and approved.		
Production house contract signed.		
Writer contract(s) prepared and approved.		
Writer contract(s) signed.		
Actor (Artist) contracts prepared and approved (if these are separate from the production house).		

(*Contd.*)

	FOLLOW-UP	DONE
Actor (Artist) contracts signed.		
Research/evaluation team selected—if this is to be different from the team who did the formative evaluation and research.		
Research/evaluation team contract prepared and approved.		
Research/evaluation contracts signed.		
Promotion agency selected (if required).		
Promotion agency contract prepared and approved.		
Promotion agency contract signed.		

Writing

Writer visits audience to gain better understanding of their culture.

Regular meeting times established with writer, editor (where necessary), and director.

Writer establishes regular writing schedule and begins writing programs.

Regular review routine established.

Ongoing preparation of support materials (where needed or possible) underway.

Promotional materials under development and tested.

Promotion campaign proposals are discussed with and approved by Program Manager.

Promotion campaign materials reviewed and approved by Program Manager.

Promotion materials are delivered to outlets on time.

Support materials proposals are discussed with and approved by Program Manager.

Support materials are pre-tested as necessary and adjusted.

Support materials are delivered to distribution points as needed.

Where necessary, training in use of Support Materials is given.

Monitoring and Evaluation

Ongoing monitoring designed.

Monitoring sites and monitoring methods are established.

(Contd.)

	FOLLOW-UP	DONE
Monitoring begins and is ongoing.		
Results of monitoring tabulated. Where necessary, changes are recommended by the Program Manager to the writer for future lessons.		
Arrangements are made for summative evaluation (post-tests).		
Summative evaluation carried out.		
Results of summative evaluation are compiled. Publicity and advocacy for the series is ongoing.		
Reports are prepared and distributed showing all aspects of project and its results, as well as lessons learned.		

Guidelines for Maintaining the Timeline and Preventing Problems

Allow Sufficient Start-up Time

At least six months—preferably more—should be allowed from the time of the decision to establish an Edu-tainment project to the commencement of script writing. This means six months of intense and continuous work, rather than doing a little bit about the project once a week or every few weeks. Establishing a project to reach out to community workers who are often in very remote and inaccessible areas of the country requires considerable work, patience and—often—ingenuity. Inevitably, the task is always more challenging than it seems at first.

Ensure that All Personnel can Work to the Designated Timeline

The very first time script writing or reviewing or production falls behind deadline, the Program Manager should discuss the problem with those concerned, and find a way of making it possible for the delay to be made up. Permitting the timeline to slip can easily encourage it to happen again.

Encourage Professional and Ethical Standards

All those working on the project should understand and acknowledge the importance of what they are doing. Educating community workers to support and encourage positive behavior change in their community is a truly important and valuable task. There should be a sense of ethical as well as professional dedication from all program staff. A big part of developing project sustainability is building a sense of personal professional pride amongst those engaged in the project. A bulletin board, displaying the 'PROFESSIONAL OF THE MONTH' has been found beneficial in some projects. Similarly, an occasional one-day professional advocacy workshop can assist all those in the project to understand the meaning and value of professionalism and how to achieve both professionalism and ethical standards in their work.

Providing professional contracts also can be helpful with those who have a subsidiary role in the project—actors, for example. The use of penalties for unmet contractual obligations can be useful in these circumstances, but it must be remembered that such penalties are unacceptable in some cultures. If penalties are to be included in the contracts, then the Program Manager must ensure that nothing on the project management side makes it impossible or even difficult for contractors to live up to their obligations. The Program Manager should also be alert to any possible impending contract breaches and assist the contractors to avoid such breaches.

Arrange Necessary Training in Advance

As earlier chapters have suggested, possible areas for training are:

- script writing for Edu-tainment programs
- production
- acting for distance education presentation
- support material preparation (especially in cases where learners have low literacy levels)

Sometimes, it is necessary to bring in consultants for these training activities and it is as well to establish dates as far in advance as possible to ensure that consultants are available.

Build Extra Days into the Timeline

For example: If the timeline requires the writer to complete three programs a week for 8–10 weeks, it is wise to add—from the outset—an extra week on the writer's schedule (in which there are no script requirements scheduled). Similarly, fallback days can be added to the production schedule to allow for illness of an actor or problems with production equipment.

Project personnel should be persuaded never to use the fallback days unless it is absolutely necessary and fully approved by the Program Manager. In this way, a bank of spare time is built up that can accommodate more serious emergencies if they arise.

Conduct Regular Meetings

At such meetings, everyone working on the scripts: writer, director, translator, typist or computer inputter, language reviewer (if one is used) and script reviewers, can raise questions and concerns before serious difficulties arise. These meetings also provide a venue for the sharing of suggestions and ideas that can enhance the ongoing work of the project.

Conduct the Review Panel Meeting

Before any script reviewing begins, a review panel meeting should be conducted so that all reviewers know exactly what their responsibilities are and how to fill out the review sheets. The importance of the review panel to the success of the project should be stressed in the initial meeting, together with the essential nature of timely return of script review comments.

Maintaining the Tracking System Rigidly

Once the continuous process of writing, reviewing, production, and editing is under way, the Program Manager must keep very close watch to be sure that quality is being maintained. A tracking system (see in the following section) should be established and adhered to rigorously from Day 1 of the writing and production cycle. The Program Manager should check the tracking system personally on a regular basis to ensure that it is working appropriately.

Be Prepared for Difficulties

There are some problems that are quite likely to arise in any Edu-tainment project. It is advisable to be aware of these and to give some thought to how they will be handled if they do arise. The most common problems that can occur are:

- **Disability of a writer.** Have a backup writer in mind. Where there is only one writer for the project (as is typical) the Program Manager should be aware of someone who can take over temporarily at short notice. This might be someone on the project staff who has writing ability and has been reviewing the scripts regularly. Alternatively, it is wise to be aware of one or two other writers who could be called upon if the primary writer has to drop out of the job permanently.

Give the new writer all previously written scripts and a copy of the design document, and allow two weeks before submission of some new scripts. This is an obvious place where fallback time will be invaluable.

- **Disability of an actor.** This can cause considerable disruption for television programs if episodes are being shot very close to the broadcast date. If there is a reasonable time lapse between writing, production, and broadcast, it is much easier to ask the writer to write out a particular character for a certain time, or indeed, if necessary, to remove the character from the story altogether. For radio, it is easier to find another actor with a similar voice who can take over the role of the disabled actor. If necessary, the audience can be told that a new actor will be taking over a certain role.

Other problems, such as electricity shortages, strikes, and political disturbances are not so easy to prepare for in advance. The biggest asset to overcoming problems of any type is keeping all aspects of the project rigidly on the timeline and maintaining some fallback time when there are no problems occurring.

Know and Use Major Checklists

Everyone involved with the project should be aware of all the steps that must be accomplished satisfactorily—many of them on a continuing basis—if the project is to reach its goal. Some Program Managers like to display in the office, prominently and permanently, the Major Checklist to encourage staff to appreciate the value of completing all tasks on time and the necessity of maintaining professional and ethical standards.

Encourage Q and A at All Times

Quality (Q) and Accuracy (A) are essential in all aspects of the Edu-tainment project if it is to have the desired positive effect on the distance education students and on the lives of their communities.

TRACKING SYSTEM SAMPLE

In order to keep reliable track of such things as script writing and review, it is helpful to create and maintain a Tracking System. The sample shows a tracking system for all aspects of script writing. Similar tracking systems can be set up for production, and for other parts of the project that requires steps to be completed in a sequence and on time.

SCRIPT TRACKING SYSTEM

PROGRAM #1	PROGRAM #2	PROGRAM #3	PROGRAM #4	PROGRAM #5	PROGRAM #6
Script to P.M. Due: Rec'd:	Script to P.M. Due: Rec'd:	Script to P.M. Due: Rec'd:	Script to P.M. Due: Rec'd:	Script to P.M. Due: Rec'd:	Script to P.M. Due: Rec'd:
Translated for reviewers (if necessary*). Due: Rec'd:	Translated for reviewers (if necessary). Due: Rec'd:	Translated for reviewers (if necessary). Due: Rec'd:	Translated for reviewers (if necessary). Due: Rec'd:	Translated for reviewers (if necessary). Due: Rec'd:	Translated for reviewers (if necessary). Due: Rec'd:
To reviewer. Due: Sent:	To reviewer. Due: Sent:	To reviewer. Due: Sent:	To reviewer. Due: Sent:	To reviewer. Due: Sent:	To reviewer. Due: Sent:
From reviewers. Due: Rec'd: 1: 2: 3:	From reviewers. Due: Jan 21 Rec'd: 1: 2: 3:	From reviewers. Due: Jan 28 Rec'd: 1: 2: 3:	From reviewers. Due: Feb 4 Rec'd: 1: 2: 3:	From reviewers. Due: Feb 11 Rec'd: 1: 2: 3:	From reviewers. Due: Feb 19 Rec'd: 1: 2: 3:
To writer after review (Rewrite as needed) Due: Rec'd:	To writer after review (Rewrite as needed) Due: Jan Rec'd:	To writer after review (Rewrite as needed) Due: Rec'd:	To writer after review (Rewrite as needed) Due: Rec'd:	To writer after review (Rewrite as needed) Due: Feb 12 Rec'd:	To writer after review (Rewrite as needed) Due: Rec'd:
To P.M. final Due: Rec'd:	To P.M. Due: Rec'd:	To P.M. Due: Rec'd:	To P.M. Due: Rec'd:	To P.M. Due: Rec'd:	To P.M. Due: Rec'd:

	1	2	3	4	5	6	7
To translator:	Due:	Due:	Due:	Due:	Due:	Due:	Due:
From translator.	Due: Rec'd:	Due: Rec'd:	Due: Rec'd:	Due: Rec'd:	Due: Rec'd:	Due: Rec'd:	Due: Rec'd:
To Media Director.	Due: Rec'd:	Due: Rec'd:	Due: Rec'd:	Due: Rec'd:	Due: Rec'd:	Due: Rec'd:	Due: Rec'd:
Recorded, edited, copied.	Due: Complete:	Due: Complete:	Due: Complete:	Due: Complete:	Due: Complete:	Due: Complete:	Due: Complete:
Archive script filed:	Date:	Date:	Date:	Date:	Date:	Date:	Date:
Broadcast.	Planned date: Actual date:	Planned date: Actual date:	Planned date: Actual date:	Planned date: Actual date:	Planned date: Actual date:	Planned date: Actual date:	Planned date: Actual date:

Notes: P.M. is Program Manager.

* In some situations, writers will prepare scripts in the local language and the scripts will have to be translated into another so that they can be read by a reviewer who does not speak the local language.

3

STARTING UP THE EDU-TAINMENT PROJECT

The first step for everyone involved in the project is to visit and get to know the audience.

CONSIDERATIONS WHEN STARTING UP THE EDU-TAINMENT PROJECT

In developing any type of distance education program, it is helpful to remember that '... education can have either a beneficial or a harmful effect on people's well-being. It can help increase people's ability and confidence to solve their own problems, or, in some ways it can do just the opposite.'* Therefore, in the creation of an Edu-tainment project, it is vitally important to ensure that everything possible is done in program planning and design to ensure that the programs increase ability and confidence. Among the most important factors to be handled with extreme care are choice of medium (discussed in detail in Chapter 2), knowledge of the audience, and lesson design.

Other important areas also require careful decision-making, such as where, how, and how often the learners will receive the programs, over what period of time the lessons will be given, whether or not to provide support materials and whether or not to undertake some type of pre- and post-test for students and whether or not to give some type of certificate or other recognition to those who complete the post-test successfully. These decisions, however, will be affected by the three major decisions that need to be made first:

---

*Werner, D. and D. Bower. 1982. *Helping Health Workers Learn*. The Hesperian Foundation.

1. UNDERSTANDING THE AUDIENCE

In order to help determine the curriculum to be taught, the following points must be examined:

(a) **Culture** plays a big role in education and in student attitude to learning. Simple things, such as the respect paid to teachers, vary widely from culture to culture; in some societies, teachers are treated almost reverentially; in others, they are seen more as friends. Some cultures still have barriers to women's education, while others are eagerly encouraging more and more women to raise their educational level. The designers of distance education programs to support general population behavior change should take these attitudes into account as they prepare the programs. They must decide if any of the current attitudes toward education need to be changed, and if so how this will be done.

   Everyday situations such as weather, working hours and family obligations differ from culture to culture, and these must be understood by the program creators in order to ensure suitable times and days for program delivery. Similarly, an understanding of the following life factors can influence the style and presentation of the programs.

(b) **The literacy level** of the audience will influence whether or not print materials can be used as a supplement to the media programs. The literacy level can also affect the language used in the audio/video presentations. In situations where the literacy level is low, writers must be extra sure to keep dialogues simple and short.

(c) **The language** of the audience is also an important factor. It is necessary that the writer (i) has a clear understanding of the language or dialect that is best understood by the audience and (ii) is capable of writing in this language or dialect.

(d) **The average age of the audience members.** Age can be a significant factor in deciding the type of entertainment background in which to place the learning.

(e) **The sex of audience members.** While both men and women typically enjoy mystery stories, it is often true that men prefer action stories while women prefer love stories. If there is to be a background story (however minimal) as the entertainment in the programs, it is important to know whether the audience will be largely male or female or whether it will be mixed, and what type of stories the audience enjoys.

(f) **Previous training experience.** It is wise to avoid turning away the audience by presenting them with knowledge they already have. Such knowledge can be reinforced in the programs, but it should not be presented as new. Determining the knowledge level of learners who are scattered throughout a large area of the country and who cannot be expected to respond to a written test can be difficult.

Chapter 11 of this book—on Support Materials—provides some guidelines on how such information can be obtained through questionnaires given via the medium to be used for the training.

(g) **The identified audience's need for further education.** In identifying the need for new or further education, project management should require adequate research on the following points:

   (i)   the knowledge the intended audience must have in order to carry out their job and support the recommended behavior change
   (ii) how much of this needed knowledge they already possess and are using efficiently
   (iii) which parts of the needed knowledge they already possess must be reinforced
   (iv) what new knowledge must be taught
   (v)   at what pace the learning should be delivered

   Care must be taken to ensure that any new practices recommended in the distance curriculum are possible in the locality in which the learners live. For example, many developing countries do not have access to all the latest medical equipment, so use of such equipment should not be taught or recommended in a distance course without first determining if it is available or when it is likely to be available.

(h) **Speed of learning.** It is also useful to have some understanding of the speed at which new knowledge can be absorbed by the audience, in order to ensure that the programs do not present the new instruction either too slowly or too quickly. Simple tests can be done with sample learner groups (where these are available) to find how quickly they can learn and remember new information.

(i) **How learners will apply their new knowledge.** A distance education course for community support workers must be based on what the learners are expected to do with the new knowledge, not just on what they are expected to be able to recall. Edu-tainment courses are not designed simply to increase academic strength, but to provide the learners with applicable knowledge and to demonstrate to them how this knowledge can be put to use immediately and effectively. The 6 T Teaching Process—described in detail in Chapter 5—explains how every lesson in an Edu-tainment course can encourage learners to make immediate use of what they have learned in a particular lesson.

2. LESSON DESIGN

Whether education is being delivered in a classroom where pupils and teachers are together for every lesson or through a distance channel, those preparing the lessons must have a thorough understanding of the following tried and tested principles of good teaching:

3. Curriculum Design

Every course of instruction (even informal instruction) should be begin with a clearly defined curriculum that is based on sound research of audience needs and culture and that adheres to the principles of good **curriculum design**, which require:

- **Clearly defined objectives.** The commencement of the design of any educational course begins with a statement of the overall goals that are appropriate for the students who will be taking the course. 'The traditional approach for writing objectives is also effective for distance education courses. Specifically, objectives should state the conditions under which learning should occur, the performance expected of the learner and the standard to which the performance will be matched. One way to write objectives is as follows:

  Given: *the conditions under which learning occurs*
  The learner will: *meet some predetermined level of performance*
  According to: *a minimum standard*

Good instructional goals should form the basis for instruction regardless of the medium used.'*

Given the background and life conditions of students of Edu-tainment programs, planners should be careful to set realistic goals. Indeed, such goals might have to be less than the project planners would like, but it should be remembered that the main aim of these courses is to attract and hold the attention of the learners and to motivate them to want to learn, and, more importantly, to want to apply what they learn within their community.

- **A lesson plan.** A clear, reliable lesson plan should be established and used in every program. This does not mean that every lesson will be exactly the same. Rather, it means that learners will know the typical shape or order of lesson presentation that they can expect in each lesson. A reliable lesson plan for distance learners can be based on the 6T Process of Teaching which is discussed in later chapters (see Chapter 5).
- **Distributed learning**, which allows for the learning of a specific topic, especially a difficult one, to be spread over time and presented more than once, both within one lesson and within several lessons.
- **Interactivity.** Interactivity between the 'teacher' and the learners should be encouraged in all distance education situations, no matter what the medium of delivery or who the audience. Interactivity allows students to be personally engaged in the lesson, through questions requiring learner response, whether

---

*Simonson, S., S. Smaldino, M. Albright, S. Zvacek. *Teaching and Learning at a Distance*, p. 129. Pearson Merrill Prentice Hall.

immediate or delayed, and sometimes through appropriate physical activities. While providing interactivity is relatively easy when students and teacher are in the same room together, the question arises of how it can be done when the teacher is in one place and the students are scattered about in numerous different locations, often learning on their own. Internet has an advantage because of the comparative ease with which students can 'talk to' the teacher or to other students. Radio and television, while they do not have the same interactive flexibility as online media, can include interactivity. Guidelines for creating and using **Interactivity** in Edu-tainment programs are given in Chapter 5.

- **Reinforcement.** When learners are questioned or tested during the course of a lesson, there should be immediate reinforcement of the correct answer. This is particularly important when learner and teacher are at a distance from each other. Guidelines on providing reinforcement in answer to questions are included with the information on Interactive Questioning in Chapter 5.

Other important factors to be kept in mind while designing the project include:

MOTIVATING LEARNER INTEREST

Motivating learner interest is significantly important in Edu-tainment programs designed to support and encourage maintenance of behavior change. In some situations, learners are eager to improve their general education or learn more about a particular topic, and they will 'attend' all lessons even if the programs are not particularly attractive. At other times, attracting and holding the interest of the students can be a challenge. When they are not required to be accounted as 'present' in the classroom, it can be tempting for students to skip one or several lessons if they are not truly interested and engaged. Learners have different interests, different abilities and different levels of concentration. On the whole, it is somewhat easier to find ways of engaging the attention of children than adults in a learning situation. Children like to sing songs and engage in physical activities. Learning is still a new and often fun activity for them. Many adults, on the other hand, lead busy lives. Asking them to take on study as well as work (and very often family responsibilities) can be daunting.

The most obvious motivators for adult advanced learning are rewards: a raise in pay or a step up the professional ladder. In many developing countries, these rewards are not possible, so other 'rewards' must be found to motivate the selected group to increase their knowledge. An attractive and 'entertaining' format can do a lot to encourage learners to 'attend' every class. Another influential motivator is increased self-esteem, and awareness of the vital role of encouraging and supporting appropriate behavior change in the community. The Edu-tainment format can contribute a great deal of support for both these needs.

Increased self-esteem can come also from the response and attitude of others. Long-range self-esteem can be powerfully strengthened by the reaction of community members to those whose professional attitude and support capabilities have improved noticeably as a result of the Edu-tainment programs. Nevertheless, most people like to receive some tangible acknowledgement for their capability. If distance learners can be given some type of recognition that is seen not only by their families, but also by their community members and leaders, this can be a satisfying reward. Often something as simple as an attractive certificate to hang in the home or workplace is enough to motivate positive community response. The award of a simple badge that can be worn while working can also boost self-esteem for those who successfully complete a professional distance learning course. Recognition in a local newspaper article is another form of reward, as is the presentation of the names on radio or television of all those who complete the course successfully.

Providing these rewards, however, requires that learners are registered and given some degree of testing before and after the course. Some suggestions on how such registration and testing can be done, even in low-literacy and geographical situations, are given in Chapter 11.

LESSON LENGTH

Typically an in-class distance education lesson lasts for about one hour. Careful consideration needs to be given to the question of whether or not this time period is appropriate for lessons delivered through the media. The decision will rest, at least in part, on the amount of time the local radio station or television channel will allow for the program, or on how much air time the project can afford to buy. It will also depend on the learners' level of concentration and the time of the day and the day of the week on which the lesson is being given. Community workers who have put in a long, hard day working with their clients might not have the necessary mental stamina to concentrate on an hour-long lesson delivered through the media. Similarly, they might not be accustomed to listening to or watching any program of that length. Project leaders must be prepared to spend time investigating just what program length would be acceptable to their students and appropriate to the subject being taught.

LEARNERS' GROUPS

These groups can provide motivation by encouraging learners who live or work in the same region to listen, watch or work on the programs together. Information on setting up Learners' Groups for Edu-tainment programs is given in Chapter 11.

Transforming Knowledge into Action

Every good instructor lets students see why new 'classroom-acquired' knowledge is relevant to their lives and how new knowledge can be used. Effective instructors demonstrate how new knowledge can be transformed into a life skill and they encourage their students to apply what they have learned in appropriate areas of their personal or professional lives. Learners should be able to understand, at all times, why the knowledge is relevant to their lives and their jobs, and how they can use it. In situations where they will be using their new knowledge to instruct others—as community workers and volunteers do—it is essential that the designers of the course keep this in mind. Every lesson must demonstrate how, and in what ways, these learners can transform their acquired knowledge into usable skills to instruct or help improve the lives of others.

The K.A.P. Gap

Designers of general behavior change communication projects often warn about the K.A.P. gap. In other words, there is always a danger that even when people gain the Knowledge (K) and acquire the right Attitude (A) about new knowledge or behavior, they might not move to the essential step of using the knowledge or putting it into Practice (P). A clear example of this is the worldwide response to anti-smoking campaigns. Virtually everyone knows that cigarette smoking is highly dangerous and results in the death of almost one in every two regular smokers. Large numbers of people who smoke plan to give it up 'one day', but the number who actually put their knowledge and attitude into practice is still horrifyingly low. Designers of Edu-tainment programs must pay equal attention to ensuring that their students actually put into practice in their communities what they are learning in their lessons.

Responses from Learners

How can teachers be sure that the students are **using** their new knowledge when they have no personal contact with them? Monitoring and evaluation can go a long way to check on success, but other specific motivators can also be employed to encourage and ensure that learners are using their new knowledge. These motivators include:

- **Newsletters:** Distance education projects that cannot include regular written instructions and assignments can publish and distribute an occasional newsletter. Learners can be invited to contribute anecdotes and questions which can be published in the newsletter together with responses from project directors who, at the same time, can clarify points that seem to have been misunderstood by some learners. The use of a newsletter, however, is appropriate only when the majority of the learners are literate. In some situations, learners are willing to dictate their comments to a child or someone else who will do the writing for them.

- **Learner Forum:** Radio and TV programs can make use of occasional Learner Forum programs (perhaps every 10th program in the series), to which listeners are encouraged to contribute with personal accounts of how they made positive use of what they have learned, or with questions about ways in which they might use their new knowledge. These contributions can come in the form of written letters, or they can be delivered by telephone, or where time and money will allow—they can be collected by project staff members when they make visits to areas in which the programs are being presented.
- **Letter Cards or Quiz Cards** are another way in which learners, especially low-literate learners, can respond to the program cheaply and easily. (For information on and samples of letter cards and quiz cards, see Chapter 11.)
- **Support Book:** Where there is a support book provided for learners, there can be pages in the book that encourage learners to record their questions or their experiences with the new knowledge and mail them to the project office. A sample of a Support Book containing a letter page can be found in Chapter 11.
- **The Internet:** Internet classes, where they exist, can establish chat rooms and blog files where learners are encouraged to share their experiences and their questions.

FIELD VISITS

Any of these approaches is difficult in places where literacy levels are low. In these situations, it is helpful for Program Managers to arrange for occasional visits to the field where learners can be interviewed and their responses or questions recorded on tape, to be used in a Learner Forum or Summary program.

With all these requirements in mind, the next major step in the creation of Edu-tainment programs is the determination of the precise curriculum to be used.

4

THE CURRICULUM GUIDE

Curriculum specialists, writers, and producers work together to determine precise lesson format and content.

DEVELOPING THE CURRICULUM

Once the points discussed in the previous chapters have been clarified, it is time to develop the instructional curriculum that will be covered in the Edu-tainment programs. Curriculum Development can be done in different ways.

Existing Curriculum

Sometimes, there is an existing curriculum—perhaps in a local school or college—that needs only minor adjustment to make it suitable for the current project. This adjustment can be done by a small group of curriculum specialists who know both the subject and the audience very well. It is almost always necessary, however, to ensure that the finalized curriculum is approved by the appropriate government ministry, and by the broadcast outlet through which it will be delivered. This last point is particularly necessary if the programs will be dealing with culturally sensitive issues, such as sexual matters or behaviors that might seem to run contrary to local religious, cultural or political beliefs.

New Curriculum

If there is no existing curriculum, or if it is evident that the existing curriculum needs considerable revision or change, it can be valuable to run a Curriculum Development Workshop so that all appropriate people can work together to reach agreement on all aspects of,

- the topics to be covered, and the order in which they should be presented, and whether they need to be divided into Units, Modules, and Topics (see page 75 for more discussion of this question).

- the academic level of topic presentation, bearing in mind that there might well be different levels of previous knowledge and experience among the learners.
- the finalized printed version of the Curriculum Guide, which will become the reliable reference for all those working on program creation and presentation and on any support materials.

Depending on the number of programs planned for the Edu-tainment series, a Curriculum Guide Design workshop will usually last four or five days.

THE EDU-TAINMENT CURRICULUM GUIDE DESIGN WORKSHOP

Those attending the workshop should include:

- The Program (or Project) Manager.
- Topic Specialists who are knowledgeable in the subject matter and how it can best be taught to the intended audience. If possible, these people should be those who have actually taught these topics previously and will have some idea of how the topics can be broken up into lessons.
- Representatives of the Behavior Change Communication project that is being conducted for the general public (if such a project has already been put in place) and that will be supported by the Edu-tainment series. Their presence helps ensure a synergistic effect between the two projects.
- The writer(s) who will be involved in preparing the programs for the chosen medium.
- The video or audio director or producer of the programs.
- In the event that Internet will be used, those who will be structuring the programs should also attend the Curriculum Design Workshop.
- Representative/s of the broadcast channel through which it is intended that the programs will be delivered. It is wise to be sure, from the outset, that the topics to be taught and indeed, the technical language to be used, are not deemed offensive to the broadcast audience. This approval particularly refers to any health-related courses that deal with sexual matters, or to new behaviors that at first might seem to be culturally or religiously offensive.
- Representatives of the audience for whom the programs will be created.
- Representatives of the appropriate local ministries; for example, Ministry of Health. It is extremely important that all education offered through Edu-tainment programs is approved and supported by the appropriate local ministries. Without their total support and approval, there is always the likelihood that the programs will be blocked while—or even before—they are broadcast.

- Support Material creators in those cases where support materials will be provided for learners. Support materials can be of various sorts. (See Chapter 11 for further information on possible Support Booklets and Learner Group Discussion Guides.)

EDU-TAINMENT CURRICULUM GUIDE CONTENTS

A Curriculum Guide usually will contain most or all of the information in Box 4.1, depending on the learners and the nature of the subject matter:

Frequently only Sections 1–12 will be completed in the Curriculum Design Workshop, with the Implementation Plans being finalized by the Program Manager and project staff members immediately after the workshop.

Box 4.1

CURRICULUM GUIDE CONTENTS

Part 1: Background and Overall Description:
1. Justification for the Project
2. Audience Information
3. Justification for the Chosen Medium
4. Overall Measurable Objectives
5. Overall Purposes
6. Attitude to be encouraged
7. Number, frequency, and length of programs
8. Scope and Sequence of Curriculum

Part 2: Individual Lessons Plans: For each lesson:
9. Measurable Objectives of the lesson
10. Purposes of the Lesson
11. Precise Lesson content
12. Glossary Entries

Part 3: Implementation Plans:
13. Support Materials, Registration, etc.
14. Research and Pilot Testing
15. Timelines
16. Evaluation Plans
17. Promotional Activities
18. Writer's Support Team
19. Script Review Team
20. Program Format Description

Curriculum Guide Details

A sample of a Curriculum Guide for an Edu-tainment project can be found in Appendix A. Details of each section of the Curriculum Guide are as follows:

Part 1: Background and Overall Description

1. Justification for the project: This section will answer the basic questions: For whom is the learning to be provided and what evidence is there that it is necessary? Why is distance education needed rather than classroom or workshop teaching? Why does Edu-tainment seem like the appropriate format for this audience? The answers to these questions will be determined through baseline research conducted by a professional research team at the outset of the project, and should be presented (in summary form) by a representative of the team at the outset of the workshop and included in this opening section of the Curriculum Guide.

2. Information about the chosen audience: This information falls into two broad categories:

(a) information about the audience's current knowledge of the topic and their interest in learning
(b) information about personal characteristics, which will include such information as:
- cultural and social background
- language and literacy level
- previous learning environment
- interest in learning the subject to be offered
- time available for lessons and assignments
- whether learners will be alone or working in a group
- motivators that might be available to encourage learning (such as certificates, badges, titles)

(See sample in Appendix A for details on audience information).

3. Justification of the chosen medium: This section will provide answers to the following questions:

- What is the preferred medium for delivery of this instruction and why?
- Is the preferred medium available to learners?
- What is the justification for using the chosen medium?
- What are the advantages and disadvantages of this medium for the learners?
- How can any disadvantages be overcome or lessened?

Perhaps, as important as the audience to be reached and the instruction to be given, is the choice of medium to be used with the chosen audience. In order to make wise and appropriate decisions on medium or media choice, as they relate to the subject being taught and the audience to be reached, it is necessary to have a clear understanding of the pros and cons of the various media.

Understanding the Media and Choosing the Medium to be Used

Whether the project will use radio, television, books, the Internet or a combination of media depends on several things:

- availability and reach of the medium
- cost
- suitability to the audience (for example, books are not appropriate with low-literacy learners)
- suitability to the topics to be taught (for example topics that must be seen to be understood are best covered on television or Internet)
- availability of trained writers, producers, and others

Currently, because it is relatively inexpensive and definitely far-reaching, **radio** is still one of the most popular ways of bringing programmed instruction to remote areas throughout the world. Radio programs are usually cheaper to produce than books and they are often more attractive than books because they offer actual voices to the audience and are therefore more like real teaching. The presence of real people on the radio (whether they are teachers or characters in a fictional drama) makes the programs seems more like real life. **Television**, or more commonly **video**, is popular for similar reasons, but has the disadvantage of more costly production. The **Internet** is clearly the direction of the future, but is still some way off for many of the poorer or more remote areas of the world. Chapters 12–15 of this book provide some guidelines on the challenges, advantages, and methods of using the Internet for distance education in those areas where it is, or soon will be practical.

The following guidelines can be useful in making a selection of the medium or media to be used for Edu-tainment programs.

Understanding the Medium—Radio

(a)   Radio is an aural medium. Everything the audience is required to understand must be conveyed through SOUND, which means dialogue, sound effects, and music. The secret of writing for radio is finding the perfect balance of enough sound to convey the message, but not so much that it results in confusion.

(b)   Radio is a personal medium. Even when listening with a group of people, each listener is in a one-on-one relationship with the radio voices. For this reason, it is important that the program 'hosts/teachers' and characters in distance education programs are presented as real people in whom the audience can believe. It is the people in the program, even more than the content, that will initially attract and then hold the attention of the audience.

(c)   Radio is a medium of the imagination. One of the joys of radio is that it allows listeners to 'see' what they are hearing in their own way. They can picture radio characters as they would like them to look, and they can imagine houses, cities, and villages to resemble their own if that is what they choose. Unfortunately, this freedom of imagination that radio allows can be a disadvantage in instructional programming. There are times when listeners require a precise and absolutely accurate picture, not one they have thought up in their own imagination. Writing instructional programs for radio requires extreme skill—to allow freedom for the listeners' imagination when appropriate, and to give precise accurate descriptions when necessary.

(d)   Radio requires simplicity. Because radio relies on one sense only—hearing— instruction given via radio must be kept simple. Distance education programs delivered by radio should aim to give the clearest, most effective instruction they can, and to ensure repetition of new or difficult concepts.
      Simplicity can be enhanced by consistency. Consistency is one of the most important attributes of effective teaching.

(e)   Radio characters, including 'teachers' or hosts in Edu-tainment programs must be more clearly 'drawn' than is necessary on video or in print (where pictures can be given) if they are to be believable. Information on the importance of clearly presented characters is given in Part 2 of this book 'For the Writers'.

(f)   Instructional points should be limited. Usually, three discrete blocks of totally new knowledge within a 15-minute program are sufficient, and even these three pieces should be repeated or used in several ways, including audience interaction, if they are to be truly learned and remembered. This measurement suggests that six new points could be taught in a 30-minute program, but this then raises the question of whether or not that is too much new knowledge for the specific students being taught.

(g)   Radio listening requires considerable attention and concentration, because radio makes use of one sense only—hearing. In instructional programs, therefore, periods of intense listening or learning should be broken up with some 'relaxed' activities. Relaxation can be achieved through the entertainment background of the programs (perhaps a mini-drama), by interspersing teaching segments with activities, humor, interactive questions, and perhaps occasional music or songs.

Radio's Disadvantage

Perhaps the biggest disadvantage of radio is that it cannot show objects, people or actions that the learners need to see to understand. This disadvantage can be overcome, to some extent by supplying learners with Support Booklets that provide the necessary pictorial images. Even for learners who are illiterate or low-literate, a Support Booklet can be designed that contains the appropriate pictures numbered, but without text. In very remote or hard to reach areas of some countries, however, the delivery of Support Books to the students is either very difficult or not possible.

Understanding the Medium—Television

In the modern world, television is very largely used as a medium of entertainment. Factual programs such as news broadcasts and weather forecasts are a necessary and expected part of the daily programming, but for the most part, people accept television or video as a major contributor to their relaxation and entertainment. Adapting this medium for instructional purposes, therefore, can be challenging.

Television is a Visual Medium

Television production is expensive and time-consuming, but television can bring into the instructional environment pictures of reality that learners might otherwise never see. Edu-tainment programs on television or video should take advantage of this and not restrict lessons to lectures or discussions that could be just as effective on radio. Television can display such things as the details of scientific experiments, complex building construction, biological details (such as the development of an embryo), or national historical sites that students might never experience in real life. Using stock footage, television can even take students to the top of Mount Everest or to the bottom of the sea, or to other places they would otherwise never see. For professional training, television or video also offers the opportunity to provide clear physical demonstrations of actions and behaviors.

Television Pictures can Distract from Learning

Where radio calls for learners to employ one sense only—hearing—TV or video offers learners the chance to watch and listen or, if the pictures are more intriguing than the message, to watch only. There is a real need to balance the attraction of the picture with the importance of the lesson. Pictorial presentations or demonstrations are certainly helpful in some learning situations, but, if the pictorial display is too exciting, student viewers might need to be reminded that the program has an instructional purpose. The use of interactive questioning throughout the program can remind the learners that the program purpose is more than entertainment. In Edu-tainment programming, the use of an entertaining story background containing a character involved in a job (or activities) similar to those of the learners can be a powerful motivator to encourage viewers to 'learn the lesson'.

Television Leaves Almost Nothing to the Imagination

The audience can see the instructors, how they are dressed, how and where they are situated, and how they are behaving. They can see the lesson demonstrations and the surroundings in which the lesson is being provided. Everything that is visible, therefore, must be correct and must be socially and culturally appropriate and acceptable to the audience.

Television Identifies Locale and Ethnicity

In a country where there are many different ethnic groups and lifestyles, there can be a problem if those appearing on the television screen seem to be from a culture entirely different from that of even some of the learners. This is especially important when the programs are being used to train community workers; if the people in the video do not resemble themselves or do not have lives like their own, the result might be a lack of audience interest or—worse still—lack of trust in the program. The use of Voice Over presentation rather than an on-screen teacher or host can help alleviate this problem for adult learners, but the presence of an actual visible instructor is always more acceptable than consistent use of an unidentified voice. Animated or digitally generated characters (like characters in comics) can be used rather than actual human beings for some programming, but this is usually an unduly expensive format for distance education purposes.

Perhaps the main element to bear in mind, when considering the use of television for teaching of any kind, is that television is a **visual** medium. So, the main accent of the lesson should be on what needs to be seen rather than on what can be learned by being only heard.

Disadvantages of Television

Clearly, the biggest disadvantage of television is cost: cost of production, cost of delivery, and cost of television sets to receive and display the programs. It should be remembered, however, that television programs can be stored on DVDs, CDs, or even video tapes, so that they can be used repeatedly in different places with different audiences. The possession of even one video van can allow the project to show the programs in a number of places without the extra cost of a large number of TV sets and the difficulty of providing power to run them.

Understanding the Medium—Internet

Information and Communication Technologies (ICTs) are increasingly attracting attention as the means for spreading education and information worldwide. The biggest advantage of the Internet is that it enables information to be disseminated—with words, still pictures, video animation and/or 'live' presentation—from virtually any part of the world to any other part. There is already considerable evidence to show that health knowledge worldwide is being significantly improved through use of the Internet.

There are, at the same time, some serious impediments to employing the Internet for distance teaching. In many places, connection to the Internet is impossible or, at best unreliable, because of the lack or unreliability of the local energy supply. Added to this is the expense of obtaining and maintaining the hardware that is needed for accessing the Internet such as computers, printers, CDs, and DVDs. At the same time, the speed of development of the Internet and its necessary accessories is so rapid that there is an almost continuous need to replace or upgrade the facilities used to access Internet programs. The Internet, however, should not be automatically discarded as a possible distance education medium. Some guidelines on acquiring and using the Internet for distance education are provided in Chapters 12–15 of this book.

4. The overall measurable objective(s) of the course as a whole refer to what it is hoped the learners will accomplish as a result of these programs. The Overall Measurable Ob-jective is a broad statement of what the distance education programs hope to achieve in terms of learners' new knowledge, their attitude to the new knowledge, and how they make use of it.

Measurable objectives refer to the changes that are expected in the knowledge, attitude and practice (K.A.P.) of the selected audience. The Overall Measurable Objective/s might be expressed in a manner similar to this sample from a Curriculum Guide for health workers.

As a result of this training course, there will be a measurable increase in the number of community volunteer health workers who will:

KNOW: How to instruct and motivate community members to provide the best possible healthcare for their children.

ATTITUDE: They will feel strongly motivated to help community members to adopt the appropriate new behaviors with regard to taking better care of their children. And they will feel proud of the help they can provide to the community.

DO (Practice): They will instruct and motivate all community members to provide the best possible healthcare for their children.'

5. The overall purposes of the course as a whole. 'Purpose' can be interpreted as 'approach' and refers to the approach the **program presentation** should take to make it possible for learners to achieve the objectives. All programs must be designed **to motivate** as well as **to instruct**, but some lessons will be designed to **teach** new topics, while others will **reinforce** important points that are already known by the audience. Some programs must clearly **demonstrate** certain behaviors, such as Interpersonal Communication skills. The writer needs to be aware of the purpose or intention of the program in order to create an appropriate episode of the story or program format to match the lesson needs.

6. The overall attitude to be encouraged in learners toward the subject and toward their role in supporting and encouraging behavior change. A learner's attitude to education has a major impact on how much is learned; similarly, attitude to a job greatly affects how well the job is done. Edu-tainment curriculum designers need to pay special attention to the **attitude** they want to encourage in learners, both toward the course and toward their work. While an attitude of **dedication** might seem very appropriate for all those engaged in supporting behavior change in general public, it should not be forgotten that **self-esteem** has a big influence on dedication. Knowing the attitude that the Edu-tainment programs want to encourage is a great help to writers who can then use the desired attitude as an underlying **emotion** in the programs they prepare, no matter what format is used.

7. The number of programs; the length of each program; frequency of presentation. This section of the Curriculum Guide is a simple statement of these practical lesson-delivery matters. Determining the length of each program will depend on:

- the time allowed by the radio or TV station. Many stations have set rules for program length, while others can be influenced by what the project is prepared to pay.
- the program length to which the audience is accustomed. If audience members generally watch or listen to programs that are no more than 30 minutes long, it might be difficult to persuade them to pay attention for a longer period of time.
- the audience's previous learning experience. If they are not accustomed to 'sitting in a classroom', it might be difficult to encourage them to listen or watch a lengthy lesson.
- the amount of time learners are likely to be able to devote to learning. In some areas, community-helpers are housewives and mothers or heavily employed men who have little free time for learning.

These considerations must be kept in mind while determining the length of the media-delivered program. Similar considerations must be borne in mind when preparing Internet or computer-based programs.

8. The detailed scope and sequence of the curriculum. This section is a listing of individual lesson topics and the order in which they will be presented. In determining the scope and sequence, program planners will need to decide if they wish to employ the Unit-Module-Topic structure, or simply list the topics in which they should be given. In the Unit-Module-Topic approach, which is commonly used in colleges, lessons are arranged as follows:

Unit: A *unit* is a significant body of knowledge that represents a major subdivision of a course's content. Often, one unit of a course would represent 4–5 weeks of instruction, and would be equivalent to a semester credit...

Module: A *module* is a major subdivision of a unit. A module is a distinct and discrete component of a unit...

Topic: A *topic* is an important supporting idea that explains, clarifies, or supports a module. A topic would be a lesson or an assignment.

Examples:

A Unit in an educational course on The Healthy Family might be 'Family Planning Methods'.

A Module on Family Planning Methods might be divided into 3–5 major components such as (a) Temporary Methods; (b) Long-term Methods; (c) Permanent Methods; (d) Methods that also Protect against Disease.

Topics in a module on 'Long Term Methods' might be (a) The Intra-Uterine Device; (b) Norplant; (c) the Injectable.'

'These three terms can be used in a variety of ways. Of importance is the idea that topics form modules, and modules form units, and units are the main subdivisions of courses.'* An alternative approach to the Detailed Scope and Sequence is to simply list the topic of each program as is done in the Curriculum Guide Sample in Appendix A.

Part 2: Individual Lesson Content

For each lesson, the Curriculum Guide must explain the following points, largely as a guide to the writer, and as a checklist for those working on the project.

9. The measurable objective(s) of this lesson. The measurable objectives will state briefly what the lesson hopes to achieve in terms of audience knowledge, attitude and practice (K.A.P.).

10. The purpose(s) of this lesson. The purpose of each lesson explains the approach the lesson should take. For instance, the purpose might be,

- to **teach** (specific facts)
- to **demonstrate** (a certain behavior)
- to **motivate** (a chosen attitude)

In each lesson outline, these points will be followed by a clear statement of,

---

*Simonson, M., S. Smaldino, M. Albright and S. Zvacek. *Teaching and Learning at a Distance*, p. 150. Pearson Merrill Prentice Hall.

11. The precise content of this lesson. Those preparing the Curriculum Guide must remember that the writers usually are not experts in the topic for which they are writing; so it is essential that the CONTENT section for each program is precise, detailed, accurate, and complete.

12. Glossary entries as needed. The glossary is intended to assist the writer by providing clear definitions of technical terms as needed, and also providing local dialect definitions of technical terms where needed.

Part 3: Implementation Plans

Although all the following points might not be finalized during the Curriculum Design Workshop, they should be added to the Curriculum Guide as soon as possible, once they are decided. The Curriculum Guide serves as the reliable 'roadmap' for everyone working on the project and also becomes the archive record of what the project provided and achieved. For these reasons, it is important for the finalized Curriculum Guide to contain all the following points.

13. Description of proposed support materials. Support materials (if they are to be used) could be one or some of the following:

(a) Support Booklet to be given to all those taking the course (this booklet might also include guidelines on how to take pre- and post-tests and how to submit assignments in cases where these materials will be used).
(b) Discussion Guide for Discussion Group leaders, where such groups will be possible.
(c) Letter or Quiz cards to be used by learners.

14. Description of proposed Pilot Testing of the programs. A copy of the pilot test and dates and places where the pilot tests will be conducted should be included, together with the name of the research organization that will be conducting the testing, if it is to be an organization outside the program office.

The pilot-test questions can be prepared by the staff of the Edu-tainment project or by the appointed research team. The main areas to be examined in pilot testing the programs should include:

(a) Are the learners comfortable with the standard of teaching they are being offered? Or do they find it too easy or too difficult?
(b) Are the learners comfortable with the amount of knowledge included in each program? Are they able to answer all the interactive test questions in the test part of the programs.

(c) Does the 'entertainment' side of the programs appeal to them? Can they recall details of the story (if there is a story as part of the entertainment) and the characters?

(d) Do they believe that the community-helpers in the programs are like themselves?

(e) Do they trust the person or persons (teacher/host) delivering the education and the knowledge being given? If not, why not?

(f) Do they believe that the characters who represent clients of the community-helper are like those in their own community?

(g) Can they name, and did they appreciate any humorous character(s) included in the programs?

(h) Do they feel that the programs encourage them to feel good about their work; increase self-esteem?

(i) How was the length of the program? Were learners able to pay attention throughout the whole program?

(j) Would they encourage others in the community to listen to and learn from the programs?

All questions, however, should be worded so that they do not require just a 'yes' or 'no' answer. It is for this reason that experienced researchers should be employed in the creation of the pilot test.

15. Timelines for all activities, include scripting, script review, production, pre- and post-testing. Keeping an Edu-tainment project of this nature on time and on budget is a major challenge, which is largely left in the hands of the Program Manager. Preparing realistic but strict timelines is an essential component of a successful project.

16. Details of evaluation plans, such as pre- and post-tests to be used with the learners to determine formative and summative evaluation.

17. Description of promotional activities and materials that are designed to attract and motivate the learners for whom the project is created and to keep them informed of times of program airing, assignment delivery (if assignments are used), and other facts.

18. Writer's Support Team. This team will consist of two or three people who can be called upon by the writers for advice or guidance as they prepare the programs. Even when the Curriculum Guide has been very carefully prepared and reviewed, it can happen that a writer will need further explanation or assistance with a particular topic to ensure that it is delivered accurately and appropriately within a program. The people nominated to the Writer's Support Team must have attended the Curriculum Design Workshop, must be familiar with all details of the project, must know the lifestyle of the audience well, and must be available as needed.

19. Script Review Team. Script review is an essential part of any Edu-tainment project. No matter how experienced and competent the writer is, there is always a chance that inadvertent errors might be made or parts of the curriculum missed. Just as every book author relies on an experienced editor, so too every Edu-tainment writer must recognize the importance of having a reliable reviewer to check the quality and accuracy of every script written. The Script Review Team should consist of a limited number of people so that production is not delayed while awaiting reviewer response. Ideally, the review team will include:

- a topic specialist (who comments only on the accuracy of the lesson and the suitability of its presentation); usually, this person can also be the audience representative who can determine that the lesson presentation and language are appropriate;
- a program format specialist (that is, someone experienced in Edu-tainment writing who can guide the writer and who comments only on the format, not on the content);
- the program director or producer who needs to ensure that there is nothing in the script that makes production difficult or even impossible; and
- a representative of the appropriate government ministry or ministries—where this is necessary—whose job is only to ensure that nothing in the program contravenes ministerial policy.

The Program Manager should delineate clearly the role that each Script Review Team member will play and encourage members to stick to their own tasks in the review process and not try to make comments on all aspects of every script.

Script Review Guidelines

The following guidelines can be used by the Script Review Team members as they regularly review scripts.

A. **Check the Curriculum Guide.** Reviewers should be thoroughly conversant with the details of the Curriculum Guide and with details of the chosen program format. They should be aware that at the script-writing stage, they cannot request changes in the Curriculum Guide information unless there has been a change in or addition to current knowledge on the topic, subsequent to the Curriculum

Design Workshop. Content reviewers should check each program against the Curriculum Guide to be sure that all points in the Guide have been correctly included in the script. Usually, each script is accompanied by a cover page that provides details of the program from the Curriculum Guide. If this page is not appended, reviewers must make it their job to refer to the Guide itself to ensure that the program is accurate.

B. **Check that the 6Ts of the Teaching Process are being correctly followed:** (Details of the 6Ts of the Teaching Process can be found in Chapter 5.)

C. **Check the Interactive Question segment** of each script to be sure that the questions adhere to the Guidelines for Interactive Questions (Chapter 5).

D. **Check the lesson presentation against the 7Cs of lesson presentation:** The 7Cs help ensure that the lesson content and the format in which it is presented are accurate and appropriate.

Box 4.2

THE 7CS OF LESSON PRESENTATION

Every lesson must be:

- **C** omplete
- **C** orrect
- **C** lear
- **C** oncise
- **C** onsistent
- **C** ulturally appropriate
- **C** ompelling

While checking scripts, reviewers should also be aware of their own **commitment** and that of the writers to **quality** and **accuracy (Q and A)** in all aspects of the scripting.

Conducting Script Review Meetings

Rather than sending the scripts to the various reviewers and asking them to respond individually, many Program Managers prefer to invite script reviewers to regular meetings where they can sit down together and complete the review of several scripts in one meeting. A script review meeting of this nature can also be helpful in reminding the various team members of their particular contribution and preventing team members from spending time commenting on those areas of the script which are not their domain.

20. Program Format Description and Sample Script. In order to create a complete archive of the curriculum, it is helpful to include in the finalized Curriculum Guide a brief description of the format that has been chosen and a copy of one sample script.

As mentioned earlier, the Curriculum Guide is the precise 'roadmap' for all those working on the Edu-tainment project. It is the essential guide for the writer/s who will rely on it for precise information about the content of each program.

PART 2

For the Writer

5

WRITING FOR EDU-TAINMENT PROGRAMMING

Writing educational programs requires talent, training, and time.

DISTANCE EDUCATION PROGRAMS TO SUPPORT AND MAINTAIN BEHAVIOR CHANGE

While Entertainment–Education programs on radio, TV and occasionally Internet do their best to motivate the general public to adopt appropriate behavior change, there is no denying that the **maintenance** of the behavior change is greatly enhanced when there are trained, real live human beings, on the ground, and right there in the community ready to answer questions and provide help and personal motivation to community members so that they can succeed in making and maintaining the proposed behavior change. Edu-tainment programs to train these important people (when training cannot be done on the ground) are the perfect partner for Entertainment–Education programs that encourage behavior change in the general public. The success of the Edu-tainment programs relies to a large degree on the program writer/s.

THE ROLE OF THE WRITER

The writer is a vitally important member of the Distance Education project team, because it is the writer who must create the programs that deliver quality teaching within an attractive and engaging program format. Indeed, the writer is a key player in the creation of both Entertainment–Education and Edu-tainment programs, but it is safe to say that Edu-tainment writing is by far the more challenging task.

Edu-tainment is not for every writer. Many writers like to have total creative freedom as they write, and clearly this is not possible in Edu-tainment. This disciplined writing requires strict adherence to the lesson details outlined in the Curriculum Guide, while providing a type of 'entertainment backdrop' against which to present the lessons. The entertainment backdrop must be culturally appropriate for the intended audience, and even the characters must be clearly representative of the people (and their lifestyles) for whom the education is being provided. Before accepting an assignment to create Edu-tainment programs, writers should be absolutely sure that they are willing to keep the educational intent of the project in the forefront of their minds and not feel 'cheated' because they do not have complete creative freedom.

Apart from being willing to accept what may seem like the restrictions of Edu-tainment creation, writers must be sure that they understand some very important aspects of educational writing:

1. Knowing the audience
2. Knowing how to use the Curriculum Guide
3. Understanding the need for lessons to follow a regular pattern
4. Appreciating the value of the **5 Es** of effective Edu-tainment writing
5. Knowing how to write for the chosen medium
6. Choosing an Appropriate Lesson Program Format

Knowing the Audience

'Helping people to begin to look at things in a new way is a teacher's chief job. This is easier, if (the teacher) looks at ideas, not in terms of general theories, but through real-life examples. It is better still when the examples come from the lives and experiences of the learning group.'* By far, the best way for the writer to find examples from the lives and experiences of the learning group is to get to know them personally. Writers should ensure that the Project Manager arranges for them to spend some time in a representative community, watching the community-helper at work and seeing how members of the community respond to her/him. It is not the writer's job to find out what should be taught in the programs, but rather to gain a solid understanding of the lifestyle of the community-helpers and how, when, where, and how often they interact with community members.

---

*Werner, D. and B. Bower. 'Helping Health Workers Learn'. *The Hesperian Foundation*, p. 1.7.

Observation

The writer's main activity on a visit to the community is **observation**. Observation of the home and family environment, the work environment, the recreation environment of those for whom the programs will be designed. Writers visiting the community should be careful not to seem as if they are prying into personal lives or questioning personal behavior. They must be extremely discrete as they observe what they need to learn.

Some writers like to use community members they meet as models on which to create characters for their programs. This is excellent way of ensuring that the characters will be understood by the audience.

Knowing How to Use the Curriculum Guide

The Curriculum Guide is the reliable reference for everyone working on the Edu-tainment project. As mentioned earlier, the writer must attend the Curriculum Design Workshop, or—if no workshop is needed—meet with the content specialists to fully understand the subject/s being taught. The writer must rely on the Curriculum Guide to develop the teaching content of every program. The writer does not have the freedom to change the content within one lesson or to change the order of the lessons. Writers who have difficulty following any part of any lesson in the Curriculum Guide must seek the help of the Script Support Team before proceeding. Writers should have a sense of commitment when undertaking Edu-tainment writing, because the lessons they are preparing will help, not only the immediate learners, but also the people in the communities where these learners work.

Understanding the Need for Lessons to Follow a Regular Pattern

Writers who are not accustomed to creating Distance Education programs might be, at first, somewhat frustrated by having to adhere to a regular pattern or shape in every program. They need to understand that having a regular pattern makes it easier for students to follow lessons when there is no teacher present who can guide the lesson direction or answer questions. If learners know that all lessons are structured on the same pattern, they know what to be prepared for and what to expect as the lesson moves along. Writers should appreciate that sticking to a regular pattern does not need to result in a boring program; variety can be introduced within each segment.

Appreciating the Value of the 5 Es of Effective Edu-tainment Writing

Keeping the 5 Es in mind will help the writer ensure that the program is not just didactic, but should have real personal appeal to the learners. This means that while the basic intent of the program is to teach, there should be

1. some **entertaining** underpinning to the programs that allows the audience to be **emotionally engaged**;
2. a character or characters with whom the learners can **empathize**;
3. a character or characters who inspire the learners with a sense of self-**efficacy**. (this often is the same character/s with whom the learners empathize);
4. some clear **example/s** of the lesson that can be used with and valuable to the community;
5. constant opportunity for the learners to acquire a sense of **ego enrichment** or personal growth because of the knowledge they are acquiring.

The first four **Es** can best be provided through a host or teacher who is also a real human being with problems, concerns, feelings that can be shared by learners, and with whom they can empathize. These first four Es can also be expressed in the *transformation* section of the script which is often presented as a mini-drama, in which regularly appearing characters can be used to engage the emotions and stimulate the empathy of the learners. The final **E**—ego enrichment—comes as learners make use, in their own communities, of what they are learning from the broadcast lessons.

Knowing How to Write for the Chosen Medium

It is always necessary for the writer to have a thorough understanding of the medium that will be used for the programs. Writing for radio is very different from writing for television; writing for either of these media is very different from writing for the stage. Writing for the Internet is again different from any of these. Writers who have had little or no previous experience in radio or television (currently, the most popular media for distance education in developing countries) would do well to study the guidelines in the other books in this series.*

All writers, whether they have previous experience in the chosen medium or not, should also learn and abide by the following points that are important in the presentation of all Edu-tainment programs.

---

*de Fossard, Esta. *Communication for Behavior Change, Vol. 1: Writing and Producing Radio Dramas*; de Fossard, Esta and Riber John. *Communication for Behavior Change, Vol. 2: Writing and Producing for Television and Film*, Sage Publications India Pvt. Ltd.

INITIAL GUIDELINES FOR WRITERS AND DIRECTORS OF EDU-TAINMENT PROGRAMS

While most of the following guidelines apply particularly to writers, some apply equally to program producers and directors.

Indicate Optional Cuts

An experienced writer knows fairly accurately how many pages of script are needed for a specific radio or television broadcast time. Even with the greatest care, however, scripts can run over time when they are being recorded. Because of the vital importance of not omitting any of the instructional parts of the program, the writer should clearly indicate what parts of the script can be omitted if necessary. Known as **optional cuts**, these segments are usually marked as follows:

TEACHER: So, my friends, you have seen how Salma overcame the difficulties in her community by applying the 3P rule: patience, politeness, persistence.

OP CUT: It seems that it was a beautiful sunny day when Salma met with the community leaders, and perhaps the sunshine helped to put them in a good mood.

Follow the Curriculum Guide Exactly

Check every script to be sure that every detail of content in the Curriculum Guide has been included correctly. Always check with a member of the Script Support Team if there are any questions—however minimal or insignificant they seem. The writer's job is always to maintain **Q and A: Quality and Accuracy.**

Number the Topic Points being Presented

The writer should adopt the habit of having the 'teacher' in the lesson list and number the main points of the lesson. Numbering greatly helps the learners to recall the main points. For example, the 'teacher' might say to the listening audience: 'There are **three** important points to teach our families about care of the pregnant woman: (1) eat nutritious food, (2) avoid heavy work, (3) get plenty of rest. Let me repeat those **three** important points ....'

Avoid Using a Comic Character to Teach the Lesson

Virtually everybody enjoys comedy and many, if not most, successful dramatists like to include some comedy in their work. Even tragedies can benefit from occasional bits of comedy as Shakespeare so aptly demonstrated in his tragedy *King Lear*. However, using a comic character to teach a serious lesson is not easy and it is usually better for writers to try and avoid doing this. Certainly, the program (no matter what the format) can include a humorous character, and certainly the 'teacher' can use small amounts of gentle humor while presenting the lesson, but using a very foolish or clown-like character as the instructor is not a good idea. It is important to remember that learners must totally **trust** the teacher and the information he or she is presenting.

Indicate within Each Script where Each of the 6T Process of Teaching is Presented

Ways in which the 6Ts can be shown within each program are demonstrated in the script samples in this book (See page 96 for a description of the 6T processes).

Use the Approved Script Layout

Radio and TV script writing each has its own approved form of script presentation. It is extremely helpful to everyone using the script if the writers abide by these guidelines.

SCRIPT PAGE LAYOUT

The pages of the sample programs in this book demonstrate how scripts should be presented. Every script—whether radio or TV—should have a cover page that is, preferably, a copy of the Curriculum Guide page for the program. At the very least, the cover page must list the objectives and purposes of the program as they were given in the Curriculum Guide.

    Radio script cover pages should also list the names of characters who are to appear in this program, and the sound effects (SFX) and music that will be needed. This information assists the director to know which actors to call and to be sure that all necessary sound effects are on file at the time of program recording.

Individual pages are all numbered showing the total number of pages as well as the individual page number (for example, 3 of 9) and each speech or dialogue is numbered on the page. Some writers prefer to start with the number 1 on each new page; others prefer to carry the numbering forward throughout the script. Either method is acceptable. With radio scripts, no dialogue should be broken from one page to the next because this can cause difficulties for the actor who is reading directly into the microphone from the script.

Page Headers. Each page should have a page header that indicates: name of the program; lesson number and topic; writer's name; page number and total number of pages. Some program managers also like the page header to include the date on which the script was written or to indicate whether it is a 'draft' or 'final' version of the script. This procedure helps avoid inadvertent recording of the wrong version of the script.

Television Script Layout can be done in one of two ways. One method, which is most typically used by film producers is the 'Page Layout' method; the other is the 'column' method (see page 92). Whichever method is used, however, there are certain standard requirements:

- **Each page header** includes the title of the drama, usually given in capital (uppercase) letters and underlined; the number and title of the episode or program and the name of the author. As with radio scripts, some program managers like the page header to indicate whether this script is a draft or final version.
- **Pages must be numbered.** Some directors prefer a numbering system like that used on radio scripts, giving the number of the current page together with the total number of pages in the complete script (for example, 4 of 44). Other directors are content with just having each page numbered at the bottom. But the important point is that every page should be clearly numbered.
- **Scene numbering and setting should be given in a standard manner.** The scene number is listed on the left-hand side of the page, perhaps in capital (uppercase) letters, together with the scene location, showing:

  Interior or Exterior
  Actual Location (for example: By the river)
  Time—in terms such as 'day', 'night', 'early morning'.

- **Description of Action.** Details about action start at the left-hand margin in lower case letters. A double space is left between the scene description and the action description. A double space is left after Description of Action before the dialogue lines start.
- **Dialogue.** The name of the character speaking is given in capital (uppercase) letters in the middle of the page. The actual words to be spoken are printed UNDER

the character's name in short lines of no more than 40 characters (including spaces). Many writers and directors prefer pica type, which they find easier to read than elite. The reason for this presentation of the dialogue in short lines is to create a script where one page equals one minute of film. All dialogue lines should be double-spaced.

- **Simultaneous Action.** If the actor is required to make some action (such as shaking hands) while speaking, the writer's instructions for this action are given in parentheses immediately following the character's name. For example:

  NURSE: (pointing to a chair)
  Please take a seat, and we can have a look at your child and his problems.

Alternate TV Page Layout

Increased use of computers for script writing has led to the development of a new page layout that many writers and directors now use for TV scripts. This layout is demonstrated in the following section of a script page:

Scene No.	Location/Action/ Time of Day	Dialogue	Notes
3	School Playground. Morning. Children are playing on swing. Teacher enters scene.	Teacher: Children, children, listen to me … There is a hurricane coming. We must all move inside.	Thunder noise in background.
	The children all begin to run in different directions … in fear. Many are shouting or calling for their parents.	Teacher (shouting): Children. BE QUIET. Do not be afraid. Just follow me into the basement … Hurry.	

The layout would continue like this through all pages of the script.

As well as these general guidelines, there are specific guidelines for writers of radio and of television, as follows: (Guidelines for Internet program writers are included in the Internet section of this book—Chapters 12–15).

WRITING FOR A SPECIFIC MEDIUM: RADIO

Guidelines for Distance Educational Writing for Radio

Locations

Restrict the number of locations that are used throughout all programs, and select an identifying **SFX** for each location. This identifying SFX should be used briefly at the commencement of every scene that takes place in that location. For example, if one of the commonly used locations is a health clinic, the introductory sound might be people talking and babies crying in the background. This SFX would be used at the commencement of every clinic scene and gradually faded under the dialogue and out. Alternatively, the location can be identified through comments from the characters in the scene. For example, a community health worker can open the scene by saying 'Good Morning Glossie. What brings you here to the Health Clinic this morning?'

Sound Effects

Sound effects should be limited and used only when absolutely necessary, such as at the beginning of a scene. It is important to remember that the emphasis of Edu-tainment programs is on the teaching more than the story. An understanding of how to keep sound effects minimal can be gained by reading the scripts in Chapters 6 and 7 of this book.

Music

Music, like sound effects, should be kept to a minimum. It can be used to introduce and close the program and to identify a change of scene. In Edu-tainment programs, it should NOT be used to provide emotional background; this is more successfully accomplished by well-constructed dialogue and good acting.

Use of Names

Because they cannot be seen by their audience, characters in radio programs should address each other by name more often than they would in real life or on television. It is particularly necessary that characters address each other by name in the opening of each scene so that the listening audience will know who is in the scene.

Short Speeches or Dialogues

Absorbing information by listening alone is challenging for many people, especially those who are not accustomed to learning this way. For this reason, all radio speeches or dialogues should be limited to no more than five or six typed lines at the very most. Instructional segments in particular should be presented in clear, concise statements. The example scripts in this book demonstrate how a teaching topic can be broken into small pieces without losing the main point of the lesson.

Revealing Personality

The writer must be sure that the teacher and characters who appear regularly in the programs have distinct personalities. In the case of radio, this personality is best revealed by the way the character talks, and by the way other characters react to her/him. Writers can learn a lot about the use of character identity through speech simply by listening to everyday conversations of the people around them. Some people speak in very brief sentences; others rattle on; some people ask a lot of questions; others repeat themselves, and so on. Good radio writers know that a great deal is revealed about personality through the way a character speaks.

WRITING FOR A SPECIFIC MEDIUM: TELEVISION

Guidelines for Distance Educational Writing for Television

Limit the Number of Locations and Actors (Artists) Needed

This has to be done in order to keep down costs and shooting time, and to avoid confusing the audience. It is a good idea to have the main teaching segment (the opening segment of the program) always in the same location. Situations that are used for showing the audience how to transform knowledge into action can be varied, but even then these should be restricted to perhaps five or six different locations (for a 52-program project). The limiting of these locations not only cuts down on time and cost, but also maintains a sense of reality: in real life, a community worker typically interacts with community members in a limited number of places.

Ensure Appropriate Action

It can be very tempting in educational programs to spend a lot of the time with the camera focused on the 'teacher' while s/he is doing nothing but stand still and deliver the lesson. This type of presentation can be very boring for the viewing audience. It is better to present the teaching segments in a setting that allows a certain amount of natural action, even if some of that action is only personal characteristic movement of one or two of the characters: writing on a blackboard; holding up pictures for the learners to see, drinking tea while teaching, and other personal actions.

Avoid 'Ping-Pong' Dialogue

Ping-pong dialogue is named after the game of table tennis, which is also called 'ping-pong' and in which the ball goes backward and forward from one player to the other. 'Ping-pong' dialogue describes the presentation of dialogue when two people are conversing and the camera jumps backward and forward from the face of one speaker to the other. Such shooting can be very distracting for the viewers and makes it difficult for them to concentrate on the teaching point. If it is necessary that two characters converse alone, the writer should ensure that they are presented in a location that makes it possible for them to be doing something together, and for the director to shoot the scene from several different directions and angles.

Pay Particular Attention to Lesson Visual Accuracy

In the presentation of certain types of lessons, it is vitally important that the director calls upon an expert to ensure that the visual presentation is exactly correct. Such activities as weighing a child, taking a person's blood pressure, giving an injection should be filmed under the watchful eye of an expert to ensure that they are done absolutely correctly. The writer should indicate in the script those places where expert guidance will be needed during the filming.

Avoid Visual Distraction

It is self-evident that viewers like to have something interesting to watch as they look at the television screen. Television writers and directors alike pay considerable attention to the picture in which the action of the program is taking place. In Edu-tainment programs, it is necessary to ensure that there is nothing in the shooting that could lead to distraction for the learners. Distraction can be avoided by ensuring that the locations selected by the writer are not likely to be interrupted by local people curious to see what is going on during the filming. Such activities as uninvited people watching the shoot in the background, young children playing within camera range, animal or traffic noises can easily override the teaching points. Care must be taken to avoid any such distraction by setting the action as much as possible in a studio or in locations where such activities can be avoided.

LESSON CONSTRUCTION PATTERN—THE 6T PROCESS OF TEACHING

Writers doing Edu-tainment writing (and other forms of Distance Education writing) for the first time are often uncertain of how to ensure that the programs they write cover all elements of good teaching. A guideline that has proved of great value to many writers is the 6T Process of Teaching.

The 6T pattern is as follows:

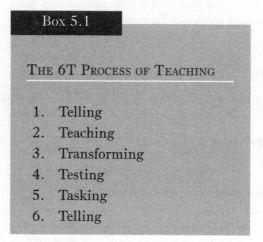

Box 5.1

THE 6T PROCESS OF TEACHING

1. Telling
2. Teaching
3. Transforming
4. Testing
5. Tasking
6. Telling

Telling

A good teacher gives students—at the outset of the lesson—a clear understanding of the topic they are about to study. The *telling* process is a simple statement of the topic together with a brief explanation of its importance. In Edu-tainment programs, the topic can be introduced by a 'teacher' or host at the beginning of the program in a direct manner, or it can be introduced more subtly in a mini-drama, as can be seen in the episode of *Under the Green Umbrella* on page 165.

This first *Telling* process can also be used to remind learners of the important points of the previous lesson, that is, what was **told** in the last lesson.

Teaching

The second step in the process is actually *teaching* the main points of the lesson. The learners should be made aware that this is a teaching segment even if it is presented in a format that is different from a typical classroom. There are a variety of ways in which the teaching can be done, several of which are demonstrated in the sample scripts in this book.

Transforming

The third process is of major importance, and all too often overlooked, even in classroom teaching. This third process is designed to encourage the students to *transform* newly acquired knowledge into practical skill and make use of that skill. All too often (even in school classrooms), students are given factual knowledge without any guidance as to how to transform those facts into use in daily life. This section, therefore, must demonstrate to learners how they can use what they have learned, either to improve their own lives or to pass it on to their community or clients. In each program, learners must be given a clear example of how they can best transform the facts they have learned into practical use. It is this transformation of knowledge into action that is the most vital part of their role as behavior change supporters.

In this **transform** part of the script, the writer has rather more creative freedom. It is also in this part of the script that the writer can include some open-ended questions to encourage learners to consider how they could transform the new knowledge for use in their own lives. (Some guidelines for open-ended questioning are included on page 98 in this chapter).

Testing

Part 4 of the Teaching Process invites the learners to be sure that they have absorbed all the necessary facts from the day's lesson. In radio and television distance education programs this testing is often achieved by the use of **Interactive Questions**. Interactive questions allow the learners to give an immediate oral response to questions from the teacher about what has been taught. Interactive questions can come in the middle and at the end of the program, or just at the end. Interactive questions must be carefully structured if they are to achieve their purpose. (Guidelines for writing and using Interactive Questions are given in this chapter on page 99.) Each of the script samples in this book shows how interactive questions are used for testing purposes.

Tasking

In this segment of the program, learners are given a simple **task** or assignment (homework) for the coming week. In the assignment, they can try out with their clients or their community what they learned during the lesson. If desired, they can be invited to provide a written report on the results of their assignment.

Telling

At the end of each program, there should be a brief announcement in which the teacher or host **tells** the students the topic for the next lesson. At the same time, there can be a brief reference to the 'story' environment in which the lessons are taking place, perhaps stressing the suspense on which today's episode of the story is ending.

Adhering to this pattern does not mean that the programs will be boring, or that there is no place for the writer's imagination. The main advantage of the 6T process is that writers have a clear guideline to follow which is designed to help learners know, eventually almost subconsciously, what to expect in each lesson. This understanding makes it easier for them to concentrate on and learn the important lesson points.

GUIDELINES FOR USING OPEN-ENDED QUESTIONS

One of the challenges of Distance Education for adults is finding a way to have learners take an active part in the lesson when there is no teacher physically present. This difficulty can be overcome to some degree by the use of questions—either open-ended questions or interactive testing questions.

Open-ended questions are those for which there is no one correct or predetermined answer. Open-ended questions invite learners to consider their personal response to a question, and for this reason open-ended questions can be used very effectively during the **transforming** process in the lesson. For example, perhaps the program shows—in the transforming process—that the community HIV counselor has learned of a man refusing to allow an HIV-infected neighbor into his house. The writer can interrupt the story at that point and have the 'teacher' pose a question to the learners. The question might be, 'What would you say to the man in this situation?' There would be a PAUSE to allow learners to think about the question and give a short oral response. Then, the 'teacher' could make a comment such as 'Yes. There are several ways in which a community health worker could respond to this situation. As some of you may have said, your answer will depend to some degree on how well you know the man and whether it is wise to speak to him alone. But, as many of you know, the important point is to be patient, speak gently and offer encouragement. So now, let us listen and see how (name of the fictional counselor in the story) dealt with this very same situation.'

Obviously, program teachers or hosts cannot hear the comments from the audience, but can respond to them in a way that suggests the answers were heard or at least correctly guessed. The use of occasional open-ended questions like this can encourage the learners to feel engaged in the lesson as they would be in a typical classroom lesson. It also encourages the learners to realize that their opinions are important and allows them to weigh their own decisions against those demonstrated in the lesson.

In creating the open-ended questions, the writer must be very sure to avoid questions that require only a 'Yes' or 'No' answer, such as, 'Do you agree with what the counselor said in this scene?' It is also important to always introduce open-ended questions with the same cue words (words that alert the learners to what is coming). For example, the 'teacher' might say, 'and now I'd like to know your opinion' every time before introducing the open-ended question. Examples of how this can be done are seen in some of the script samples in Chapters 6–10.

GUIDELINES FOR INTERACTIVE QUESTIONS FOR THE TESTING PORTION OF THE PROGRAM

One of the easiest and most successful ways of providing an immediate test of what learners have gained from the program is the use of **Interactive Questions.**

All **Interactive Questions** should be based on the content of the lesson heard in the current program. The questions are carefully designed to allow and encourage the listening audience to respond immediately and orally, and to give them a sense of confidence in their ability to learn and recall important information. The following guidelines can be used for Interactive Questioning:

1. A cue (or prompt) is used to alert listeners that a question is coming to which they are expected to respond. Cue words should be simple, like 'Tell me', or even more simply, 'Question'. These same words are used immediately before each question for which the learners are expected to give an immediate oral answer. For example: 'Tell me, how often must a woman take the oral contraceptive pill in order to prevent pregnancy?' or 'Question: What are three childhood diseases that can be treated easily at home?' Learners quickly become accustomed to the cue and are ready to listen to and answer the question.

2. Questions are based only on information that has been taught in the current program. The interactive question session always comes after the instruction has been given and demonstrated in the program. There are two reasons for this: (a) listeners have a better chance of answering the questions correctly, and (b) the interactive session serves as a reinforcement of the learning and a way for learners to correct any information they might have misunderstood in the program.

3. There is a brief Pause for the Listener Response (PLR) immediately after each interactive question. The media director must time these pauses carefully so that they are long enough for a response, but not so long that there is 'dead air' left before the answer is given. Generally a 2 second pause is long enough for a one or two word answer. An answer requiring a longer sentence may need 5 seconds. No question should require more than a 5 second oral response.

4. The expected answers are short. Interactive questioning sessions in distance education programs should require clear, short answers from the listeners. The aim of these interactive question sessions is for listeners to check quickly and simply that they have heard and absorbed correctly the important information being offered. For example: In the Nepal script 'Service Brings Reward', (page 145) Bimal asks the question 'What do we call a man who cares for his wife and takes her as an equal partner with equal rights?' The listeners are expected to give no more than two or three words in the answer: 'Vibeke Logne'

or 'A Vibeke Logne'. If there is more than one point required in any answer, the host should make this clear. For example: 'Tell me the FOUR things a family should do to prepare for a safe birth.' The expected answers must be four brief points.

5. Answers are given in the words listeners are likely to use. Generally, learners will give brief, one or two word answers to interactive questions. They do not normally answer with long, correctly structured sentences.

For example. After the question, 'Tell me, who are the family members most likely to be affected by malaria?' listeners would be likely to respond with the answer 'Women and young children'. They would be unlikely to give the answer as a whole sentence: 'Family members most likely to be affected by malaria are women and young children.' The host, therefore, should give—after the pause—the brief answer that learners are most likely to give.

6. **Questions are worded in a language very similar to that in which the instruction was given.** For example: If a character in the teaching or transforming part of the script says: 'The first thing we health workers do to detect malnutrition in children is to take the child's weight,' the interactive question would be, 'TELL ME, what is the first thing that health workers do to detect malnutrition in children?' The wording of the question and the wording in which the information was taught are very similar, making it easier for listeners to give correct responses. Encouraging correct responses motivates the audience to keep listening and to keep learning.

7. The actual brief answer is given immediately after the pause. Listeners need to and want to hear the correct answer as soon as possible; so the brief, correct answer must be given immediately following the PLR. Words of encouragement can be added after the answer. For example. 'Thirteen or fourteen. That's right ...' Or 'Thirteen or fourteen. Yes.' Avoid using the words, 'You are right,' because this might inadvertently reinforce a wrong answer that a listener has given. It is safer to say,

'Yes' or 'That's right' FOLLOWING the teacher's statement of the correct answer.

8. Avoid questions requiring only 'yes' or 'no' for an answer. If listeners are required to give only 'yes' or 'no' for an answer, they have a 50 percent chance of being correct no matter which word they use. The point of interactive questioning is to have listeners recall important information that they should be learning.

9. **Rhetorical questions are avoided throughout the program.** Rhetorical questions are those that do not require an answer, such as 'I think we've all had that sort of experience, haven't we?' A comment like this, stated as a question, usually does not require an answer. Rhetorical questions should be avoided because listeners can become confused easily and think they are being called upon to give an answer. In fact, questions addressed to the learners should be avoided altogether except in the Interactive Question on Open-ended Question segments.

10. **Questions addressed to other people in the program are clearly identified.** For example, if one host (or teacher) in the program asks a question of another host (or teacher), the questioner should address the respondent by name. *For example*: 'Frank, what is our topic going to be next week?' This makes it quite clear that the question is addressed to Frank, and not to the listeners. Care should be taken also to avoid using the cue words (such as 'tell me') in questions that are addressed to other people in the program. The cue words should be used **only** for questions addressed to the learners.

Selecting an Edu-tainment Program Format

One of the most interesting, and often most challenging decisions to be made in preparing Edu-tainment programs for distance education courses is the program format in which the lessons will be presented. The selected format will have an obvious effect on the way the program is designed, written and presented to the learners. The challenge for the writer in all formats is to create a simple, but engaging and culturally appropriate background into which the clear educational points can be inserted.

Distance education programs designed to fit the requirements of Edu-tainment can be presented in a number of different formats, most of which differ to some degree from formats used for Entertainment–Education.

Format Differences for Entertainment–Education and Edu-tainment

Entertainment–Education programs are designed to encourage individual behavior change leading to overall social change. For this reason, most successful behavior change programs for the general public are presented in the serial drama format that portrays characters in the various stages of accepting the change. Audience members identify and empathize with those characters most like themselves and can be motivated thereby to move gradually and naturally toward accepting and practicing the change themselves. A serial drama can present a variety of characters, all in different stages of moving toward permanent change. These stages include:

- having no knowledge of the change
- having knowledge but no approval of the change or no clear motivation to make the change
- having tried the change and found it either hard to maintain because of lack of resources, or of no obvious advantage to their own lives
- having adopted the change and being now eager to encourage others to adopt it.

Edu-tainment programs, on the other hand, are not designed so much to encourage behavior change as to **teach** certain professional or semi-professional people how to encourage and maintain appropriate behavior change in their community. These programs therefore come straight to the point of being a teaching tool, and—for this reason—they do not have to be presented in a serial format. They can be equally successful in a variety of other formats. Whatever the chosen format, however, there are guidelines that can assist the writer to create a program that is successful at educating the chosen audience while attracting and holding their attention.

Guidelines for creating the following Edu-tainment formats for radio or television are provided in later chapters, together with a sample script of each format:

- The fictional workshop
- The drama series
- The drama serial
- The modified (or fictionalized) magazine
- The case study

The 6T processes of teaching can be worked comfortably into any of these formats as is demonstrated in the sample scripts.

Reality Programming which is gaining popularity in some behavior change circles can be used—with certain limitations—for Edu-tainment purposes. Reality programming makes use of real people, telling their own real-life stories. There is no doubt that such stories can be very powerful emotionally as well as inspirational for audience members and can be used to inspire behavior change. For distance education purposes, however, where lesson accuracy is vital, the reality format should be used with caution. Consistency and Correctness of message are important in all behavior change programs; in teaching programs, message (or lesson) precision is essential. Modified versions of reality programming can be used, as is seen in the example in *Under the Green Umbrella* where real stories of actual health workers are used, but with some modification and editing. (Details of this are given in the introduction to the program in Chapter 9.)

Sample Scripts

The purpose of the scripts in the following chapters is to provide new or inexperienced distance education writers with some samples of program formats that they can follow or adapt as they learn the skills of Edu-tainment writing. This is not to suggest that these are the only possible formats, but each of those demonstrated in the following chapters has proved to be relatively easy to learn, and successful when applied correctly.

Guidelines for creating Internet programs are included in the Internet section (Chapters 12–15).

6

EDU-TAINMENT FORMATS—RADIO
The Fictional Workshop

Radio programs are cheaper and easier to produce, and can be
every bit as effective as television for Distance Education.

THE FICTIONAL WORKSHOP: RADIO

The fictional workshop is more suited to radio than to television because radio can more easily present a believable workshop even with a limited number of actors. The idea of setting Edu-tainment programs in a workshop might seem at first to be boring. After all, Edu-tainment is supposed to deliver the clear instruction in an entertaining setting and a workshop does not, at first, sound very entertaining. There are ways, however, in which this fairly obvious setting can be made attractive. The secret lies in the variety of characters who are present at the fictional workshop and in the addition of a minimal background story that truly attracts and holds the attention of the audience.

GUIDELINES FOR WRITING THE FICTIONAL WORKSHOP

Workshop Characters

A good writer enjoys creating fascinating, but believable characters and the fictional workshop is an ideal setting for character creation. The characters in the workshop should be typical of the type of people who would be likely to attend such training in the area to which the programs are being broadcast. The writer, therefore, should learn as much as possible about the intended audience before establishing the characters. It is also helpful for the writer to think about personality differences that would allow the characters to interact in an entertaining, but believable manner. This suggests that characters should be:

- limited in number so that the audience has a chance to get to know each one personally
- varied in personality
- varied in age to some degree
- both men and women (if this is appropriate to the learning audience)

- varied in their reasons for attending the workshop
- of different levels of experience with the main topic of the workshop

It is usually advantageous to have one character who is humorous, but who certainly is not a complete idiot or clown, and who does **not** provide the main teaching points.

Workshop Personalities

Attendance at an actual workshop (not necessarily related to the topic of the project) can assist the writer to learn how different people, including the facilitator or teacher, behave when in a learning group with others. Typically, the following personalities can be found in almost any workshop:

- the dominant, the participant who believes s/he already knows more than anyone else and wants to make everyone aware of this,
- the shy person, who tries to avoid being called upon to give answers, and who sometimes must be asked to speak up so that others can hear what s/he is saying,
- the critic, who tries to show that s/he knows more than others in the room, perhaps even more than the teacher, by criticizing their comments,
- the comic who, knowingly or unknowingly—keeps others in the workshop happily amused,
- the reluctant learner, who did not want to attend the workshop but was required to by a boss or someone else. Sometimes this person can become increasingly enthusiastic about the topic and perhaps finishes up as the star student,
- the helper, a learner who is called upon by the facilitator to help with small tasks, such as writing on the blackboard, but who otherwise plays a small role.

The personalities of the various participants can be revealed in the way they respond to the general topic and to questions put by the workshop facilitator. Various personal characteristics also can be revealed as the characters chat together before and after each workshop session.

Limiting the Characters

An actual workshop might typically have as many as 20 or 30 participants, but it is not advisable to have that many characters in a radio fictional workshop. The audience needs to get to know several characters very well so that they can anticipate how each of them will behave and how each one will respond to the teaching. The advantage of doing this type of workshop on radio is that it is relatively easy to suggest that there are many more characters in the workshop than are actually heard in the drama. Certain characters can be referred to by name quite frequently, even though they never speak. Others (like Charles in the sample script) can make an occasional brief comment, which is actually performed by one of the main actors adopting a slight voice change.

Character Profiles

In creating characters for a fictional workshop Edu-tainment series, it is valuable for the writer to create a clear character profile of each of the characters, including such details as:

- age
- sex
- general appearance
- marital status
- number and age of children, if any
- reason for attending the workshop
- past, present and future life as it relates to the workshop
- behavior habits (always being late; eating in the workshop; forgetting other people's names; singing or humming the same tune when entering the workshop, etc.)
- speech idiosyncrasies (always saying 'excuse me' before giving an answer, or 'I'm sorry' before asking a question; giving very brief answers or giving unnecessarily lengthy answers) and so on.
- attitude towards others in the workshop.

The Role of Each Character

Each of the main characters in the fictional workshop should have a specific role to play in helping deliver the 'lesson' as well as in the background story. One of the characters should be the least experienced of the participants and is the one who, quite naturally, can ask very obvious questions (which some of the audience might well need to or want to ask). Another character, perhaps, always gives very, clear brief answers to the facilitator's questions and these answers constitute the main points that listeners are expected to recall at the end of the program. If one character is particularly designed to be really humorous, s/he should not be one that the audience relies upon for correct topic knowledge. A humorous character should concentrate on being humorous rather than also trying to be reliably knowledgeable.

The Background Story

As well as relating the activities within the workshop where the serious learning is taking place, the fictional workshop should contain an entertaining 'background story', which takes up very little of the broadcast time of each episode, but which provides the enticement that keeps listeners in suspense. This background story is like a very minimal serial drama, in that it provides a certain degree of suspense that keeps the learners wanting to come back for the next program in order to find out how the story will end.

In this fictional workshop script sample from the series *Our Neighbourhood* from Zambia, the ongoing background story is a mystery involving the workshop facilitator, Sister Evalina. The following script shows how the mystery is mentioned just enough to attract and hold the listeners' attention without detracting from the main educational points of the program.

SAMPLE: FICTIONAL WORKSHOP

Introduction to Episode 9 of 'Our Neighbourhood' Written by Nikki Ashley:

'Our Neighbourhood' is an Edu-tainment series that was produced in Zambia to provide new knowledge and skill-upgrading for community health volunteers. In true representation of these volunteers in Zambia, the characters are of varied ages, experience and backgrounds. Those who appear in this episode appear in all episodes of the series. Because each script in this series had to be produced in eight different ethnic languages, the number of characters was limited to facilitate ease of production and to help keep production costs down.

The characters are:

Robert: the host who introduces and 'presents' the program every week.

Sister Evalina: the workshop facilitator. She is about 40 years old, an attractive personality with considerable knowledge. But, she has a secret that is only finally revealed in the final episode of the series: she has a daughter who had problems with drugs and who became a prostitute. This young girl is thrown into prison and contracts HIV/AIDS. Without knowing about her daughter, the participants in the workshop realize that something is troubling Sister Evalina and they try hard to find out what it is. In this episode, the participants are aware that their 'teacher' is distracted and not paying attention. They (like the audience) become more and more curious to find out what is going on in her life.

Lumbiwe: a young girl of about 19 years of age who truly wants to be of service to her community. She is shy and always afraid that she is going to give the wrong answers to Sister Evalina's questions. Everyone in the workshop likes Lumbiwe and they are very angry when, one day, she is attacked and almost raped by a young vagrant. From that moment on, Bashi Lulu insists on seeing her safely to her home after each workshop meeting. Everyone at the workshop refers to her as 'Lumbi'.

Bo Nyambe (Bo = Mister): an ex-policeman. He is egotistical and suspicious of everyone. He is convinced that Sister Evalina is implicated in something criminal, and that it is his business to find out what it is. He thinks that he knows everything and often contradicts what others in the workshop say.

Bashi Lulu: an elderly man, gentle and shy, who has the habit of saying 'who ... me?' every time Sister Evalina asks him a question. He used to work in an office, but now he spends his time learning as much as he can about how he can help improve the health of his community.

Charles: The role of Charles is played by the same actor who plays the host, using a different voice. The script writers wisely limited the number of characters in the drama, by having certain members of the workshop who hardly ever speak. Charles is one of these. Other workshop participants and Sister Evalina refer to these 'invisible' characters by name, so that listeners have the impression that there are many people in the workshop. The few words or lines that these characters occasionally have are spoken by other cast members using slightly different voices.

The 6 Teaching steps have been identified in this script to show how naturally they are blended into the program.

SCRIPT COVER PAGE

Our Neighbourhood—Episode 9: Program Duration: 30 minutes
Writer: Nikki Ashley

Measurable Objectives: After this program, Neighbourhood Health Committee (NHC) workers will:

KNOW:
- The value and importance of breast-feeding.
- How to encourage mothers to exclusively breast-feed for the first six months of the child's life.

DO:
- Encourage and promote exclusive breast-feeding for six months among community women.

- Advise mothers that they can get correct advice about the relationship between breast-feeding and HIV/AIDS from the Health Center.

HAVE AN ATTITUDE OF:
Feel confident discussing breast-feeding with the community members and feel assured to encourage mothers to seek advice from Health Center or trained community members about breast-feeding-related questions.

PURPOSE:
The purposes of this program are:

- To teach NHC workers how to instruct mothers to breast-feed their children correctly, and
- To motivate NHC workers to encourage mothers to go to the Health Center for correct advice on all matters relating to breast-feeding.

Cast of Characters	SFX and Music
Host-Robert	Pg. 1. L. 1 Intro Song
Sister Evalina	Pg. 1. L. 4. Music break
Lumbiwe	Pg. 2. L. 6. Chair moving
Bo Nyambe	Pg. 8. L. 1. Workshop Music
Bashi Lulu	Pg. 8. L. 4. Workshop Music
Charles	

OUR NEIGHBOURHOOD: Program No. 9
Writer: Nikki Ashley
Part A: Breast-Feeding   Final: Page 1 of 8

1/1 INTRODUCTION SONG:
In our neighbourhood, to be happy and healthy,
We must all work together, we must all work together.

1.	ANNOUNCER:	'Our Neighbourhood' is a series of programs for Neighbourhood Health Committee members. 'Our Neighbourhood' looks at common health issues and how Neighbourhood Health Committee members can help their communities to overcome them.
2.	HOST:	Hello NHC members. Welcome to OUR NEIGHBOURHOOD. I'm your host, Robert. Today, we'll join the Golide NHC Workshop in their lesson on Child Health.

OUR NEIGHBOURHOOD: Program No. 9
Writer: Nikki Ashley
Part A: Breast-Feeding   Final: Page 2 of 8

---

3. HOST: As always, I hope you'll take an active part—by answering
                        my questions, and writing down important points. You'll
                        need pencil and paper. If you have the booklet, 'Health Care
                        in The Community', and—or—a 'Simplified Guide', you may
                        want to get them as well. Okay, let's have some music while
                        you get everything together.

4. **MUSIC BREAK—SCENE CHANGE**

5.   Now, let's go over to Golide NHC Workshop. Our facilitator,
                        Sister Evalina should be just about to arrive ...

6. **WORKSHOP MUSIC IN AND UNDER**

7. **SFX**   **CAST CHATTER (AD LIB)**

8. Sr E: (COMING IN—PRE-OCCUPIED) Hello everyone.

9. **CAST RESPONSES (AD LIB)**

10. Sr E: Are Robert and our radio guests here?

11. HOST: We're here, Sister Evalina

12. Sr E: (INTERRUPTS) Ah, yes, there you are. Good. In that case, we
                       can begin. I hope you all have 'HealthCare Within the Com-
                       munity' pages, pages 10 ... and er...(HESITATING)

13. **SFX PAGES TURNING**

14. Sr E: Yes ... 10 and 11. Good. (Pause) Umm—Charles, yes Charles—
                       can you come and write on the board for us today please?

15. **SFX CHAIR BEING MOVED**

    (CAST: WORRIED MUTTERS)

16. LUMBI: (WHISPERS OVER) Bashi Lulu—what's wrong with Sister
                       Evalina? She looks so worried today...

OUR NEIGHBOURHOOD: Program No. 9
Writer: Nikki Ashley
Part A: Breast-Feeding   Final: Page 3 of 8

TELLING:

17. Sr E:

Right. Settle down everyone. Our topic for the next six sessions is 'Child Health'. In Zambia, many children die before the age of five from infectious diseases. **In this session, we see how correct breast-feeding can help protect children from some of these diseases.** Charles, please write 'Breast-feeding' on the board. (PAUSE) Now, Bo Nyambe, how soon should a mother begin breast-feeding?

TEACHING:

18. BoNy:

Immediately after birth, Sister Evalina. A mother should breast-feed immediately, within one hour of giving birth. But—but the first yellow milk. It is dangerous for sure!

19. CAST MIXED REACTIONS. (AD LIB)

20. Sr E:

(OVER) That is not true, Bo Nyambe. The 'yellow milk' is very, very good. It contains natural 'medicine' that helps protect the new baby from diseases. I cannot stress this strongly enough to you all. A child must be put to the breast within one hour of birth. The 'yellow milk' is very special and protects the child from diseases, so the baby must have it.

21. BoNy:

Does this 'yellow milk' have another name, Sister Evalina?

22. Sr E:

Oh—didn't I mention that Bo Nyambe? It's proper name is 'Colostrum'. Charles, please write it for us. (SPELLING IT) COLOSTRUM. We must tell our community members that Colostrum helps protect the child from infection, so the baby must have it. All right, let's move on. How often should the child be allowed to breast-feed?

23. BLU:

Well, Sister Evalina, I think a mother should breast-feed as often as the child wants.

24. Sr E:

Yes, Bashi Lulu. A mother should breast-feed as often as the child wants. And the child must be allowed to breast-feed long enough to empty at least one breast! And at least eight times a day.

OUR NEIGHBOURHOOD: Program No. 9
Writer: Nikki Ashley
Part A: Breast-Feeding   Final: Page 4 of 8

25. CHAS:	(DISTANT) Um—what do I write on the board, Sister Evalina?
26. Sr E:	Oh, sorry Charles. What do you write on the board? Umm—write ... um ... 'Breast-feed whenever the child wants. At least eight times a day'. Now, what's next ... Where are we? Oh yes. Before we continue, maybe someone can review what we've talked about so far. Bashi Lulu, please.

REPETITION	*TEACHING*
27. BLU:	Who? Me? Breast-feeding should start within one hour of birth, beginning with the first yellow breast milk—'colostrum'— It contains natural protection against infection. Mothers should breast-feed whenever the child wants, at least eight times a day.
28. Sr E:	Thank you, Bashi Lulu ... Any questions?
29. LUMBI:	Sister Evalina, at the market I have seen mothers feed their newborns with bread, dipped in a cup of fizzy drink. That's bad isn't it?
30. Sr E:	Very bad, Lumbiwe. Breast milk contains everything the child needs for the first six months of life. No other food. No other liquid. Not even water. So when **should** a mother begin giving other foods and liquids?
31. Mr B:	When the baby is one year old.
32. LUMBI:	Not two years, Mr Beenzu?
33. BoNy:	Six months, Lumbiwe!
34. Mr B:	One year, Bana K!
35. LUMBI:	But my mother...
36. BoNy:	Back to focus please. Sister Evalina ... Sister Evalina?

OUR NEIGHBOURHOOD: Program No. 9
Writer: Nikki Ashley
Part A: Breast-Feeding   Final: Page 5 of 8

TRANSFORMING—INTRODUCTION

37. Sr E: Oh ... sorry, Bo Nyambe. Six months is correct. When we visit our community members, we must make sure they all understand that mothers should begin giving their babies other foods or liquids **only** when the babies reach six months of age. Charles write '6 months' so that we don't forget. We must help everyone in the community remember that at six months—and not before—a mother must slowly start giving the baby small amounts of other foods and liquids.

38. LUMBI: Does the mother stop breast-feeding then Sister Evalina? No I don't think so. Sorry. Silly question.

39. CAST TITTERS (AD LIB)

40. Sr E: It is not silly Lumbiwe. You did well to ask. We must remind mothers that as well as starting to give solid food, they must continue breast-feeding until the child is at least two years old. So Charles write 'two years' on the board. Umm—has anyone got questions?

41. LUMBI: Some people say that if a mother gets pregnant while she is breast-feeding, the milk gets poisonous and the child will die.

42. Sr E: Breast milk does not become poisonous Lumbiwe. (Pause) I think you can all see from this discussion, that there are many strange beliefs to do with breast-feeding. And it is OUR job to ensure that all our community members know the FACTS about breast-feeding.

43. CAST MURMURS (AD LIB)

44. Sr E: That is why it is so important that YOU know the facts, and YOU give the true information to your community. You may help to save a child's life!

OUR NEIGHBOURHOOD: Program No. 9
Writer: Nikki Ashley
Part A: Breast-Feeding   Final: Page 6 of 8

45. BoNy:	Sister Evalina, may I ask something—because my niece has problems. She told my wife that it hurts when she breast-feeds her baby.
46. Sr E:	And what did your wife tell her niece, Bo Nyambe?
47. BoNy:	She advised her to go to the Health Center for help.
48. Sr E:	That is right Bo Nyambe. Service Providers and Health Center staff will give mothers advice on breast-feeding ... including how to deal with problems. Anything else before we do our review?
49. BLU:	Last week, Sister Evalina, you mentioned that today we would also discuss breast-feeding and HIV/AIDS.
50. Sr E:	Oh—yes, Bashi Lulu. I seem to have forgotten that. What I wanted to say is that if a new mother knows she is—or thinks she may be—HIV positive, we must tell her to get advice from the Health Center about breast-feeding her baby.
51. LUMBI:	Surely, it is our duty as NHC members to advise ALL mothers that information about breast-feeding and about HIV and AIDS can be obtained from the Health Center.
52. Sr E:	That's right Lumbi. Now is there anything else? (PAUSE) No? (PAUSE) Bashi Lulu—maybe you can give us a quick review of this session?
53. BLU:	Breast-feeding should begin within one hour of birth. The first, yellow, milk, 'colostrum', must be given to the child. Breast milk is all that a child needs for the first six months. Then other liquids and foods must be introduced gradually. Breast-feeding should continue until the child is two years old. A mother must not stop breast-feeding if she becomes pregnant. If she suspects she is HIV positive, or if she has breast-feeding problems, she should go to the Health Center for help.

OUR NEIGHBOURHOOD: Program No. 9
Writer: Nikki Ashley
Part A: Breast-Feeding   Final: Page 7 of 8

TESTING:

54. Sr E:	Thank you, Bashi Lulu. Now dear radio listeners, it's testing time. **I will ask you some questions about breast-feeding. After each question I will pause, so that you can say your answer aloud.** Then I will say the answer, so that you can check if your own answer is correct. I will ask each question only once, so listen carefully.

55. SFX: BELL

56. Sr E:	Here's Question One: Tell me—what is the name of the first yellow breast milk that protects a newborn child's health?
57. *PLR*	*5 SECONDS*
58. Sr E:	Colostrum. Yes. Colostrum. Question Two: Tell me—at what age **must** a mother begin to give her child other food and liquid?
59. *PLR*	*5 SECONDS*
60. Sr E:	Six months. Yes. Six months. Question Three: Tell me—for how many years should a child be breast-fed?
61. *PLR*	*5 SECONDS*
62. Sr E:	Two years. Yes. Two years. And Question Four: Tell me—where must community members go for advice on breast-feeding?
63. *PLR*	*5 SECONDS*
64. Sr E:	The Health Center. Yes. To the Health Center. All right, that's our test for today. I hope you got the answers correct, so that you are now ready to advise **your** community members about correct breast-feeding.

65. CAST POSITIVE (AD LIB)

TASKING:

66. Sr E:	Very good. This week, my task for you is that you spend time teaching **your community** about breast-feeding and encouraging everyone in your community to encourage all mothers to breast-feed their babies correctly.

OUR NEIGHBOURHOOD: Program No. 9
Writer: Nikki Ashley
Part A: Breast-Feeding   Final: Page 8 of 8

67. **SFX: BELL**

68. Sr E: Now, it's time for a break. When you come back, our storyteller
                       Augustine will be here. His story will help us understand how
                       we can **transfer** our knowledge to our community members....
                       Unfortunately, I must go. I have some urgent business. So I
                       will leave you in the hands of Robert, our host.

69. **CAST CHATTER IN AND UNDER (AD LIB)**

70. LUMBI: (WHISPERS OVER) Bashi Lulu! Look! Bo Nyambe's packing
                       his things.

71. **WORKSHOP MUSIC UNDER**

72. BLU: Maybe, he has some urgent business, too, Lumbi.

73. LUMBI: Or is he following Sister Evalina because he's suspicious of her?

74. **WORKSHOP MUSIC UP AND FADE UNDER LINE 5**

75. HOST: So I'm in charge for the rest of the session! I hope I do as well
                       as Sister Evalina! Remember that you can find information
                       on Breast-feeding in your booklet, Health Care Within the
                       Community on pages 10 and 11...

76. **WORKSHOP MUSIC UP.**

These programs were originally designed not only to **teach** *community health volunteers
some of the basics of their trade, but also to* **demonstrate** *how community life can be greatly
improved through the work of volunteers. The second part of each program, therefore was presented by a storyteller, Augustine, whose weekly story was about a community health volunteer
and some of the difficulties he faced while working in the community. The idea of using a story
for the second half of each program came about for the following reasons:*

- *it is culturally appropriate in Zambia where storytelling is a traditional form of
  entertainment*
- *the programs had to be produced in 8 languages, so having one actor only—to read the
  story—rather than having many actors as would have been necessary in a drama, saved
  production costs and time*
- *so that the two halves of the program could be used separately in re-broadcasts, if desired.*

7

Edu-tainment Formats—Radio or TV
The Drama Series

A good TV Edu-tainment drama closely reflects the lives of the intended audience.

THE DRAMA SERIES: RADIO OR TV

A drama **series** is similar to a collection of short stories, with a new adventure being presented in each story, with its own suspense, question or climax coming to an end within one program. The drama **series** is different from a drama **serial**. A drama **serial** is an ongoing story. Each episode moves the story forward just a bit, in the same way that the chapter in a novel moves the story forward. Some degree of suspense or question is maintained from the very beginning of the serial, until the climax is reached at the end or very near to the end. The drama **serial** is very appropriate for Entertainment–Education projects where an ongoing story can demonstrate how members of a community can move—gradually—towards a new behavior. The drama **series** can be very effective in Edu-tainment programming because each separate 'story' can contain an individual lesson.

The stories in a drama **series** can involve the same main characters every time. Rather than being involved in an ongoing story, however, as they are in a serial, the characters appear in a new, complete story in each broadcast. Generally, there are one or two extra characters in each program who contribute to the story (and lesson) of the day, but have no role in any other program. The series format, therefore, works well for Edu-tainment distance education programs where a different topic or sub-topic is taught each week.

CHALLENGES OF WRITING A SERIES

The challenges of creating Edu-tainment programs in the series format include:

- creating an engaging story that can be completed within one program length (usually 20–30 minutes) while still allowing room for the actual teaching to be completely and adequately delivered
- telling the main part of the story through a limited number of regular characters

- limiting the number of 'extra' characters who are introduced into each program
- encouraging the learners to tune in to the next program when there is no ongoing suspense (as there is in drama serial) to hold their attention

THE IMPORTANCE OF CHARACTERS

In the writing of a series, as with the fictional workshop, a great deal of the success of the programs lies in the character presentation. Because there is usually no ongoing story suspense from episode to episode in a series as there is in a serial, the audience must be so strongly attracted to one or more of the characters, that they want to come back and 'meet' these characters again every week. In the following sample of an Edu-tainment series from India, it is the character of Badshah who has very strong appeal to the audience. Although he is employed in the somewhat humble position of a doctor's driver, he is a fascinating combination of wisdom and humor. Interestingly, it is his wisdom revealed in a very realistic and simple manner (often through analogies with aspects to real life), that makes him more appealing than does his humor. Wisdom is an essential part of Badshah's character. If he were humorous only, he could not play such an important role as he does in the drama. It is Badshah's serious concern for other people that allows him to be a positive role model for the Indian community health workers for whom these programs were designed. While it is Doctor Sahib who does the actual teaching, it is Badshah who reinforces the value of the work done by the health workers (the **transforming** part of each lesson).

REGULAR LOCATIONS

A successful drama series, whether delivered through radio or television, limits the locations in which the stories take place. The use of the same location for the teaching centerpiece of the story provides the audience with a type of 'anchor' that establishes some sense of permanence, even when each story is new and complete each week. On radio, sound effects can be used effectively to help the listening audience recognize when the action is taking place in a familiar location. For example, the *Pum Pum* sound of Badshah's car horn lets the audience know they are in the vicinity of the Doctor's house where each program begins.

DRAMA WITHIN A DRAMA

This Indian Edu-tainment series *Darpan* also illustrates effectively the use of a mini-drama within the main drama of each program. Each program involves the Doctor and his assistant, Behin ji didi as they deliver the 'lesson of the week' to the community nurses. The mini-drama which usually involves Badshah's interaction with various community citizens, provides the example of **Transformation** as the listeners see how Badshah, who is also learning from the doctor's teaching, encourages the villagers to learn, how to improve their own lives.

DRAMA SERIES: 'DARPAN' FROM INDIA

'DARPAN' is a Hindi word meaning 'Mirror'. The title is very fitting because the intention of these teaching programs is to encourage the learners to look at or reflect on their own lives as they listen to and learn from the programs. This 26-part distance education radio drama series was written with the main objectives of increasing the knowledge of Auxiliary Nurse Midwives (ANMs) and other Health Service Providers (HSPs) in Uttar Pradesh, India, about Family Planning, Maternal and Child Health, the importance of the girl child, and Reproductive Tract and Sexually Transmitted Infections. At the same time, the goal was to improve the Midwives' and Health Providers' use of Interpersonal Communication (IPC) skills and increase their self-esteem.

The main **attitude** or emotional focus the series aimed to encourage in HSPs was **confidence** in their ability to provide quality healthcare services, and **pride**, resulting from their improved self-image and appreciation from the community.

Each program in the series is an individual story involving the main characters, various HSPs and village community members.

The main characters in the drama series are:

SANGEETA—the main narrator/teacher for the series.

DOCTOR SAHIB—the rural doctor in charge of training the health workers. He lost his wife tragically during childbirth and ever since then, has devoted his entire life to helping people. He is a simple man of few words; he understands people, and is a good teacher.

BEHIN JI DIDI—the Assistant Nurse Midwife who assists the doctor in organizing training sessions for other health providers. There is a love–hate relationship between her and Badshah. She thinks he gets more than enough attention from the doctor and that he should remain 'within his own shoes'.

BADSHAH—a typical modern rural youth, 26+ who wanted to become a cine star, but ended up being a taxi driver instead. Now, he drives the vehicle owned by the health department and used by Doctor Sahib. He is a fun-loving person, but very wise, a great storyteller, who loves to sing and mix with people. He provides gentle humor in the story.

HARIYALI-VEHICLE—Badshah's old jeep, which serves as a symbol of 'life'. Like people, the vehicle needs looking after and proper 'food'; requires 'health' check-ups and has ups and downs, but manages to find its way along the road of life.

OTHER MINOR CHARACTERS appear in the drama each week; these include health service providers who are attending the various training workshops led by the Doctor and Behin ji, and various villagers whom Badshah meets when he and Hariyali go off on their own affairs while the training meetings are taking place.

DARPAN Episode 3: Final
Topic: Determination of Sex of the Child
Writer: Raj Khumar Jha

Objectives: After listening to this episode, the audience will:

KNOW:
A family is complete with no more than two children, even if both are girls.
Biologically, the father determines the sex of the child, and the mother should not be blamed if the couple has no son.
The importance of a girl child in the family and in the society.

DO:
Explain the relevance of a well-planned family to community members and encourage well-planned families.
Encourage all community members to appreciate the importance of girl children.
Explain to community members that the father determines the sex of the child and therefore the mother cannot and should not be held responsible.

ATTITUDE:
To have a sense of responsibility for encouraging all community members to appreciate the value of a small family and the preciousness of girl children and to have confidence in their ability to encourage acceptance of girl children.

PURPOSE:
The purposes of this episode are,

- to encourage health workers to sensitize the community toward the benefits of a well-planned family, regardless of the sex of the child
- to discourage the practice of blaming the woman for delivering girl children
- to educate health workers on how to educate the community about the fact that the father determines the sex of the child
- to demonstrate to health workers how to encourage families to treat girl children as equally important as boy children

CAST	MUSIC and SFX
Sangeeta	Pum Pum
Doctor Sahib	Opening Song
Behin ji	Scene Change Music
Badshah	
Sukhram (villager)	
Sukhram's wife	
Man	
Community-based Health Worker 1	
Community-based Health Worker 2	

Darpan.   Page 1 of 13
Episode 3: Topic—Benefits of Small Family
          Determination of Sex of Child
Writer: Raj Khumar Jha   Final

1. MUSIC   OPENING THEME SONG

2. OPENING STANDARD ANNOUNCEMENT

3. MUSIC   OPENING MUSIC. FADE AND HOLD UNDER
                  SANGEETA

4. SANGEETA: Namaskar (SALUTATIONS) from me, Sangeeta, in this third
                  program of Darpan. This mirror is lets us know the truth;
                  gives us an opportunity to teach and learn, makes us aware
                  of the knowledge and ways and means that help us do our
                  work.

TELLING   Now ... the subject of today's lesson. Today Badshah and
                  Behen ji are going to tell us more about the benefits of a small
                  family. They will also help us understand that whether it's a
                  son or a daughter, a baby is always a precious addition to the
                  family. And we will learn one more very important point:

TEACHING INTRO How the sex of the child is determined. So, come on ... let's
                  hear what is cooking today. We find Badshah standing beside
                  Hariyali talking to Behin ji.

5. MUSIC   OPENING MUSIC UP. FADE UNDER AND OUT.

Darpan.   Page 2 of 13
Episode 3: Topic—Benefits of Small Family
            Determination of Sex of Child
Writer: Raj Khumar Jha   Final

---

6. BADSHAH: Please hold on to this letter for me, Behin ji. It has to be sent
                  to Hasanpur. We will mail it wherever we find a post office.
                  A cousin of ours is putting up a shop, as the festivals are about
                  to come. This letter relates to festival time. So I don't want it
                  to be misplaced lying around in the vehicle.

7. BEHIN JI: Shame on you Badshah! You think of earning even in festival
                  time. I ask you, are you scared of anything in life or not?

8. BADSHAH: What are you saying Behin ji! If we are able to earn a little in
                  these festivals then we will also be able to light up our houses.
                  Everything is under God's control. (*PAUSE*) Aha, I see Doctor
                  Sahib has arrived…

9. DOCTOR: (*COMING IN*) Are we late? Come on, let's move; let's not get
                  delayed. Hope your Hariyali is feeling good today.

10. BADSHAH: Rightly pointed out. Hariyali is after all a female; getting upset
                  at times is her inbuilt nature. What do you say, Behin ji?

11. BEHIN JI: I never discriminate between man and woman, Badshah. It's
                  only people like you who talk like this.

12. DOCTOR: Ok, Ok … now enough. Both of you. Don't begin to banter so
                  early in the morning. Let's go; let's go or it will be late.

13. **SFX**   **PUM PUM PUM**

14. SANGEETA: Today's journey begins with Doctor Sahib, Behin ji, Badshah's
                  Hariyali and the sound of pum pum. After dropping Doctor
                  Sahib and Behin ji at their meeting, Badshah went to look for
                  a post office and to buy tea for the doctor and Behin ji. We will
                  catch up with him a little later. But first, let's join Doctor Sahib
                  and Behin ji as they meet with their health provider students
                  in the workshop.

15. DOCTOR: So dear friends, today we are here to talk about what we can do
                  to help our community members to understand that girl chil-
                  dren are every bit as important as boys, and that they should
                  welcome girl children into their homes.

Darpan.
Episode 3: Topic—Benefits of Small Family
        Determination of Sex of Child
Writer: Raj Khumar Jha   Final

16. BEHIN JI:	The sadness is that even in today's society, so many people still consider the family incomplete without a son. How can we convince them otherwise?
17. DOCTOR:	We can tell them the truth. Today women are working at places that once nobody would have imagined. They are in the army, flying airplanes, they are doctors, politicians and engineers; doing everything.
18. H.P.* 1 (MALE):	True. In Delhi recently, I saw a petrol station where girls were pumping the petrol. I was a bit surprised, then got to know that there are some women who drive trucks—even three wheelers. In Bhavnagar, most of the porters are also women.
19. BEHIN JI:	Now, health provider friends, please share with us any other experiences on this subject.
20. H.P. 2 (FEMALE):	I come from a nearby village. At our place, having to provide dowry is the reason for discrimination against daughters. That's why, too often, as a woman gets pregnant, the couple has the sex of the baby determined. If it's a daughter, abortion is carried out.
21. BEHIN JI:	And abortion is definitely illegal. We must all remember that. Those who have the sex of the child determined before birth are criminals in the eyes of the law. It is absolutely wrong.
22. DOCTOR:	And the results of this cruel and ignorant behavior are coming out in the open. There are several places today where girls are so few that finding a wife for a boy is getting difficult. And that leads to an increase in sexual crime. Girls are bought and sold. There will be a time—soon—when boys will not have sisters and aunts. The balance of male and female ratio in the society will topple. Indeed, this is already beginning to happen.

---

*H.P. = Health Provider.

Darpan.
Episode 3: Topic—Benefits of Small Family
            Determination of Sex of Child
Writer: Raj Khumar Jha   Final

---

23. BEHIN JI: This is very true, Doctor sahib. But people so often think that their one personal action cannot make a big difference. Such people do what they feel like, even if it's not right.

24. DOCTOR: It's in fact injustice. Actually, I feel if there is a girl in the home you get a different line of thinking altogether. There is no life without them. Society *MUST* change its attitude and behavior.

25. H.P. 2: But Doctor Sahib, if somebody wants to determine the sex of an unborn child, what can we do to stop it?

26. DOCTOR: It would be untrue to tell them that determining sex before birth is not possible. What you *MUST* do is tell them it is illegal and wrong and—most importantly—totally unnecessary.

27. H.P. 1: So why did someone make a machine that can even examine the unborn child? That's probably the real cause of all the trouble.

28. DOCTOR: No, not really. Actually the machine was made for good purposes. When a child grows in the mother's womb, the machine helps doctors find out if proper growth is happening or not. So the machine can be used to help save the life of an unborn child. The problem is that now it's being misused too often. Aborting the fetus because it is a girl, is wrong. It is murder. We must stress that fact to our communities.

29. BEHIN JI: Yes. We health workers have got to make people understand this.

30. H.P. 3 (FEMALE): Doctor Sahib, I believe if we can change our people's attitude toward girls in the society, our job will be much easier.

31. BEHIN JI: What you are stating is right. It's necessary that you talk to those who are old and respected; those who are revered in the society. If they are on your side, it won't take so much time to convince the younger generation.

Episode 3: Topic—Benefits of Small Family
        Determination of Sex of Child
Writer: Raj Khumar Jha   Final

---

32. DOCTOR:	Yes. If you put some examples in front of them, about how the whole environment is changing, it will help. To do this, you health providers will need to meet with your community members regularly and make them aware of the benefits of change.
33. BEHIN JI:	How should they do that Doctor? What does the community need to be told?
34. DOCTOR:	Well, we can talk about how much has changed around us. Ways of farming have changed; behavior in the society is changing. Employment of women is changing. There is definitely change occurring in many areas. They will have to agree.
35. H.P. 3:	But when talking about girls, I find that sometimes even women raise their eyebrows. Women get enemies even from other women.
36. DOCTOR:	That's probably because a mother, who suffered as a daughter, doesn't want to give birth to a daughter of her own who would undergo the same suffering.
37. BEHIN JI:	That's why some terminate the pregnancy. They do not understand the fact that doing this is harming both themselves and other daughters in the society.
38. DOCTOR:	Even I believe that people have to be motivated, have to be inspired to educate their daughters. Our people must be motivated to understand that if they prepare their daughters to take on the future, everyone will benefit. And all of you health providers can help teach your community members these things.
39. BEHIN JI:	Eventually, people *WILL* understand the wisdom of a small family, instead of having more and more children, just in the hope of having a son.

Darpan. Page 6 of 13

Episode 3: Topic—Benefits of Small Family
Determination of Sex of Child

Writer: Raj Khumar Jha Final

---

40. H.P. 2:	In my area, however big a family is, it's considered small. Yesterday I went to someone's place. There are 14 people in the family but all of them have migrated to earn a livelihood, only three people remain at home. So, they claim that their family is small.
41. DOCTOR:	The real definition of a small family is that there is proper balance between family size and family resources. Everyone in the family should be educated and have the best possible chance of good health. Everyone should have leisure time. But because our nation is already seriously overpopulated, every couple would do well to limit the number of children they have to one or two.
42. BRIEF MUSIC	
43. SANGEETA:	While Doctor Sahib and Behin ji answer the questions from health providers, Badshah went to the market to buy some tea. There he saw a man complaining aloud. Wondering about the reason, Badshah moved toward him. Come on, let's go and hear what went on.
44. MUSIC	**BRIEF SCENE CHANGE MUSIC**

TRANSFORMING:

45. SUKHRAM:	(*OFF MIC A BIT*) I am destroyed, my luck is broken into pieces. This woman has put an end to my lineage. Oh God! There will be no one to put fire on my dead body when I die.
46. BADSHAH:	(*SLIGHTLY ASIDE*) What a wonderful person is he? Not even sure about living, he's worried about who will give him fire when he's dead ... Who is he ... and who is he scolding so much?
47. MAN:	Oh brother don't ask, he always complains. While hoping for a son he has two beautiful daughters, and he scolds his wife for this. Every evening he starts scolding her. Now who will make him understand the truth?

48. BADSHAH:	What's his name, brother?
49. MAN:	He's Sukhram. He is in service. But he doesn't have any wisdom.
50. BADSHAH:	Let me talk to him ... (*GOING OUT*) see if I am able to convince him (*COMING IN*) Oh! brother Sukhram ... Is that your name? Look ... the court has issued a summons on you. Listen to me. I, Badshah, am talking to you.
51. SUKHRAM:	Yes, my name is Sukhram. What is this nonsense about the court? I have not harmed anyone. In fact I'm suffering myself. My world has deserted me. Now this notice from the court! I'm clueless.
52. BADSHAH:	If the court comes to know, it will definitely take some action. Ok, come on, let's get inside the house ... I need to speak with you ... it's a matter of the court of law ... if we are able to solve it ourselves, it will be better.
53. SUKHRAM:	My fortune has deserted me ... come on brother come ... that's my house ... come on and help me out brother ... I have nobody.
54. SFX	**DOOR OPENING AND CLOSING (AS THEY GO INTO THE HOUSE)**
55. BADSHAH:	That's the reason I'm here ... but why are you saying time and again that nobody is yours ... are these beautiful daughters not yours? And this lovely lady I see. Is she your wife or no?
56. SUKHRAM:	What good are they? They are females. This house has no son ... and all because of this woman ... she could not give me a son. Now, you tell me who will be the support in my old age?
57. BADSHAH:	Old age! You will pass it very nicely in jail. What support will you need there? Your own work, own labor.
58. SUKHRAM:	Why in the jail? ... I have not stolen anything ... have not oppressed anyone till now. Then what are these charges against me?

Darpan.   Page 8 of 13
Episode 3: Topic—Benefits of Small Family
            Determination of Sex of Child
Writer: Raj Khumar Jha   Final

---

59. BADSHAH: You seem to be an expert! The entire village will file a report against you. You are blaming everything on your wife. That's one problem, and moreover you have destroyed the peace and…

60. SUKHRAM: What have I done? … this is a mischief to victimize me … do I have no rights to present my sorrows also?

61. BADSHAH: Wonderful … you said just now that because of your wife you had daughters. Now, listen to me with open ears … Whether the baby is a boy or a girl, depends on the father alone and not on the mother.

62. SUKHRAM: How's that possible brother? She has given birth to the kids, not me.

63. BADSHAH: You seem to be a real convict, Sukhram. Listen: mother is like a piece of farmland. Her job is to carry the unborn baby, give birth to the baby, to nurture and nourish her … but men sow the seeds on that land. Now if you sow paddy, from where will you get wheat? You got two beautiful daughters from the seed you had sown. It is the man's seed that decides if the baby will be a boy or a girl. Now why should women carry the burden of men?

64. SUKHRAM: No … No … You are trying to trouble me, what is this? I thought you were going to help me out of my troubles.

65. BADSHAH: I'm helping you out by putting things right in your mind. If you do not believe me, check out with any doctor you want to. If I am wrong, Hariyali, my vehicle is yours. But if you lose, you will have to say sorry to your wife in the village square. Just think about it …

66. SUKHRAM: But the trouble is, there is nobody to carry forward my lineage and now you say the fault is mine.

Darpan.
Episode 3: Topic—Benefits of Small Family
              Determination of Sex of Child
Writer: Raj Khumar Jha   Final

---

67. BADSHAH: It's not a fault at all! Now you tell me, don't you have your part in these beautiful girls? Is their lineage not yours? Will you not be a grandpa to their kids? You are not ready to embrace happiness while you're alive, but you're worrying about who will come to see who has given you fire after you die.

68. SUKHRAM: It's a mistake brother, it's a mistake. I will never do it again. Now please save me from the rigmarole of the court. I do not want to go to jail. Please save me.

69. BADSHAH: What can I do in this? Nobody's above law. If you discriminate between a son and a daughter you are gone. O.K. Not in front of the whole crowd but just in front of me. If you apologize to your wife, I'll write on this paper that the report was false. What do you say, madam?

70. WIFE: What apologies do I need? … I just want him to love his daughters, and be happy. His own children are scared of him. They do not talk with him. Even the neighbors laugh at him. Do I like all this?

71. BADSHAH: Don't you worry. Now Sukhram brother has understood everything. It's never too late to begin. In today's world where is the difference between boy and girl? Educate them both properly and make them both successful.

72. WIFE: You are right brother! But the society doesn't always agree with you.

73. BADSHAH: But remember, people like you and me also *MAKE* this society.

74. WIFE: That's true. But we people just manage to eke out a livelihood. How can we change society? What can we do? Just somehow…

Episode 3: Topic—Benefits of Small Family
            Determination of Sex of Child
Writer: Raj Khumar Jha   Final

---

75. BADSHAH: That's the problem, we surrender before the battle has begun. God is there to see us through. You keep doing your duties. Oh ... what am I doing? I came here to fetch some tea.

76. WIFE: Tea will be ready in a minute. You be seated please.

77. BADSHAH: No, no, I am not alone, the entire team is there and I have to fetch tea for all. Everyone must be waiting there. I'll take my leave, but brother Sukhram, whatever God has given, take it as his plan and remain happy. And remember, daughters are yours, every bit as good as a son. If you insult them, you insult the Almighty.

78. WIFE: (*GOING OUT*) I am making tea for everyone. Just give me two minutes.

79. MUSIC

TESTING:

80. SANGEETA: So, we have heard what kind of misconceptions many people have. I come from a small village; and until recently, people there thought on these same lines. But now things are changing. Girls are being educated and are standing equal to boys. The law has also given women equal rights. So let me ask you a question. I hope you are ready to answer. *QUESTION*: who determines whether the baby will be a boy or a girl?

PAUSE FOR LISTENER RESPONSE (PLR ... 5 SECONDS)

81. SANGEETA: The father. Right. The father's sperm determines the sex of the child. It is not the mother's body at all. And you should know, there is scientific evidence of that fact. Whether the baby will be a son or a daughter depends on the man's sperm alone. So the woman cannot be held responsible for this. We must help everyone in our community to understand this important fact. (*PAUSE*). So Badshah once again showed us how he transforms the knowledge he learns from Doctor Sahib into life improvement for the people he meets. On this day, he came back with the tea in time to join the discussion. Let's hear what is happening.

The Drama Series   **135**

Darpan.   Page 11 of 13
Episode 3: Topic—Benefits of Small Family
                Determination of Sex of Child
Writer: Raj Khumar Jha   Final

82. MUSIC

83. SFX GENERAL CHATTER OF PARTICIPANTS.

84. DOCTOR: One thing we must all agree on Badshah, that everything you told Sukhram is the truth.

85. BEHIN JI: If only everyone knew that. Many people still believe that whether they have few or many children, somehow everyone gets brought up, somehow, so why talk about the rights or resources?

TEACHING:

86. DOCTOR: It's not like that. Let's take an example of a jungle. Small animals are more in numbers than the big ones. Every big animal preys on the little ones and gets food because of that. Now, if bigger ones multiply in excessive numbers, in time there will no longer be enough prey food for them all. And then even the big ones will die.

87. BADSHAH: (*COMING IN*) If there is more than one tiger in the same territory in the jungle, a fight is inevitable because the space is not be enough. What do you think Behin ji!

88. BEHIN JI: Your talk is invariably disjointed, Badshah. You haven't even heard all the discussion, so now what are you talking about?

89. BADSHAH: You have problems whenever I open my mouth. So, I will not speak up.

90. DOCTOR: No ... No Badshah, you are right. Slowly and gradually resources, not only people, but also national resources are bound to deplete when the population grows too large. In our nation, that is already happening. It's the same with a family. In a small family, everyone can be looked after properly. And most importantly, the mother's health has a better chance of being good if she does not have too many children.

91. H.P. 1:   Mother's health? What must we tell our communities about that?

Darpan.   Page 12 of 13

Episode 3: Topic—Benefits of Small Family
                  Determination of Sex of Child

Writer: Raj Khumar Jha   Final

---

92. DOCTOR: We must help them understand that if a woman has children too close together, she becomes weak. She cannot look after all the children properly, and she cannot take care of herself or her husband properly.

93. BEHIN JI: We can explain that small families have many, many benefits. Both mother and father can give more affection to son or daughter if the family is small.

94. BADSHAH: I was going to say something more, but it's better for me to keep my mouth shut. Anyway, it's time for us to make a move now. I will go and get Hariyali ready. On the way, we need to return Sukhram's wife's tea utensils also.

95. SFX   **PUM PUM PUM PUM PUM**

TESTING:

96. SANGEETA: So dear listeners, you heard how not just Sukhram, but many others are lost in their own world of ignorance. Let's think about that and how we can bring knowledge to people in our own communities. (PAUSE). So now, it's time for a QUESTION: What should we tell our community members are the advantages of having a small family?

97. PLR ... 10 SECONDS

98. SANGEETA: Improved resources, improved education, improved health for everyone in the family—most particularly improved health for the mother. That's right. And today, we also learned that Indian law gives both boys and girls equal rights. So let me ask you again. *QUESTION*: If a couple tells us that they want to know the sex of their child before birth, what should we tell them?

99. PLR ... 10 SECONDS

100. SANGEETA: That it's a legal offence and they themselves will end up losing.

Darpan.   Page 13 of 13
Episode 3: Topic—Benefits of Small Family
          Determination of Sex of Child
Writer: Raj Khumar Jha   Final

TASKING   Let us all work hard *in the coming week* to try to convince all
                         our community members to educate their daughters so that
                         people will recognize daughters as equal in every way with sons.
                         Please write to us and let us know what you do in the coming
                         week to encourage sex equality in your community.

TELLING:

101. SANGEETA: We end today's episode of DARPAN here. See you again. Same
                         day, same time next week, when our topic will be 'How to en-
                         courage community leaders and elders to support the Small,
                         Well-Planned Family. Till then, Ram Ram (BYE BYE)

102. SFX   **PUM PUM PUM PUM**

103. MUSIC   **CLOSING MUSIC**

CLOSING STANDARD ANNOUNCEMENT

MUSIC: CLOSING MUSIC.

8

EDU-TAINMENT FORMATS
The Drama Serial and Synergistic Programming

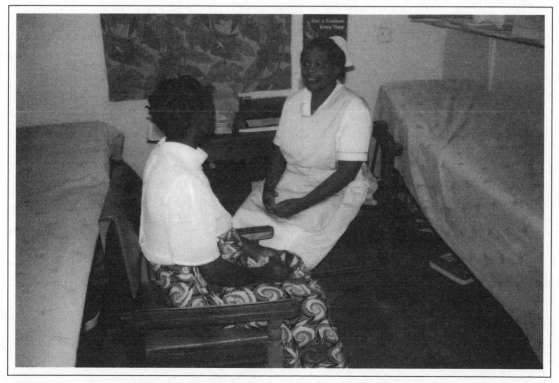

Synergistic programming reaches out to both community members and community workers.

THE DRAMA SERIAL FOR EDU-TAINMENT

A well-written drama serial always has the potential of being very attractive to an audience. With each episode ending on a note of question or suspense, the audience is eager to find out what will happen and so they willingly tune in for the next episode. At the same time, audience members become closely acquainted with various characters whose lives are developing gradually as the ongoing story unfolds and there is always the fascination of wondering whether the unfolding lives will move into success or disaster.

A well-written drama serial usually also contains several plots: a main plot and two or three sub-plots which, in effect, provide the audience with several fascinating stories at the same time. Clearly, the drama serial is a very powerful tool for encouraging positive behavior change in the lives of a general audience or even several discrete audiences. Where the main plot of a serial drama can reflect and affect the lives of a general adult population, one of the sub-plots can attract and hold the attention of an adolescent audience, for example, while yet another sub-plot can reach out to a specific audience group such as community leaders.

While the drama serial is an excellent Entertainment–Education medium for encouraging appropriate behavior and social change in a general audience, the question arises: How appropriate or effective is the drama serial, for Edu-tainment purposes?

CHALLENGES OF THE DRAMA SERIAL FOR EDU-TAINMENT

Handled with considerable care, the drama serial can be used effectively for Edu-tainment purposes, but it requires some serious adjustment. The main purpose of Edu-tainment is to teach a lesson. The main purpose of a drama serial is to tell an ongoing story. Blending these two elements successfully is a very challenging task. All too often, the story predominates and the lessons are—at best—unclear or incomplete, or the lessons predominate and the story is—at best—uninteresting. Writers who want to consider the use of the *drama serial* format for Edu-tainment purposes, should keep the following guidelines in mind:

GUIDELINES FOR USING THE DRAMA SERIAL FOR EDU-TAINMENT

- the *main plot* should be about the life of a character who is representative of the learning audience for whom the programs are designed, for example, a health worker. This plot can present a fairly simple, but engaging story of this person's life. For example, in the set of programs of the Nepali serial *Service Brings Reward,* the main plot told the story of the personal difficulties faced by health worker, Ganga, whose husband, had always been a caring and loving 'Vibeke Logne' (responsible husband) suddenly left home without any explanation. Ganga is a devoted Female Community Health Volunteer (FCHV) who is determined to continue her work despite her personal difficulties. The mystery of her husband's strange behavior provides the necessary amount of interest and suspense for the audience, without in any way interfering with the important lessons being taught.
- the *sub-plot* should show this main community-helper involved with her/his teacher in the learning environment (for the segments of the **Teaching** process) and then in the community or work environment for the **Transforming** process. In the following episode, the first scene shows Ganga in the **Teaching** environment with Romesh, the Senior Health Worker, and her teacher. This first teaching scene is followed by a brief **Test**, which is—in turn—followed by another brief teaching session. Then the listeners go with Ganga to the **Transforming** scene where she is using her new knowledge to help improve the lives of a young couple who are having some trouble making a harmonious decision about the size of their family.
- the *ongoing story* should rest to a large degree on the main character's response to her/his job as a result of what is being learned in the **teaching** segments of the program, even while facing personal problems.

All of this suggests that the drama serial is perhaps not the best, and certainly not the easiest format to use for distance education or Edu-tainment purposes. The biggest challenge posed by trying to blend clear teaching into the drama serial format is obtaining the appropriate balance of an engaging personal, ongoing story with clear unambiguous instruction. It can be done, but it requires considerable skill, knowledge and patience from the writer. The inexperienced writer would probably find it easier to use one of the other formats discussed in this book.

SYNERGISTIC PROGRAMMING

Service Brings Reward is a radio Edu-tainment distance education drama *serial* that ran for many years in Nepal, with one new 15-minute program each week, for 52 weeks at a time.

The really interesting fact about *Service Brings Reward* is that it was one 'half' of a synergistic project. The other 'half' was a drama serial designed for the general public and named *Cut Your Coat According to Your Cloth*. The adjective 'synergistic' means 'working together' and derives from the noun 'synergy' which means 'the cooperative action of two or more bodily organs or the like.' This Nepal project is, therefore, a perfect example of one program designed to encourage positive behavior change in the general public, working in harmony with a distance education program designed to bring the FCHVs up to date so that they could support, encourage and help maintain the behavior change. Both the general audience and the FCHVs lived in remote rural areas of Nepal and the FCHVs had no access to regular classroom instruction.

Each year, the distance education programs went on the air several weeks ahead of the drama serial so that the FCHVs had the chance to upgrade their skills *before* the general public listeners were invited to turn to them for advice. All the programs could be heard by anyone (including the general public) who turned on the radio, and this provided a further incentive for the health workers to upgrade their skills because they were aware that their clients might be checking to see if their health workers had learned what was being taught in the radio programs.

This synergistic approach was very successful. *Cut Your Coat According to Your Cloth* encouraged couples to go to the Health Centers for advice and counseling, while *Service Brings Reward* ensured that the FCHVs were up to date with their knowledge and counseling skills. Those evaluating the programs had the following comments:

'To what can the success of the project be attributed? On the program side, the design was developed with unusual rigor and attention to theoretical explanations of the effects. Specific behavioral objectives were defined from the outset and formative research identified plausible objectives, social, psychological, and structural changes that would be most likely to support these changes. Scripting and production of program materials, particularly the two radio dramas, were done by skilled, trained Nepalese dramatists with sensitivity to the nuances of local arts and culture. The dramas themselves, while technically accurate, had *higher production values and were less didactic than previous radio development projects*, a fact that undoubtedly enhanced their appeal. The fact that improvements in actual health worker performance through the distance education serial accompanied the promotion of increased client–provider interaction may have had a reinforcing effect: People who went to the clinics seeking better services than they were used to in the past were less likely to be disappointed, and this may have reinforced attitudes and behaviors that were beginning to change. Finally, the use of a dramatic format for the distance education series was an innovation that clearly pleased health workers and made that serial accessible, even popular, among the general public as well.'*

There is a growing interest in providing synergistic media projects to promote behavior change. The organization of such projects requires very careful planning and precise co-ordination among the organizers, writers and producers of both programs. There is little doubt, however, that this hand-in-hand approach to behavior change communication and behavior change maintenance has obvious advantages in places where providing on-site training—either to the general public or to the community workers—is difficult, if not impossible.

SAMPLE: *SERVICE BRINGS REWARD*—NEPAL—RADIO

Episode Introduction

The following episode of *Service Brings Reward* is a good example of using serial drama to *demonstrate* to Health Workers how they can transform their academic learning into appropriate interaction with their clients. Dramatic demonstrations like this not only encourage appropriate behavior in Health Workers, but also help the general public to understand the type of treatment they should expect from trained Health Workers, so that they will be encouraged to turn to them for help.

The characters in this episode are:

BIMALA—the male host of the program who introduces the topic each week and asks the listeners interactive questions designed to ensure that they were learning correctly.

GANGA—the female Health Worker in Ranikhet village, who is dedicated to her work and is always eager to learn more.

ROMESH—the senior male Health Worker in charge of the clinic; Ganga's teacher and 'boss'.

KHAIRE—a young husband who is having trouble deciding how to agree with both his wife and his parents.

*Boulay, D.M., Y. Karki, K. Heckert and D.M. Karmacharya. 1999. 'Impact of the Integrated Radio Communication Project in Nepal, 1994–97'. *Journal of Health Communication*, 4: 271–94. Taylor and Francis.

Service Brings Reward
Episode #7: Final
Topic: Husband and Wife Communication
Writer: Ganesh Singh

Measurable Objectives: After listening to this episode, the FCHV will:

KNOW:
The importance of communication between husband and wife and among family members.

- What a Vibeke Logne (responsible, caring husband) is.
- How to help couples and families to communicate more comfortably with each other.

DO:
Teach couples how to communicate more effectively with each other.

- Encourage men to become Vibeke Logne (responsible, caring husbands).
- Encourage other family members to have intra-family communication.

HAVE AN ATTITUDE OF:
Feel and appreciate the importance of the vital role of communication in improving the quality of life of couples, families, and communities.

PURPOSE:
The purposes of this episode are:

- To educate the FCHVs about the importance of communication between husband and wife and among family members; the concept of Vibeke Logne and to encourage them to promote communication.
- To demonstrate how the FCHV can encourage effective communication between husband and wife, and among family members.

MUSIC/SFX/CUTS (in order in which they appear in the program)

CAST	Page#	Line#	MUSIC/SFX/CUTS
1. Bimala	2	1	Music: Theme music 5 seconds hold under
2. Ganga	2	4	Music: Theme music up and out
3. Romesh	2	6	SFX: Sound of the health post

4. Khaire	2	7	SFX: Moving of the chair
	4	12	Music: Interactive session
	5	6	Music: Interactive session
	7	7	Music: Transition music
	7	8	SFX: Sound of village Ranikhet
	8	10	Music: Transition music
	8	12	Music: Interactive session
	9	5	Music: Interactive session end
	9	7	Music: Transition music
	9	9	Music: Theme music up 05 seconds and hold under
	9	11	Music: Theme music up and end

Episode #7: Final   Page 1 of 10
Topic: Husband and Wife Communication   Date: January 23
Writer: Ganesh Singh   Final

1. **MUSIC**   **THEME MUSIC 5 SECONDS HOLD Under Announcer**

2. **ANNOUNCER:**   Namaste (GREETINGS)! Welcome to the Distance Education Radio Program *Service Brings Reward*, which is presented for FCHVs by Ministry of Health.

3. **MUSIC**   **THEME MUSIC UP AND OUT**

TELL

4. **BIMALA:**   Dear FCHV friends, Namaste from me, your host, Bimala. Last week we learned about the three interpersonal communication skills we FCHVs must use: listening, questioning, and rapport building. Today, we'll learn more about important communication: this time between husband and wife ... Let us go to the Ranikhet health post where Romesh, the Senior Health Worker and teacher is waiting for FCHV Ganga to arrive.

5. **FX**   **SOUND OF THE ENVIRONMENT OF HEALTH POST**

6. **ROMESH:**   (FADE IN) Ganga Didi should be here any moment ...

7. **GANGA:**   (COMING IN AND LAUGHING LIGHTLY) I'm almost here, Romesh Bhai ... Namaste ... Namaste ...

8. **ROMESH:**   Namaste Ganga Didi ... please come ... take your seat here ...

Episode #7: Final   Page 2 of 10
Topic: Husband and Wife Communication   Date: January 23
Writer: Ganesh Singh   Final

9. GANGA:	(DRAGGING THE CHAIR) Thank you Romesh Bhai ...
10. ROMESH:	Ganga Didi, I was thinking of you when you came in ... With all your energy ... (TEASINGLY) You will live hundreds of years ...
11. GANGA:	Oh ... that will be nice, Romesh Bhai ... (SAD) But it would be nicer to live a hundred years with my husband in peace and happiness ...
12. ROMESH:	You will Ganga Didi ... I don't know what has gone wrong now that Khemnath has left home and not been in touch with you. He has always been a really responsible husband, a loving and caring father ... He is truly a good example of a Vibeke Logne ...
13. GANGA:	Romesh Bhai, I also used to think of my husband as a Vibeke Logne ... (BECOMING EMOTIONAL) But now I have not heard from him ... I'm confused what a Vibeke Logne should be.
14. ROMESII:	Oh, I think you really know what it means ...
15. GANGA:	(GETTING CONTROL OF HERSELF) Yes Romesh Bhai, you are right. We FCHVs should be able to help hundreds of families if we encourage Vibeke Logne. (LAUGHING) So let us review the facts.

TEACH

16. ROMESH:	(SERIOUS VOICE) A Vibeke Logne is a 'responsible husband'. He has responsibilities both toward his wife and his family ...
17. GANGA:	What responsibilities toward wife, Romesh Bhai?
18. ROMESH:	Understanding, respecting and caring for his wife ...
19. GANGA:	Understanding ... respecting ... caring for wife ... Are these sufficient to become a Vibeke Logne?

Episode #7: Final   Page 3 of 10
Topic: Husband and Wife Communication   Date: January 23
Writer: Ganesh Singh   Final

20. ROMESH: Understanding, respecting, and caring for the wife are import-
                 ant parts of being a Vibeke Logne ... And a Vibeke Logne also
                 recognizes his wife as an equal partner with equal rights in
                 all aspects of life.

21. GANGA: So to put it together ... a Vibeke Logne is a husband who under-
                 stands, respects and cares for his wife ... And he recognizes her
                 as an equal partner with equal rights in all aspects of life ...

22. ROMESH: You're right Ganga Didi ... Also, remember, a Vibeke Logne
                 also takes care of his children and family ...

23. GANGA: But, what do men need to learn so that they can be a Vibeke
                 Logne?

24. ROMESH: (ADMIRING) Ganga Didi, you have asked a very relevant
                 question ... There are four things ... by which men can take
                 on the role of a Vibeke Logne by learning and practicing ...
                 these ...

25. GANGA: (INTERRUPTING) Romesh Bhai, would you remind us of
                 these four things one by one so that we can all take them in.

26. ROMESH: Yes Ganga Didi, I will do that ... Men can understand the role
                 of the Vibeke Logne by learning and practicing: *ONE*: mutual
                 respect and care between husband and wife. *OK*?

27. GANGA: So men need to act in such a way that husband and wife are
                 mutually respecting and caring to each other ... That's fine.

28. ROMESH: Similarly ... *TWO*: sharing responsibilities between husband
                 and wife and among all family members when necessary.

29. GANGA: So to be a Vibeke Logne, men need to share responsibilities ...
                 between husband and wife ...

30. ROMESH: Yes ... to be Vibeke Logne men need to share responsibilities
                 between husband and wife ... And *THREE* ... by which men
                 can understand their role of a Vibeke Logne is—providing
                 financial resources for women's healthcare and other needs.

31. GANGA:	(LAUGHING LIGHTLY) Oh, that's important … To be a Vibeke Logne a man should provide his wife access to financial resources for her healthcare and other needs … That also I understand.
32. ROMESH:	Similarly, the *FOURTH* is: relationship … in order to create a conducive environment between husband and wife, the husband must ask for her opinion and listen carefully to her …
33. GANGA:	Well, I suppose it is up to husband and wife to decide what kind of relationship … environment … they want to create for themselves.
34. ROMESH:	But it is up to FCHVs to teach, promote and encourage the role of a modern Vibeke Logne … so that couples can be happy together. Now let us see how much we have learned about these roles so far …

TEST

35. MUSIC	**INTERACTIVE SESSION**
36. ROMESH:	Dear FCHV friends, it's question time. Till now we discussed four things that FCHVs need to teach men about the role of the modern husband … Now Question 1: What do we call a man who cares for his wife and takes her as an equal partner with equal rights?
37. PLR	**05 SECONDS**
38. ROMESH:	Vibeke Logne. That's right. A Vibeke Logne is a husband who understands, respects and cares for his wife … Now Question 2: In what way will decisions be made in a family having a Vibeke Logne?
39. PLR	**05 SECONDS**
40. ROMESH:	By husband and wife together. That's right. A Vibeke Logne invites his wife to share in all decision-making.
41. MUSIC	**INTERACTIVE SESSION END**

TEACH

42. GANGA:	From the discussion, till now, what I understand Romesh Bhai … Communication is an important part of everyone's life … In case of husband and wife, good communication between them is a must …
43. ROMESH:	Good communication is good for the family, isn't it Ganga Didi?
44. GANGA:	Yes … Increased communication between husband and wife will strengthen the relationship … and it will have a positive impact on their life, and on the whole family.
45. ROMESH:	You are perfectly right …
46. GANGA:	(SIGHING) That's the way it used to be with my husband and me … But, (PULLING HERSELF TOGETHER) I must stick to my work. FCHVs must encourage husband and wife to establish a good communication.
47. ROMESH:	Yes, Ganga Didi … FCHVs should inform couples and families about the advantages of communication with each other … and with *ALL* family members. A Vibeke Logne initiates discussion and joint decision in all aspects of family lives …
48. GANGA:	That we FCHVs can do Romesh Bhai … But what advantages can we tell clients they will gain from good communication between husband and wife?
49. ROMESH:	Mainly, we can point out six advantages … One is: When husband shares decision-making with his wife, the outcome is usually better.
50. GANGA:	Because, in this case, the decision will be a joint decision. The result of their joint decision will also be stronger … Then another …
51. ROMESH:	Two is: Better communication between husband and wife makes the couple increasingly comfortable to discuss sensitive matters together.

Episode #7: Final
Topic: Husband and Wife Communication
Writer: Ganesh Singh

52. GANGA: Well, when we communicate with each other, we know each other better ... knowing each other better makes us more comfortable to discuss even sensitive matters openly ...

53. ROMESH: That's right. Then three is: When husband and wife are united in their decisions about such matters as family size, it is easier to get support from in-laws and parents.

54. GANGA: That's true ... If couples are together in their decisions, others are more likely to support them ... Then the fourth advantage?

55. ROMESH: Four is: When a husband supports his wife in contraceptive choice there is more effective use of contraceptives.

56. GANGA: Both need to discuss the choice of contraceptive method ... husband needs to be fully supportive as well ... For this also, a good communication between husband and wife is essential ...

57. ROMESH: Similarly, five is: Communication among all family members also reinforces equal responsibility in all aspects of family life.

58. GANGA: Good communication between husband and wife will be helpful in a good communication within the family as well ... This is also an advantage.

59. ROMESH: Advantage six is: When a husband respects and loves his wife and her opinion ... when in-laws also value this, there will be a more loving, closer relationship among all family members.

60. GANGA: This will be helpful in creating loving and closer relationship ... as well as a better quality of life for all ... Isn't it Romesh Bhai?

61. ROMESH: Yes, Ganga Didi ... this will be helpful for better quality of life for all as well.

Episode #7: Final   Page 7 of 10
Topic: Husband and Wife Communication   Date: January 23
Writer: Ganesh Singh   Final

62. GANGA:	Today, we have reviewed things that will be helpful in my own life as well ... (DETERMINED) Now I will head straight to my house ... I need to see if I can find out my husband's whereabouts.
63. ROMESH:	Oh yes ... You help everybody else to solve their problem ... but ...
64. GANGA:	The problem of my own house remains unsettled ... Darkness under the lamp ... (GOING) ... I will call on Khaire Babu on the way home ...
65. MUSIC	**TRANSITION MUSIC HOLD UNDER TILL LINE 8**
66. SFX	**SOUND OF THE VILLAGE RANIKHET**

TRANSFORM

67. GANGA:	(COMING) What's this Khaire Babu ... What are you doing in the courtyard ... holding your head.........
68. KHAIRE:	(UNHAPPILY) See Ganga Kaki ... my wife, Silu is such a headache ...
69. GANGA:	What happened Khaire Babu? I am your neighbor ... and I have never heard you two quarreling before ...
70. KHAIRE:	What to say Kaki ...
71. GANGA:	Well ... Whatever is the matter husband and wife need to talk together ... discuss together ... Then only you can find the right solution ... Anyway ... may I ask ... what is the problem?
72. KHAIRE:	What to say ... My mother wants us to have another baby ... she wants another grandchild ... Silu wants to wait for three years before having a second child ... It is I who am grinding in between ...
73. GANGA:	I will talk with your mother. But Babu, what Silu is saying is the right thing ...

74. KHAIRE: I also know we need to space for three years before a second child ...

75. GANGA: So you—husband and wife—need to discuss together ... An educated person like you should behave like a modern Vibeke Logne ...

76. KHAIRE: Kaki, I am not neglecting what Silu is saying. It's not that ... She is right, I agree ...

77. GANGA: Khaire Babu, what I mean is it will be good if husband supports decisions taken by wife ... When husband and wife take decisions together, then it is easier to get support from in-laws and parents ...

78. KHAIRE: (THINKING ABOUT IT) Yes, that is true, Ganga Kaki ... If I had also told my mother that we need to wait for three years before giving birth to another child ... Silu wouldn't have to suffer this much ...

79. GANGA: That's why I am reminding you that husband and wife need to be open and communicate with each other ... When there is good communication, you can take decisions together ... And that will be good for everybody in the family as well ...

80. KHAIRE: (ENCOURAGED) I now feel stronger after talking with you, Ganga Kaki ...

81. GANGA: Better, call Silu as well here into the courtyard ... Show her that you are a Vibeke Logne ... And together, you can decide how to help your parents understand your decision ...

82. KHAIRE: (CALLING) Silu ... Silu ...

83. MUSIC   TRANSITION MUSIC

TEST

84. ROMESH: Dear FCHV friends, while Ganga Didi is talking with Khaire Bhai and Silu about 'Vibeke Logne', and husband and wife communication, let me invite you to take part in the interactive question session ...

Episode #7: Final
Topic: Husband and Wife Communication
Writer: Ganesh Singh

Page 9 of 10
Date: January 23
Final

85. MUSIC	**INTERACTIVE QUESTION SESSION**
86. ROMESH:	A few questions on husband and wife communication ... Now Question 1: What does a Vibeke Logne do when important family decisions are to be made?
87. PLR	**05 SECONDS**
88. ROMESH:	Invite wife to share in decision-making. That's right. When husband supports the wife in decision-making, the outcome is better. Now Question 2: What will you suggest your clients to do, so that they get support from in-laws and parents in their decisions about their reproductive health?
89. PLR	**05 SECONDS**
90. ROMESH:	Husband and wife make decisions *TOGETHER*. That's right. When husband and wife are united in their decisions, there is more chance that others in the family will also support them.
91. MUSIC	**INTERACTIVE SESSION END**

TASK

92. ROMESH:	Dear FCHV friends, you need to encourage each of your male clients to be a Vibeke Logne and encourage husband and wife communication in your community ... This will be a good assignment for all of you this week ...

TELL

93. MUSIC	**TRANSITION MUSIC**
94. BIMALA:	Ganga used to think her husband Khemnath to be a Vibeke Logne ... She is now sad over his behavior of keeping himself mute and not letting her know where he is ... But, she is determined to find him and learn what is going on. Let us see what happens next time when we will be discussing Safe Pregnancy.
95. MUSIC	**THEME MUSIC UP 5 SECONDS AND HOLD UNDER**

Episode #7: Final
Topic: Husband and Wife Communication
Writer: Ganesh Singh

96. ANNOUNCER: Dear FCHV friends, if you need further information on today's topic, please consult the reference manual or do write to us …To know new things, tune in to our upcoming programs… Till then, Namaste.

97. MUSIC   **THEME MUSIC UP AND END.**

9

EDU-TAINMENT FORMATS—TV OR RADIO
The Magazine and Reality Programming

True stories from real people in the community can be powerful motivators for change.

THE MAGAZINE FORMAT

The Magazine Format (sometimes called the Variety Show) is a format in which the program is made up of a number of different segments, such as interviews, talks, music, mini-drama and quizzes. On the surface, this format sounds like a fascinating way of attracting and holding the attention of many different audiences, but the format has challenges that can make it difficult to use for instructional programming such as Edu-tainment. The varied format of the magazine program might at first seem to be ideal for passing on knowledge through the use of experts, interviews and testimonials, interspersed with relaxing moments of music, general chat, and perhaps a mini-drama.

The Consistency Challenge

The challenge, indeed the danger, of this format lies in trying to maintain message or lesson **consistency** in the various segments, especially in interviews and talks. Finding interviewees and testimonial givers who can not only grab and hold the attention of the audience, but who can present the knowledge in a manner consistent with the Curriculum Guide is often difficult. There is also the challenge of maintaining the lesson process in clear and understandable steps while presenting a whole range of program segments.

THE SEGMENTS AND THE CHALLENGES OF A MAGAZINE PROGRAM

Segments: The Host or Anchor

The first essential ingredient of an audience-attracting magazine program is an outstanding host or anchor; someone who has a strong appeal to the intended audience and who can become—in effect—the teacher, presenting the teaching points of the program in a clear, but friendly manner. Many magazine programs have two hosts or anchors (often one man and one woman) who can introduce the lesson topic of the day in a natural conversational manner, even when using a script. Hosts or anchors must be good actors who can sound as if they are indulging in natural conversation even while they are working from a prepared script that allows the information they give to be absolutely accurate and in line with the Curriculum Guide. Allowing the hosts to 'ad lib' or create their own dialogue can result, all too easily, in inconsistency or even inaccuracy in lesson presentation.

The 'Experts'

While there would appear to be obvious advantages in using real doctors or other specialists to provide the **teaching** section of each program, it must be remembered that **consistency** is an essential ingredient of successful education. Sometimes, it is better to work with only one expert who provides the main lesson points in every program in the series. Even in this case, however, it is essential to ensure that the expert consistently and correctly abides by the lesson points as they are laid out in the Curriculum Guide. It is equally important to be sure that the chosen expert has a clear speaking voice and an attractive personality that will appeal to the audience.

An alternative approach to the use of actual experts in the magazine program is to create what might be called 'fictional experts.' In other words, the program writers create the character of a doctor or other expert, and script his or her dialogue to accurately present what is given in the Curriculum Guide. One advantage of the fictional expert, apart from message accuracy, is that the writer can give the expert an interesting and attractive personality that the audience will like, and this attractive personality can be presented by a competent actor.

Reality Programs and Interviews

Reality Programming makes use of real people telling their own stories, either as interviews or as monologues. Sometimes, the reality programs take the form of diaries, in which the same person appears on a regular basis, giving details of how an ongoing problem is developing or being solved in her or his life. Reality Programming like this is commonly used in programs for the general public—especially programs related to very personal topics such as HIV/AIDS stigma. There is no doubt that real-life stories and diaries can have a strong emotional effect on the audience and can be powerful in motivating an audience to adopt a new behavior. There are, however, obvious dangers to reality programming when used for teaching purposes. These dangers include:

- poor presentation skills of 'real' people
- message inaccuracy
- repetition leading to audience boredom (if several people give almost identical stories), or if a diarist repeats parts of the story many times over
- lack of truthfulness. Sometimes, people are tempted to enrich their own stories in order to make them seem more exciting or more dramatic. Obviously, when this happens, the presentation is no longer 'real'

In presenting a distance education program for community workers, there might appear to be some advantage in interviewing real people who work in this field, or who receive care from them. Frequently however, those being interviewed or telling their stories are not particularly good at being interviewed or at public speaking. Shyness, lack of speaking experience, nervousness in front of a microphone: all these things combine to make it very difficult for some people to give an attractive and convincing interview, or to relate a personal story in an attractive manner. It is possible, with considerable time spent in putting the interviewee at rest and considerably more time on editing the finished product, to create some compelling interviews or stories. It must be recognized, however, that obtaining compelling interviews from members of the general public is a real challenge and can take a lot of time. Some guidelines for editing interviews and personal stories are given at the end of this chapter (page 189). Another approach to the use of real-life stories in television programs is as follows: The storyteller is filmed on location walking around, going about typical daily duties, greeting clients, and so on, but with no dialogue being recorded. The storyteller then does a sound recording of her or his story. This sound recording can then be scripted, edited as needed and presented as a Voice Over the picture, read by a professional actor. This method of real-life story presentation ensures message accuracy and quality presentation. Similarly, in situations where it is impossible to record frequent interviews or personal stories (because of time or distance restrictions), it can be effective to have learners mail in their stories. These contributions can then be edited and presented by an actor.

Vox Pop

Many producers turn to Vox Pop comments in place of lengthy interviews. The Vox Pop (From the Latin *Vox Popularis* meaning 'Voice of the People') format uses short comments of one sentence or less from a number of different people in response to a question related to the topic of the day. Typically, the host of the program, or an appointed interviewer, will go out on to the street, to a school, a factory or some other place where there will be many people congregated, and pose a question. The interviewer will then collect several unrehearsed (preferably short) responses. For example, the interviewer might ask a number of HIV counselors, 'What do you find is the hardest thing for people living with HIV to cope with?' The answers will vary: 'stigma', 'lack of a job', 'remembering to take medication', 'fear that my family will be left alone when I die,' and so on. The Vox Pop provides what is, in effect, a series of miniature interviews that can give the audience a quick overview of people's feelings about the topics to be covered in the day's lesson. Nevertheless, it must be remembered that recording and editing effective Vox Pop takes time and money, and again there is the problem that many people are not very effective when it comes to giving quick, brief, and powerful answers.

Mini-Drama

Almost always the most popular segment of a magazine program is a well-written and well-performed mini-drama. The mini-drama can be used to demonstrate the **transforming** process of the distance education program, but it is also an attention-grabber because it can be carefully designed to allow the lesson to appear within an entertaining format. The fact that the mini-drama is often the audience's favorite section of the magazine, perhaps suggests that creating the whole program as fiction could be a better guarantee of success than trying to use reality segments throughout the magazine.

Music

A magazine program invariably contains two or three musical inserts, based on the belief that most people like music and that music provides a relaxing break from the topic under discussion or the lesson being taught. This idea of a relaxing break might seem appropriate in a lesson, but consideration should be given to the fact that the inclusion of music can also create a break in concentration and thus make it more difficult for learners to hold on to the main points of the lesson. Indeed, there is evidence to show that when learners are truly engaged in the topic of the lesson, they do not like to be interrupted with even two or three minutes of music.

THE FICTIONAL MAGAZINE

Bearing in mind the constraints and challenges of the magazine program for use as a teaching tool, it is clear that it is not necessarily an ideal vehicle for Edu-tainment programming. However, if there is strong reason to believe that the magazine format is the one most likely to appeal to the intended learners, it might be as well to consider using a 'fictional magazine' format.

The 'Fictional Magazine' is a program in which all (or most) segments, including reality segments, are very carefully scripted, structured, and rehearsed prior to recording, and edited as needed before going on the air. Alternatively, it can be that everything is entirely fictional, meaning that the various experts, interviewees, diarists or storytellers are actually actors presenting dialogue that has been carefully scripted by writers and then reviewed to ensure that it is educationally sound and based on the exact content contained in the Curriculum Guide.

The obvious advantages of the fictional magazine are:

- instructional material given by 'experts' can be consistent and correct
- personalities of 'experts' can be created to appeal to the learners
- interview or Vox Pop comments can be structured to correctly support the lesson purpose
- recording or filming and editing time and cost are considerably shortened, especially in situations where the lessons have to be created and presented in several different languages

The following script is an example of a fictional magazine Edu-tainment program designed to provide training and skill-upgrading to health workers in Bangladesh.

'Under the Green Umbrella'* Introduction

This television script demonstrates how the magazine format can be fictionally adjusted to suit Edu-tainment needs. The 'teachers'—Tara and the Doctor—are both fictional characters; so it is possible to ensure—through scripting—that the teaching process is accurate and consistent every time, and that the teachers' personalities are attractive to the audience.

The program requires very little by way of locations. The opening scene of every program can be shot in the same small field. The kitchen from where Tara and the doctor address listeners' questions can be a simple room or an inexpensively constructed set.

---

*This series was originally written for radio, but is shown here in the video adaptation as an example of how a modified magazine format can be used to good effect in TV Edu-tainment programming.

Using Tara's kitchen as the setting from which she and the doctor address the audience came about as a result of the desire to make the field-worker audience feel relaxed as they learned. A home kitchen seemed much less formal than a classroom or a studio.

The scene for the Case Study portion of the programs was done with actors rather than using the actual people who sent in the letters. Using actors in these scenes made production easier and ensured a better presentation. These Case Study scenes were presented with Voice Over, which cut down filming costs and time and ensured quality vocal presentation.

The only part of this type of program that requires time for preparation and location shooting is the mini-drama, but a series like this can be easily arranged so that several of the mini-dramas take place in the same location—for example, the clinic or a particular client's home. Because each drama is no more than 10 minutes long, several of them can be shot in one day on the same location.

The overall objective of *Under the Green Umbrella* series was to increase and upgrade the health knowledge and Interpersonal Communication skills of health workers (known as Field Workers) in Bangladesh, so that there would be an increase in:

1. the number of rural community members who have complete faith in and respect for the field-workers
2. the number of rural community members who look to the Field Worker to assist them in matters of family health, particularly reproductive health (including family planning) and infant health
3. the number of Field Workers who demonstrate increased self-esteem and professional self-respect and acknowledge themselves as 'Social Teachers'.

The characters in this program are:

Tara—the community health nurse (Field Worker)
Nana—Tara's father
Nani—Tara's mother
Rakhal—Nana's farm assistant (age 15)
The Doctor
In the **mini-drama**, there are these extra characters:
Mother
Manju (her daughter, aged 8)
Her young son, aged 3 (a non-speaking role)
A baby, several months of age

Under the Green Umbrella   Page 1 of 25
Episode #16   Draft # 2
Writers: Dr Selim Alden; Giasuddin Selim   Date: March 2

OPENING SCENE—OVER WHICH TITLE AND MAIN CREDITS ARE SHOWN

Outside Tara's house. Night time.

> Nana and Rakhal are barely seen as they move around. The
> Instructor's voice is heard over the Scene.

TELLING

1. INSTRUCTOR:

Voice Over (V.O.)

Now we begin today's program of our special magazine, 'Under
the Green Umbrella' for health workers engaged in assisting
their clients with family planning and maternal and child
health programs. Today, our topic is

Montage: Topic title appears on screen: 'Common Diseases of Childhood'.

The scene becomes a little lighter. Characters are seen dimly in the night light.

2. NANA:

Rakhal, it's getting dark and you haven't put the cow in the
pen yet.

3. RAKHAL:

I have brought the two oxen, master ... I don't see the cow,
Nana ...

4. NANA:

What do you mean, Rakhal! You don't see the cow? Go look

for her. Here, take my torch.

Rakhal moves off into the dark, calling the cow.

5. RAKHAL:

Shamli, O Shamli … say ham-ba-a-a-a

6. NANA:

I'll go and mix some fodder in the bowl. (TO HIMSELF) That

will make the cow come. It's so dark. Oh well, I can manage

in the dark.

Rakhal walks up quietly behind Nana, grumbling softly. It is clear that he cannot see where he is going.

7. RAKHAL:

Where could the cow go? … I don't see at all at night … (TRIPS)

… ah … here, I have got you, darned cow … I'll beat the hell

out of you … My God! (SCUFFLE) …

Rakhal has grabbed Nana, thinking it is the cow, and pushes him to the ground.

8. NANA:

Hey … hey … what are you doing … !

Under the Green Umbrella
Episode #16
Writers: Dr Selim Alden; Giasuddin Selim

Page 3 of 25
Draft # 2
Date: March 2

9. RAKHAL:

Er ... r ... Sorry Nana, I thought it was the cow...

10. NANA:

You, good for nothing ... you took me for a four-footed animal!

You are fired.

11. RAKHAL:

Please forgive me Nana—I fall at your feet.

SCENE 2: KITCHEN, TARA'S HOUSE. MORNING

Tara's mother, Nani is talking with Nana

1. NANI (LAUGHING):

What did you say? Rakhal took you for the cow last night!

2. NANA:

It's a shame. He had the torch with him ... and yet he grabbed me, thinking I was the cow!

3. NANI (LAUGHING):

I think he did the right thing.

Under the Green Umbrella   Page 4 of 25
Episode #16   Draft # 2
Writers: Dr Selim Alden; Giasuddin Selim   Date: March 2

4. NANA:

What do you mean ...?

5. NANI:

I have been telling you that Rakhal has not been seeing well at night lately ... he needs treatment. But you never listened.

6. NANA:

I don't know where to take him ... who to go to. That's why I haven't done anything yet.

7. NANI:

Why, don't you hear anything? Tara told us you must take him to the clinic for help. I've been telling you that night blindness is quite common in children and adolescents around here.

8. NANA (JOKING):

I see, you are becoming more intelligent day by day.

9. NANI:

Stop frolicking. Rakhal eats nothing but fish and meat. I have told him so many times. He must eat lots of green and yellow vegetables, like lal shak, kachu shak, sweet pumpkin ... They contain Vitamin-A which helps prevent night blindness.

Under the Green Umbrella   Page 5 of 25
Episode #16   Draft # 2
Writers: Dr Selim Alden; Giasuddin Selim   Date: March 2

10. NANA:

So, you will cook all these every day and I will make him eat …

I'll beat him with this stick I use on the cows until he learns

the lesson.

Nana leaves the room. Nani puts the kettle on the stove and then she leaves the room.

SCENE 3:

Tara is in the kitchen. She is making tea, from Nani's kettle and then turns to the audience

1. TARA (C.U.):

Greetings, field-worker friends. I hope you are all in good health.

And I hope your children are well, too. Helping families keep

their children healthy is a very important part of our job. And

it's not just night blindness we must teach our communities

about. There are many diseases that children can be protected

from if their parents know how to do it.

Nana comes in.

2. NANA:

Tara, I have come.

Under the Green Umbrella   Page 6 of 25
Episode #16   Draft # 2
Writers: Dr Selim Alden; Giasuddin Selim   Date: March 2

---

3. TARA:

So you have, Nana. ... Tea is almost ready ... I am sure you will

have some.

The sound of a rickshaw bell is heard off.

4. TARA:

There ... that is doctor uncle's rickshaw.

The doctor comes into the kitchen.

5. DOCTOR:

How are you Tara dear? And how is your health, Nana?

6. NANA AND TARA (SPEAKING AT THE SAME TIME):

I am well.

Tara pours tea for the doctor and for herself as they talk. Then they both sit down at the table where there is a pile of letters.

7. DOCTOR:

How many letters have come for us this week?

8. TARA:

Many. Look at this pile.

9. DOCTOR:

Good. Let's open the letters, let's see what our health-worker friends have written about this week.

10. TARA:

Doctor uncle, how about this letter.

Tara picks up and reads one of the letters.

TEACHING

11. TARA:

Health worker Jahanara Begum has written from Harbang Chokoria—She says 'In my areas, some mothers have complained that their children have no appetite. They do not want to eat anything. They almost throw up when food is offered. Sometimes, they talk of pain in the stomach. What would I advise them in such circumstances?'

12. DOCTOR:

Usually, children lose appetite when they are infested with worms. This may cause nausea, pain and loose motion. First, you give the medicine for treating worms. If their condition does not improve after taking medicine for worms, then refer them to the hospital for further treatment.

Tara picks up the manual and opens it at page 20.

13. TARA:

Doctor uncle, on page 20 of our health workers' manual, there is a lot of information on today's main topic: keeping children healthy in the home. We can use this while giving advice to the parents.

14. DOCTOR:

You have said it correctly, Tara … now, please, read the next letter.

Tara searches through the envelopes and picks up another letter.

15. TARA:

This one has been sent by an NGO health worker from Kushtia, Tahmina Khatun. She wants to know … if a child suffers from acute malnutrition, then what is to be done?

16. DOCTOR:

Due to malnutrition, a child loses disease-resistance power and may suffer from many diseases. A child may die too if acute malnutrition persists; so necessary measures have to be taken to feed the child balanced and nutritious food on a regular basis.

Under the Green Umbrella
Episode #16
Writers: Dr Selim Alden; Giasuddin Selim

Page 9 of 25
Draft # 2
Date: March 2

17. TARA:

(TARA HOLDS UP PICTURES OF THE VARIOUS FOODS
AS SHE MENTIONS THEM.)

Yes, doctor. To avoid malnutrition, children between five months and two years of age should be given soft 'Khichuri' with potato, green vegetables and fish, meat and egg, if possible, along with breast-milk every day. This food has to be given regularly, in small amounts every time.

18. DOCTOR:

A child suffering from malnutrition may get infected by other diseases easily; therefore, the parents have to be advised to take special care. If there is sign of minor cold or cough, the child should be referred to the clinic for treatment. The child's weight must be recorded every month. And let us remember that Vitamin-A supplement must be given to the child to prevent night blindness.

Tara and Nana exchange amused glances at the mention of night blindness.

19. TARA:

And as long as the child is still on breast-milk, then the mother should also be advised to take available but nutritious food to help maintain her supply of milk. (PAUSE) Doctor uncle, while listening to you, I remembered an incident. Its very interesting.

Nana steps forward excitedly in front of the camera.

20. NANA (HAPPILY):

That means ... drama time!

The camera moves CU on doctor.

21. DOCTOR:

Dear listeners, please watch our drama with attention. Let's particularly watch the way Tara interacts with the mother on this occasion. And remember, Tara will have a few questions for you after the drama.

The drama begins.

SCENE 4: INSIDE A SMALL HOUSE. DAYTIME

TRANSFORMING

The mother is seated and the young girl, Manju, is playing with some toys.

The mother has a baby on her lap, about 6–7 months old.

1. MOTHER:

O ... my jewel ... my new little baby, I shall buy a rattle from the fair for you to keep. Let the fairy of sleep come now and put my jewel to sleep.

Under the Green Umbrella   Page 11 of 25
Episode #16   Draft # 2
Writers: Dr Selim Alden; Giasuddin Selim   Date: March 2

Tara's voice is heard outside the house.

2. TARA (CALLING):

Manju's mother … O Manju's mother…

3. MOTHER (QUIETLY. ANGRY):

Ah … she has come again … that Tara Begum… Manju, go

and tell her that mother is not home. Tell her to go.

Manju jumps up and runs outside. We hear them talking outside the room as the mother
watches anxiously. She puts the baby on the floor.

4. MANJU:

Tara auntie …

5. TARA:

Upon my word! … Manju has such lovely hair.

6. MANJU:

Mother told me to tell you that she is not home.

7. TARA (LAUGHING):

Oh, is it so? Go and tell mother that I won't take long. I'll

just say a few words.

Mother walks toward the door as she speaks ...

8. MOTHER (CHANGING HER TONE):

Manju, I told you to give your auntie a seat.

9. MANJU:

But you said...

10. MOTHER (ANGRY):

Quiet ... you little brat ... leave us alone ...

Tara comes into the room calmly. Manju comes with her.

11. TARA:

Let it go, she is only a kid ... maybe, she did not understand
you well ... please don't scold her.

12. MOTHER:

Well, Manju, go to play now ...

13. TARA:

Manju's mother, why did you put the baby on the floor? She's
such a cute little thing ... won't she get all dirty?

14. MOTHER:

My floor is not dirty. Not any more dirty than any other floor.

15. TARA (PICKING UP THE CHILD):

Manju's mother, if you allow me, I would like to examine the child more carefully.

16. MOTHER:

Yes ... no! Well, no problem. Go ahead, ... but we often go to the doctor.

17. MANJU:

But, when did we go to the doctor, mother?

18. MOTHER (ANGRILY):

Ah, keep quiet!

A young boy comes into the room. About 3 years old.

19. TARA:

And there's Ranju, Manju's brother. Come to me, little man ... what a beautiful outfit you are wearing. So, Manju's mother, how is your son, Ranju's appetite?

Under the Green Umbrella   Page 14 of 25
Episode #16   Draft # 2
Writers: Dr Selim Alden; Giasuddin Selim   Date: March 2

20. MOTHER (HESITANTLY):

Yes, ... very good ... he can eat a lot ...

21. MANJU:

But mother, Ranju can't eat anything ... he always complains
of stomach ache ...

22. MOTHER (ANGRY):

Be gone ... you ... Stay out of my conversation.

23. TARA (GENTLY):

She is just a child ... we shouldn't scold her ...

Mother gets up and begins to walk out of the room...

24. MOTHER:

Please wait, sister Tara, I'll bring some paan.

25. TARA:

I can see some beautiful sandals over there, Manju ... why don't
you and your brother wear those? Do you know what happens
if you walk around bare-footed?

26. MANJU:

What happens, auntie?

27. TARA:

If you walk bare-footed, lots of dirty things cover your feet, isn't it? And there is a type of worm that enters the body through the feet if you walk bare-footed. Children suffer a lot when they get infested with worms. So, never walk bare-footed, OK?

28. MANJU:

Yes, auntie. Come now Ranju, put on your sandals.

The children sit down and put on their sandals as mother comes back into the room with the paan and tea.

29. MOTHER:

Leave us now, children ... let us talk. Here, take some paan.

The children exit.

30. TARA:

Manju's mother, please don't mind ... you have three lovely children ... but all of them have some kind of health problem. It seems your son, Ranju has worms. The baby has a skin disease. That beautiful girl Manju is also suffering from malnutrition.

Under the Green Umbrella   Page 16 of 25
Episode #16   Draft # 2
Writers: Dr Selim Alden; Giasuddin Selim   Date: March 2

31. MOTHER:

But these are not serious diseases.

Tara takes a book from her bag.

32. TARA:

If you have some time, I would like you to look at this book. These diseases can cause serious complications. But, if timely measures are taken, then there is nothing to fear. What do you say, will you take some time to look at this?

33. MANJU'S MOTHER:

All right ... let me see ...

Tara gets up and moves towards the door.

34. TARA:

I will come back tomorrow, if I may. And I would like to invite you to come with me to the clinic tomorrow morning with the children.

The scene fades as Tara leaves the house. Then the scene dissolves into

Under the Green Umbrella
Episode #16
Writers: Dr Selim Alden; Giasuddin Selim

Page 17 of 25
Draft # 2
Date: March 2

SCENE 5: MANJU'S HOUSE. DAY

Mother is in the room with the children. Tara is heard outside the door.

1. TARA (CALLING):

Manju's mother ...

Mother picks up the book when she hears Tara's voice. She keeps the book in her hands as she goes to the door and welcomes Tara inside...

2. MOTHER:

Please wait, I am coming.

3. TARA:

You promised yesterday that you would come to the clinic with

me this morning. Are you ready?

4. MOTHER:

Yes, let me dress up this little one. (CALLING) Manju ...

Ranju... let's go ... your Tara auntie is already here.

The children come in. Manju has on sandals. Ranju does not. He puts on his sandals after his sister speaks to him.

5. MANJU:

Ranju, don't walk bare-footed. Put on the sandals. We are going

to the satellite clinic with Tara auntie. Isn't it fun?

6. TARA:

So, Manju, what happens if you walk bare-footed?

7. MANJU:

We get worms.

8. TARA:

You have already learned. That is very good. So, if we're all ready

let's go to the clinic. (THEY ALL GO OUT THE DOOR)

SCENE 6: TARA'S KITCHEN. DAY

1. DOCTOR:

Health-worker friends, I hope you have watched our little drama

with attention. Let's discuss what the drama reminded us.

The doctor taps a glass with a spoon to make a 'gong' sound

Under the Green Umbrella
Episode #16
Writers: Dr Selim Alden; Giasuddin Selim

Page 19 of 25
Draft # 2
Date: March 2

TESTING

2. DOCTOR:

The audience sees relevant still shots from the drama as the doctor asks the questions.

So, tell me, when Tara first went to meet Manju's mother, what did Mother tell Manju to say to me?

The doctor pauses for 3 seconds

3. DOCTOR:

That mother was not home. That's right. Tara's client wanted to avoid meeting Tara. But Tara did not take any offence for that.

4. TARA:

As 'social teachers' we must never take offence if clients behave in this manner. We have to keep our cool and perform our duties of providing service and advice. Health-worker friends, at one stage I told Manju's mother that one of her children had worms, one had skin disease and one was suffering from malnutrition.

The doctor taps the glass again.

Under the Green Umbrella   Page 20 of 25
Episode #16   Draft # 2
Writers: Dr Selim Alden; Giasuddin Selim   Date: March 2

5. DOCTOR:

Tell me, what did Tara tell Manju's mother about these diseases?

Pause, 3 Seconds

6. DOCTOR:

That these diseases can cause serious complications. That's right. We must clearly explain to our clients that, even if these diseases do not seem bad, they can cause serious complications. But we must do it gently, as Tara did.

The doctor taps the glass again.

7. DOCTOR:

Now tell me, why did Tara tell the children not to walk barefooted?

Pause, 3 Seconds.

8. DOCTOR:

Because that could cause worm infestation. Correct. If we can give children health education in simple language, then they can learn to adopt good health practices at an early age.

Tara picks up the support book and opens to page 12.

9. TARA:

Health-worker friends, on pages 12 and 13 of our manual,
information on childhood diseases is given. Please make use of
the manual. The symptoms, causes, complications, prevention
and treatment of each disease are given there. You may explain
these to the clients with the help of the manual.

10. DOCTOR:

Children in Bangladesh too often suffer from scurvy, worms,
night blindness and so on. Parents sometimes don't realize how
bad these problems can be and so do not take them seriously.
So we must explain to them carefully how dangerous these may
become if timely treatment is not given.

11. TARA (PICKING UP A LETTER):

And that's something we health workers can do. In fact, our
success story of the week is about how to help children learn
important health facts. Today's success story comes from
health worker Latifa Begum of Amgaria Union under Kustia.
She writes:

As Tara reads the story, the scene fades to

Under the Green Umbrella   Page 22 of 25
Episode #16   Draft # 2
Writers: Dr Selim Alden; Giasuddin Selim   Date: March 2

SCENE 7: THE VILLAGE WHERE WE SEE THE ACTIONS THAT TARA IS DESCRIBING. DAY

1. TARA (V.O.) (READING THE STORY):

Once I gave medicine to the children of Progpur village under Alamdanga Thana for the treatment of worms. After one month when I went to a satellite clinic in that same village, I noticed that all the children were running to their mothers saying that the 'Worm Doctor' has come. I learned from the mothers that last time when I gave them the medicine for worms, plenty of worms had come out and because of that the children were frightened of me and running away. I told them not to be frightened as I was not going to give them any medicine right away. Rather, I was going to show them some pictures. On hearing this about 50 to 60 children came near and I explained with the help of pictures that their abdomen gets large if they have worms, that worms eat up everything they eat and as a result they will feel weak.

They will always feel sick, and not feel like studying or playing or even run away seeing me. The children understood, with the help of the pictures, what I said and they agreed to take medicine for worms. I told them that

I would come back after five or six months to give medicine again.

The scene fades back to the kitchen.

SCENE 8: TARA'S KITCHEN. DAY

1. DOCTOR:

Latifa Begum's success story is inspiring. We enjoyed listening,

and perhaps we all learned something useful: the value of using

pictures as we teach. So, if you would like to share with us your

ideas or experiences on keeping children healthy, please write

to us. But right now we have a quiz for you.

2. NANA (JUMPING UP EXCITEDLY):

I want to give the quiz question today.

3. TARA:

Ok, go ahead. Dear friends, don't forget to write down today's

quiz question.

Nana picks up the card on which the question is written. He stands very straight and tries to look very important as the camera moves in C.U. He clears his throat.

4. NANA:

So, my health-worker grand-sons and grand-daughters, tell me ... Tara Begum had identified three childhood diseases when she went to Manju's house ... *QUIZ QUESTION*: what are those diseases? I repeat the question: what are the three childhood diseases Tara Begum identified at Manju's house?

5. TARA:

Send your answer, and your opinions and letters to:

Here, the address is shown on the screen as Tara reads it.

TELLING:

6. TARA:

We shall meet again next week, same day, same time when we will learn more about home treatment for malaria and diarrhea.

7. TARA AND DOCTOR:

Good-bye for today.

8. NANA:

OK, Tara, as we go, let's hear a song to cheer us up.

Under the Green Umbrella
Episode #16
Writers: Dr Selim Alden; Giasuddin Selim

Page 25 of 25
Draft # 2
Date: March 2

9. TARA:

Sure Nana ... (*at this stage, Tara mentions the name of a listener who has requested a particular song. She gives the name of the song and the artists and the song is played under the closing credits of the program.*)

PROGRAM END

GUIDELINES FOR REVIEWING RECORDED INTERVIEWS, REAL-LIFE STORIES, AND REALITY PROGRAMS

When recording of interviews or other types of real-life presentations is done in the field rather than in a studio, it is wise to review the recording immediately and undertake the following steps before leaving the area:

1. Ensure **quality of sound** throughout the recording. If any areas are of poor sound quality, re-record them. For television presentations, it is equally important to check that there is no background activity going on that can distract from the speaker.
2. Listen carefully to the **lesson**. If the speaker/interviewee is supposed to be making, strengthening or reinforcing a teaching point, it is very important to ensure that what the speaker says is accurate and matches the instructional message that has been prescribed in the curriculum; and if necessary, have the host of the program add a short 'epilogue' after the interview or real-life story to stress the main educational points.
3. Ensure that all **NAMES** are given and correctly pronounced. The interviewee should be introduced by name unless he/she has requested that the name not be used. If the name *IS* used, the interviewer or the host who introduces the guest should use the name more than once, so that the audience can clearly hear and recall the name. If the name is *NOT* to be used, the interviewer or host must explain to the audience that the name is deliberately not being used at the request of the interviewee.

4. Ensure that the **length of the interview** is appropriate to the program in which it will be used. If the interview is too long, care must be taken in the editing to ensure that no parts of the lesson are erased, and that no emotionally powerful parts of the interview or story are erased.

If the lesson is too short, the program host should ask the interviewee or storyteller a question or two that will enrich the presentation. In cases where the interviewee or the storyteller has nothing more to add, s/he can be asked to select a favorite piece of music. The interviewer or host can then say something like, 'And so let's end today's interview (story, diary,) with some of ....'s (name of person) favorite music (then name the music and the presenter).

Recording 'Real People' in a Studio

If reality program recording is being done in a studio, it is helpful to bring the intended presenters to the studio well ahead of recording, so that they have a chance to understand how the recording will take place and to feel comfortable in the studio environment. The producer should spend time putting the presenters at ease and encouraging them to ask any questions they may have before the recording begins.

Rehearsing in the Studio

The question of rehearsing a 'reality' presenter is tricky. Many people give their best performance on the first run. Rehearsing can lead them into sounding unnatural when the actual recording begins. At the same time, with many inexperienced presenters, it is helpful to give them time to 'get comfortable' in front of the microphone. This can be done by the producer (in the control room) engaging in a normal, simple conversation with the presenter in front of the microphone for a few minutes. In the course of this conversation, the producer can ensure that the presenter is properly placed in relation to the microphone. At the same time, the presenter becomes accustomed to the microphone, the studio and the activities in the control room.

Mistakes during Recording

As much as possible, presenters should be encouraged to 'keep talking' even if they make mistakes during the recording. People with little or no microphone experience usually feel more comfortable with this approach than being told to stop every time they make a mistake. Most errors can be removed during post-recording editing. If a serious error is made, the producer can take note of it and ask the speaker to repeat that particular section after the main recording is finished.

10

EDU-TAINMENT FORMATS—THE CASE STUDY
TV, CD, DVD or Video

Distance Education programs can be created for special groups, such as soldiers or police officers.

INTRODUCTION TO THE CASE STUDY

Some distance education programs are made for a specific professional, semi-professional or community-helper audience and not designed to be broadcast on a public medium. Most frequently, this type of program, made for a specific audience, is presented on video or DVD. Such programs, when used for training sessions, can be structured with occasional 'stops' during which the facilitator can encourage participants to answer questions and share their points of view during open discussion.

The Case Study is an effective Edu-tainment format that can be used to educate groups of a specific audience in an entertaining way. The **Case Study** format for teaching purposes typically follows a pattern like this:

- Scene 1: presentation of a situation related to the topic being taught. The learners are asked to consider, while watching the situation, if any of the characters are doing anything that is wrong, or is likely to cause problems later
- *PAUSE* for audience discussion of the situation and possible solutions
- re-presentation of Scene 1 in which certain changes have been made that correct the mistakes or provide for avoidance of follow-on problems
- *PAUSE* for discussion of the improved scenario
- presentation of guidelines for viewers on what they should learn from the presentation and how they can make use of it in their own lives and professional activities

WRITER'S GUIDELINES FOR CASE STUDY PRESENTATION

The following guidelines can assist writers in creating successful Case Study programs:

Know the Audience

Because Case Study programs are usually designed for a very specific audience, writers need to be knowledgeable about the learners: their lifestyles; what their job requires of them, and the degree to which they are interested in increasing their knowledge. Program Managers should ensure that writers have an opportunity to visit and talk to the prospective learners and watch them on the job. Directors and producers also can benefit from spending time with the learners.

Adhere Strictly to the Curriculum Guide

Writers should always ensure that they are provided with precise guidelines on what is to be taught in the program. Even though the Case Study is often just one program, and is therefore not created in a Curriculum Guide Workshop, it is essential that the writer be given clear guidelines on precisely what is to be taught in the program.

Prepare the Program Segments Carefully

This has to be done so that the question and discussion breaks come at the point where the learners are involved in the action of the story and keen to see what is going to happen next. Making the breaks at these points will help ensure that learners remain engaged throughout the entire program.

Pay Attention to Comments from Script Reviewers

The Script Review Team will include people who are well acquainted with the learners and their needs, and so their comments should be designed to strengthen the programs. Writers should always ask if they are not sure how to use or interpret comments from the reviewers.

Be Committed to the Task of Writing an Important Educational Program

Writers of all Edu-tainment programs should recognize and respect the valuable role they are playing in upgrading knowledge and improving behavioral standards among the learners for whom the programs are being created.

THE COMMON PATTERN OF A CASE STUDY PROGRAM

Case Study programs tend to follow a common pattern. Generally, the topic is introduced and led by a host/teacher who guides the audience through the steps of the case study; the host/teacher explains the main points of the topic and invites the audience to think about how they would react or behave if faced with a similar situation. The common pattern of the case study, therefore, is as follows:

1. The first scene, following the introduction, shows the main character—representative of the audience—faced with or involved in a situation common to members of that audience, where he/she has to make a decision or a choice and act upon it.
2. The teacher interrupts the story when the main character has made the decision or begun to take action and invites the audience to answer some questions about or discuss together the possible outcome of the decision the character made, and whether they think it was right or appropriate.
3. The teacher invites the audience to watch the next scene which shows what happened because of the character's choice.
4. The teacher invites discussion on the outcome of the character's decision and then invites the learners to suggest other decisions or actions that the character could have taken.
5. The beginning of the opening scene is shown again, but this time the main character (or another character) takes a different decision or action—in line with what the program is trying to teach. Again, the audience does not see the final outcome of that decision at this point.
6. The host interrupts the story to invite the audience to consider and discuss what the outcome might be this time.
7. The video returns to show (a) what happened as a result of the first decision and (b) what happened as a result of the second decision.
8. The host closes the program by inviting the audience to apply the lessons of the Case Study to their own lives and to make a clear decision about how they should behave when similar circumstances arise in their own lives.

Although the Case Study is not as tightly structured as the other Edu-tainment programs, it still follows the 6T processes of lesson presentation. The program stops from time to time to allow learners to think about what they have learned and how they would transform that learning into life skills of their own. At the same time, the various 'demonstrations' in the story show how individuals can have a positive effect on the lives of others.

The video, *The Song of Life,* written by Sunil Pokarel, was designed for policemen in Nepal, but the script was also designed to be easily adjusted for use with other male groups such as soldiers. This version was intended to be shown only to policemen in their barracks. Its aim was to give that audience clear, straightforward knowledge about sexually trans-mitted infections (including HIV), and to teach them how to protect themselves and others from the infections. The video aimed to encourage married policemen to remain faithful to their wives while away from home, and to encourage all policemen—whether married or not—to use condoms if they visit sex workers.

This particular case study invited the learners to examine two different situations: one involving a married man and another involving an unmarried man, so that it would be applicable to all police force members watching it.

COVER PAGE

Program Title: The Song Of Life   Duration: 15 mins
Format: Case Study   Topic: Safe Sex
Audience: **Men Away from Home (Police/Army)**   **Draft 2.**
Writer: Sunil Pokarel

Measurable Objectives: After viewing this program, the chosen audience will

KNOW:
- About the importance of personal responsibility for Safe Sex.
- How to always ensure 'safe sex'.
- Safe Sex (using a condom correctly) protects them and their loved ones from STIs/HIV/AIDS.

DO:
- Be faithful and/or practice safe sex and encourage others in their profession to adopt the same safe behaviors.

ATTITUDE:
Viewers will develop a sense of personal responsibility to themselves, to their wives (or future wives) and to their important role as policemen.

PURPOSE:
The purposes of this program are:

- to educate policemen about safe sex and
- to encourage a sense of sexual responsibility in members of the police force.

Cast (Characters)   **Locations**
S.P. Thapa   Office
Ram Bahadur   Village of Ram Bahadur
Suntali (wife of Ram Bahadur)   Police Post (near highway)
Harka Bahadur
Binod   Bhatti Pasal (Local inn)
Some policemen   KANCHHI'S House (indoor)
Youth-1
Youth-2
Kanchhi
Hari Bahadur
Bir Bahadur

Title: The Song of Life   Draft 2.
Writer: Sunil Pokarel   Page 1 of 16

Title song: The Song of life
Credits will be shown over the song and over a montage of short clips from the film. The final credit shot shows Senior Policeman (S.P.) Thapa—in the uniform of an S.P.—strolling near the police post along the Mahendra Highway. Scene 1 follows.

SCENE 1: EXTERIOR. NEAR THE POLICE POST. EVENING

S.P. Thapa is strolling along, observing the evening life. The camera follows him awhile. Then he turns to the camera and speaks directly to the audience:

1. S.P. THAPA:

Like a sweet song, our life is also beautiful and precious. Of all

the living beings, human beings have the most conscious and

superior life. So, we have responsibility toward life as well. A

slight mistake can ruin our life and that of our loved ones.

He sees a young couple 'flirting'. The camera watches them awhile as S.P. Thapa talks.

TELLING:

2. S.P. THAPA (V.O.):

Sex is an important and essential part of human life. Sex can make life as sweet and enchanting as a song—as long as it is *SAFE* sex. Unwise and unsafe sex, on the other hand, can completely destroy this invaluable life of ours. So, we must learn about *SAFE* sex. It's easy enough to make mistakes in life, especially when our feelings are involved. You see that young man over there...

The camera picks up Ram Bahadur who is walking towards the police post. He seems happy and is walking cheerfully. He is looking at something in his hand.

3. S.P. THAPA (V.O.):

That young man is Ram Bahadur. He was married only two months ago and he loves his wife very much. His life with her is indeed a sweet song.

Ram Bahadur stops walking. He looks down at what is in his hand. The camera goes in for a close up, showing Ram's wife on their wedding day. Then he continues towards the police post.

4. S.P. THAPA (V.O.):

Ram Bahadur also loves his country very much. He has a strong

desire to serve the country—and attain personal progress—by

joining the Nepal Police. His friend from the same village,

Harka Bahadur, works in the Nepal Police at a police post along

the Mahendra Highway.

Ram Bahadur and Harka Bahadur meet outside the gates of the police post. They walk in together. Various shots of activities at the police post during a regular day. Both Ram Bahadur and Harka Bahadur are involved in the activities.

5. S.P. THAPA (V.O.):

Ram Bahadur has come to visit Harka Bahadur in order to

observe police life and also with a hope of joining the force.

So far, Ram Bahadur is finding police life interesting and

challenging. He stays with his friend Harka Bahadur the whole

day and observes his activities.

We see *RAM* in bed at night, sleeping and then he wakes up suddenly.

Teaching begins and continues as the two versions of the case study are shown.

6. S.P. THAPA (V.O.):

But Ram Bahadur finds the evenings difficult to pass. He often remembers his wife at night. The night before yesterday, he saw his wife Suntali in the dream—sitting with her eyes full of tears. He woke up and couldn't fall asleep again.

S.P. Thapa steps in front of the camera and addresses the audience directly.

7. S.P. THAPA:

And this is the point at which our story becomes a question. One slight mistake right now could change Ram Bahadur's sweet song of life into a miserable hell. Watch closely my friends. Will Ram Bahadur make a mistake that could ruin his life? If so, what will that mistake be? And would *YOU* make that mistake?

The video can be paused at this stage for discussion.

SCENE 2: INTERIOR. RAM AND HARKA'S ROOM. EVENING

Harka is finishing dressing in casual dress. Ram, bored to death, is lying on the bed, gazing at a photograph of his wife.

1. HARKA:

Come on, Ram. Why do you look so miserable? Thinking of your wife, or what?

Title: The Song of Life

Writer: Sunil Pokarel

2. RAM:

(WITH A SLIGHT LAUGH TO COVER THE LIE)

Oh, no...It's just...well. It's interesting enough throughout the day. But...don't you find it...a bit difficult to pass the evenings?

Harka is combing his hair and tidying his clothes, as he speaks.

3. HARKA:

That's just because you're not used to it. And you're not really working here yet, either. For me, it's no problem. We're on duty the whole day, and in the evening it's great to get some free time. You know...playing volleyball, writing letters to home... singing. I never notice the time.

4. RAM:

Ugh...I'm bored to death.

5. HARKA:

So, why are you sitting alone? Sitting alone gives you too much time to think. You'd better come and play volleyball with us.

6. RAM:

No, thank you. I don't want to play volleyball. Binod and his friends have invited me to some entertainment. I'd rather go with them.

7. HARKA:

Let me tell you, Ramjee. Binod and his friends are no good. If you go with them, you'll be keeping BAD company. If you want a life like mine, don't follow them! No, don't go to them. They'll say, 'Let's have fun. Let's drink' ...and you'll drink.

8. RAM:

So, what's wrong with a little drink now and then?

9. HARKA:

One drink is never enough. Next thing you know, you'll be intoxicated. And that's when you lose your power to make good judgments, and to decide what's right and what's wrong. And then...

10. RAM:

I didn't quite follow you. Just some entertainment or so ...

11. HARKA:

Yes, but a momentary enjoyment can ruin your entire life. And maybe your wife's, too. Look, you want to join the police force. How can you expect to control other people's crimes when you can't control yourself?

12. RAM:

What can happen to me? I just want to see some friends and have some talk to kill this monotony.

13. HARKA:

That's fine, but there are good ways to pass the time. You shouldn't be just sitting like this. Come on, play volleyball with us. Time will fly past, you'll see. You'll enjoy it, and it will make you tired, so you'll have a sound sleep.

14. RAM:

I'll be back after seeing my friends. Volleyball, I've always played. I want something new. Don't worry, I'll come back intact.

Ram Bahadur goes out the door. Harka follows him. The door closes behind them.

SCENE 4: EXTERIOR. VOLLEYBALL COURT. EVENING

Harka Bahadur and Ram go toward the volleyball court. Beyond the volleyball court, Ram Bahadur is met by his friends who are laughing and obviously planning to have a 'good time'. The frame freezes and the word 'MISTAKE' appears, followed by a question mark (MISTAKE?).

S.P. Thapa walks into the shot and speaks directly to the camera.

1. S.P. THAPA:

So, my friends, what do you think? Did Ram Bahadur, a happily

married man with a beautiful wife make a mistake by going

off with a group of so-called friends who obviously want to get

drunk? What do YOU think could be the worst result of his

'evening of fun'?

PAUSE FOR DISCUSSION

2. S.P. THAPA:

Let's watch!

SCENE 5: INTERIOR. INN. NIGHT

In the local inn, Ram Bahadur and his new friends, all drunk, are talking loudly. They
are intoxicated.

1. BINOD:

How did you like it? Isn't our Saili's liquor tasty?

2. RAM:

Yes, it's tasty. After so many days ... today ... greatly

enjoyed.

3. YOUTH 1:

That's it. A person of such an energetic age, yes, one should enjoy.

4. YOUTH 2:

Binod, I'm feeling drowsy. Isn't it time to go now? (WINKS AT BINOD)

5. BINOD:

Why not? They say there is also a fresh one come today. Shall we go Ram Bahadurjee?

6. RAM:

It's getting late, too. Yes, now we should go. Harka Bahadur might be waiting for me.

7. BINOD:

(LAUGHING) What the hell, Harka Bahadur? Ugh, such an energetic young man. You know, Saili...Maili ... you know, it's fun (WINKS AT HIM SUGGESTIVELY)

I mean going to 'them'.

8. RAM:

(STAMMERING) No ... Not for me ... wife at home ...
I mean ...

9. YOUTH 1:

Wife at home is at home. Since you are a man, you've got to
act like a man, you know. Why this dilemma? Let's go. You
say you're going to join the police force, and yet you talk like
a eunuch?

10. RAM:

(DRUNKENLY) Who's a eunuch? Call me eunuch?

  What do you think of me? ... Like this ... Let's go.

11. YOUTH 2:

Maybe, it's getting too late for him. Let's leave him ...

12. RAM:

No, it's not late. Who's eunuch? eunuch? Let's go. If it means
going, I'll go.

13. BINOD:

Yes, let's go. Let's go, Ram Bahadurjee.

All get up. We see a dimly lit inn in the background. They
stagger toward the dark in which they are buried. Freeze frame,
showing '*MISTAKE 2*?'

Title: The Song of Life   Draft 2.
Writer: Sunil Pokarel   Page 11 of 16

SCENE 5A: CLOSE UP S.P. THAPA

1. S.P. THAPA:

(SPEAKING DIRECTLY TO AUDIENCE)

Respected friends, what do you think? Did you observe the

second mistake made by our young friend? What do you think

will be the outcome of this mistake?

PAUSE FOR DISCUSSION

2. S.P. THAPA:

Let's watch together.

TRANSFORMING:

SCENE 6: INTERIOR: A ROOM IN A HOVEL. NIGHT

Kanchhi and Ram Bahadur enter the room. By appearance and make-up, Kanchhi looks like a professional sex worker. Poverty has left its marks in the room. Once in, Kanchhi closes the door, at the back of which a poster with the message 'Let's use condom and prevent AIDS' can be seen. Ram Bahadur is excited.

1. KANCHHI:

(POINTING TO THE POSTER) Got it?

2. RAM:

What? Money? Yes, I've got it. I'm a male, you understand?

I'm a male. I earn money.

Title: The Song of Life   Draft 2.
Writer: Sunil Pokarel   Page 12 of 16

3. KANCHHI:

No, I wasn't talking about money. Binod has already paid it.
(POINTING TO THE POSTER). That one, I mean. Got it?

4. RAM:

No. What's this and that? What do you want? No, we don't
need anything like that... It's paid, isn't it? That's all. Come
here, right away.

Ram closes the door with a kick. Camera moves outside the door. Frame freezes, showing
'MISTAKE 3?'

SCENE 7: C.U. IN FRONT OF CAMERA

1. S.P. THAPA:

Did you observe Ram Bahadur's activities? How do you feel?
Did he do the right thing? Is he engaging in safe sex? Did you
notice the mistakes he's made? ... Let's talk about that.

PAUSE FOR DISCUSSION. Then the video picks up:

Now I'll show you Hari Bahadur's story. See what Hari Bahadur
does in a situation similar to Ram Bahadur's, okay...Let's see
if he makes the same mistakes or if he finds a sensible way to
avoid them.

Title: The Song of Life   Draft 2.
Writer: Sunil Pokarel   Page 13 of 16

SCENE 8: INTERIOR. HARKA'S ROOM. EVENING

(This is the same scene as Scene 2 of the drama but with Hari in place of Ram. The dialogue and actions are the same until we come to the following change:)

There is a loud knock at the door. Binod and his friends burst in. It is obvious that they have already been drinking.

1. BINOD:

Hey, Hari, we've been waiting for you. When you didn't turn

up we thought we'd better come and rescue you from old

stick-in-the-mud, Harka here.

2. HARI:

O.K. O.K. I'm ready. Let's get out of this place.

Hari and Binod and the others head for the door. Harka calls after him and holds up the picture of Hari's wife (this is a different picture from the one of Ram's wife)

3. HARKA (CALLING TO HIM):

Oh Hari...Hari...

(HE HOLDS UP THE PICTURE AND SPEAKS

QUIETLY) Aren't you forgetting something?

Hari stops...he sees the picture...he hesitates and then turns to the door again. Binod and his friends are already through the door.

4. HARI (CALLING):

Right, Binod. You go ahead and enjoy yourself your way... (HE

TURNS BACK TO HARKA) I'm going to play volleyball.

Hari goes to Harka and takes the picture of his wife in his hands. Both men are smiling happily.

Freeze frame. S.P. Thapa walks into the scene and speaks directly to the audience.

SCENE 11: THAPA. C.U TO AUDIENCE

TESTING

1. S.P. THAPA:

So now, dear friends, you have seen the stories of two married

men away from home: Ram Bahadur and Hari Bahadur.

Which of the two men do you think behaved more wisely?

PAUSE FOR DISCUSSION. THEN THAPA COMES ONTO THE SCREEN AGAIN.

2. S.P. THAPA:

Hari Bahadur. Right. In these days, when the dreaded fatal

disease, HIV/AIDS, is all around us, we cannot be too careful.

The married man who remains faithful to his wife will never

run the risk of dying of this terrible disease. Nor will he ever

put his wife and family at risk either.

Title: The Song of Life   Draft 2.
Writer: Sunil Pokarel   Page 15 of 16

S.P. Thapa walks out of the picture and into the inn as he speaks.

SCENE 11A: INTERIOR. IN THE INN. EVENING

Binod and his friends are already there, drinking. With them is a new character—Bir Bahadur.

1. S.P. THAPA:

But what about the young and restless unmarried man who

has no beautiful and loving wife to be faithful to? Let's look at

Binod and his friends again. This time, it is not Ram Bahadur

who is with him, nor even Hari Bahadur. Tonight, it is Bir

Bahadur who is drinking with Binod. Bir Bahadur is a healthy,

young, unmarried man.

(From here, the Case Study continues, but this time examining and questioning the behavior of two unmarried men, the first of whom behaves foolishly and puts himself at risk of HIV while the second makes sure to protect himself from HIV infection with the correct use of a condom. The Case Study ends as follows):

1. S.P. THAPA (SPEAKING DIRECTLY TO THE AUDIENCE):

Friends, please take care of yourselves. Learn the song of life.

When away from home, let's keep ourselves busy in the evenings,

or do some constructive work. Let's avoid alcohol. Because

alcohol adversely affects our power of right judgment.

Title: The Song of Life   Draft 2.
Writer: Sunil Pokarel   Page 16 of 16

Married men ... let's be faithful. Let's remain honest and faithful to our wives. The safest sex is the one that is limited to one faithful and uninfected partner only.

In other circumstances, let's use condoms correctly and consistently. HIV/AIDS is a killer. Once we get it, there's no alternative to death. Your life is not simply yours.

Your life also means other people: your wife, your children, your partner—present or future; family, society, and even our country. For them all, you must protect your life. Protect yourself and your loved ones from HIV/AIDS. Please always have safe sex so that we can all continue the beautiful Song of Life.

S.P. THAPA turns and walks off into the night, mingling with the people around him.

'Song of Life', the title song, is played and rises in volume as the credits are run.

END

Those who have been watching the Case Study are then invited to discuss in detail the various points it raised and give their own ideas and suggestions for overcoming the problems highlighted by the Case Study.

PART 3

Auxiliary and Support Materials

11

Support Materials for Edu-tainment Programs

Support materials, such as flip charts, are valuable aids for community workers.

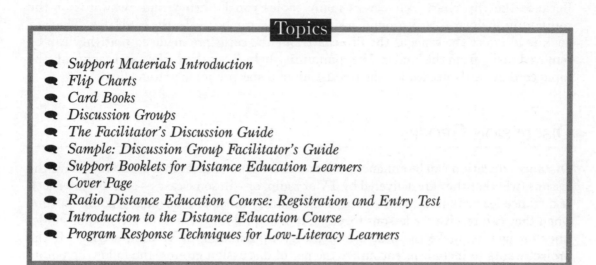

SUPPORT MATERIALS INTRODUCTION

It has long been realized that in behavior change communication, one medium alone is never enough. There is always a need for some type of support materials. This is as true for distance education programs as it is for behavior change programs for the general public. Support materials for community workers might take the form of flip charts, picture books, discussion guides, text books/booklets or other printed matter.

FLIP CHARTS

These can be created and distributed to the community-helpers so that they have pictures which can help them describe important points to their clients. Typically, a flip chart is a series of pages or cards that are held together with a plastic binding comb. One side of the page will be a picture that the community-helper will show to the client; the other side will have brief, clear statements about the topic that can guide the community-helper's discussion with the client. Even in cases where the community-helper might be illiterate or low-literate, the pictures on the flip chart can provide a valuable reminder of the main points to be shared with the client.

CARD BOOKS

Because the flip chart that covers many topics can be heavy and awkward for the community-helper to carry around, a simpler model can be used—the card book. The card book is in effect the same as the flip chart, but the cards are made so that they can be removed easily from the binder. The community-helper can then select and carry only the topic card or cards needed for the discussion of a specific topic with a client.

DISCUSSION GROUPS

Distance education can be enhanced if learners are able to meet in a group to receive the lessons (whether they are delivered by TV or radio, or—in some cases—even by Internet). If distance learners in a specific area of the country are able to arrange a common time when they can receive the lessons together, it is helpful for them to be given some guidelines on how to make the best use of the group-listening or viewing activity. If the project wants to include or encourage the use of discussion groups, the following points should be considered:

Preparing for Discussion Groups

1. Determine the main purpose of the discussion groups. Is it to encourage learners to keep listening to or viewing the lessons, or to encourage them to talk about ways in which they can apply what they have been learning, or both?
2. Know who the members of the group will be, so that the discussion questions can be formulated appropriately. Are they likely to be learners for whom much of the topic matter is quite new, or are they more likely to be experienced learners for whom the discussion could be a way of further enhancing their knowledge and practice, by inviting them to share lessons learned on the job and reinvigorating their interest in using their knowledge?
3. Determine whether the group members will be actually listening to or watching the programs together, or whether they will listen or watch in their own homes or workplaces and then get together at a later date for the discussion. This will make a difference to the way the discussion group is handled.
4. If they are listening or viewing together, determine where they will be and who will provide the radio or TV. Encourage the group to make sure that they have power (electric, battery or even solar) for the radio or TV and that the venue is such that everyone in the group can clearly hear the radio or see the TV screen.

5. Determine if there will be a designated discussion group facilitator, and whether there will be any training for the facilitator.
6. Decide if there will be a discussion group facilitator's guide booklet. Where it is not possible to give on-the-ground training for discussion group facilitators, the guidebook can provide detailed instructions on conducting the discussion group.

THE FACILITATOR'S DISCUSSION GUIDE

The facilitator's discussion guide booklet, whether it is for groups with trained leaders or not, should contain:

1. An outline of the lesson format together with some brief information on the structure of the given format. If an Edu-tainment serial drama format is being used, the Discussion Guide should include a brief outline of the entire story (without giving away the ending) and main characters. Where a series is being used, the guide should contain a brief description of the main characters and the location in which the various stories occur. This outline will give the discussion group necessary knowledge in the event that any of the broadcasts are missed by the whole group.
2. A list of the main characters in the programs, whether they are teachers or characters, their names, who they are, how they are related to each other, and so on.
3. The main teaching points for each lesson; these will be taken from the Curriculum Guide and listed in easy point form. Even if learners have been provided with a Support Booklet of their own, it is advantageous for the Facilitator's Guide to contain these main points again, in case there are occasions when none of the learners has brought the Support Booklet to the meeting.
4. Some questions to start discussion on each day's lesson. These questions will relate to the lesson, rather than to the story.
5. An address to which participants' questions and comments can be sent.

If there is no training for the discussion group leaders, the Facilitator's Guide book should begin with information on such matters as:

- how to set up the venue
- how to encourage people to listen to or view the lessons on a regular basis
- how to encourage learners to open or join in discussion
- how to respond to comments from group members
- how to open and close the meeting
- how to avoid dominating the discussion

Running the Discussion Group

The Facilitator's Guide should contain the following guidelines:

If learners are listening to or watching the lesson together in the same venue:

1. Invite listeners to come at least 15 minutes ahead of the broadcast.
2. When all are present, remind them briefly of what happened in the last lesson and what main teaching points were covered.
3. Advise learners briefly of what today's lesson will be and ask them to listen specifically for the main points of the lesson.
4. Invite listeners (if they are literate) to take notes on what they hear if they choose to. (The discussion group leader should also take notes.)
5. Listen or watch the day's lesson together.
6. After the broadcast, ask if anyone in the group would like to open the discussion with a comment or a question.
7. If there are no volunteers to start the discussion, the discussion group leader should make use of one of the questions provided in the discussion guide.
8. While some group members might want to talk a lot about other experiences they have had, the discussion group leader should encourage learners to concentrate on the main points of the lesson and how these can best be used in their work. Group members should also be encouraged to keep comments brief so that there is time for others to contribute to the discussion.

If learners have been listening to or watching the lesson separately and then come together for discussion:

Begin by reminding learners of the content of the lesson to be discussed, which will be outlined in the Facilitator's Guide. Then pick up from Point 6 in the list given above.

SAMPLE: DISCUSSION GROUP FACILITATOR'S GUIDE

Page 1

The Facilitator's Guide should begin with a general introduction on the value of Discussion Groups, such as the following:

Introduction to Discussion Facilitation

It is important to encourage people to listen or watch this program (give program name) in groups so that they can talk together about different points that are raised in the lessons. Discussion Groups are always more successful if there is a facilitator who can ask the group questions and direct the discussion. This *Facilitator's Guide* is designed to assist you, the group facilitator, to hold group discussions and to encourage the members of your group to talk openly and to respect each other's ideas and opinions.

Running a Successful Discussion Group

To run a successful discussion group, it is recommended that you review the one-page guide for each lesson prior to meeting with your group each time. This will help you become familiar with the topic and the questions you can ask to help start a discussion. If you are unsure of anything about the topic, this advance reading will give you time to obtain answers from an organization or individual who is knowledgeable about the topic.*

Reporting

As discussion group leader, you should keep notes on the discussion each week, so that you can write down any interesting questions or points that are raised and send them to the program producer. Reporting on the results of your discussion group is important because the opinions and suggestions of learners will help shape future programs, and give producers an idea of where the focus should be in future programs.

---

*The Discussions Guide should include a page providing names and contact numbers of local people who can give the discussion leader further information on the topic if needed.

Guidelines for Conducting a Successful Discussion Group

Page 2

Guidelines for Setting up the Discussion Group

1. Find and establish a regular place for the Discussion Group to meet each week. This could be in a school, a religious meeting place, or any other quiet location where a group can sit together and meet every week. Be sure it is a quiet environment so that all group members will be able to hear/see the radio or TV.
2. Encourage members of your intended audience to come to the Discussion Group each week. You can notify them by:
   - sending letters of invitation to local organizations with which they are in contact, describing the program and asking organization leaders to tell people about the Discussion Group
   - putting up notices in places that are frequented by your intended audience
3. Ensure that you have a good radio, TV or video player, and that it is placed such that everyone in the group can hear or see it.
4. If you are using batteries, be sure that you have extra batteries on hand, so they can be replaced quickly if needed.
5. Invite people to arrive at the Discussion Group venue at least 15 minutes ahead of the broadcast, so that you can prepare them for the upcoming program.

Discussion Guidelines

Page 3

The following guidelines will help you make sure that your group has successful discussions after each lesson:

1. Ensure that no one person dominates the discussion. You can do this by directing questions to or asking for comments from specific people, rather than always asking for an open response and waiting for someone to respond.
2. Respect all answers and comments, and encourage all group members to respect one another, even if they disagree. It may be useful to have the group members set rules for the discussions that everyone can agree on.
3. Encourage members to keep their comments and answers brief, so that everyone has a chance to join in.
4. Pay close attention to the person speaking. Keep side conversations to a minimum, so that everyone can hear the person who is talking.
5. Encourage participants to listen carefully to each other, and consider the opinions of others before offering their own comments and opinions.

6. Encourage learners to try to find solutions to concerns and problems, rather than just listing their complaints.
7. Encourage group members to let you know what ideas and suggestions they would like to forward to the program producers; include these in your regular report.

Before Each Program

1. Welcome the participants. Remind them that the purpose of the Discussion Group is to give everyone a chance to think about and discuss the topic and to raise questions and ideas of their own. Encourage participants to pay close attention to the program and make notes if they would like to.
2. State the topic of today's lesson. Even before the program begins, invite participants to begin to think about (and talk about, if there is time) their own responses to the topic, so that they can compare their own feelings with what they hear in the program.
3. Turn on the radio or TV several minutes before the program is timed to start to be sure that that it is working properly, that everyone is able to hear or see it, and that everyone is ready to pay attention.
4. At the end of the session, remind participants that you can provide them with names and telephone numbers of organizations that can help them with problems or questions (*Note: This point should not be included if there are no appropriate organizations available to help the learners*).

After Each Program

1. Invite participants to open the discussion by commenting on any part of the program that particularly interested them. (Remind them to listen respectfully to each other and to give everyone a chance to speak.)
2. Use the questions provided for each program as a way of opening up discussion if participants do not initiate their own discussion.
3. At the end of the discussion, wrap up by summarizing the main messages of the lesson. You can ask one of the participants to do this.
4. Make a note of the attendance for the day at the bottom of the page.
5. Make notes on the most interesting comments or questions in the space at the bottom of the page.
6. Provide any comments of your own that you think would help to make the lessons more beneficial for future learners.

    Fold the sheet so that the address is correctly placed, and mail it to: (*Give the address here*)

Introduction to *(Program Name)*
Distance Education Course

Page 4

This page will give a simple but clear outline of the program explaining the following points:

- the title of the program
- the day, time and length of broadcast and number of broadcasts in the project
- intended audience and overall major topic; for example, 'Teaching Adolescent Life Skills'
- format of the program
- brief description of main characters or hosts
- suggestions on how learners can interact with the program—if that is possible

The Lessons

Pages 5 and 6

*There will be a **lesson guide** for each program. Each **lesson guide** occupies two pages (back to back) and is designed as follows. On one side will be:*
Program #: (Give the number and the topic to be studied)

Here will be a brief listing of the main points to be covered (taken from the Curriculum Guide)

Before the Program

1. Explain what the topic of today's program is and briefly explain the nature of the main points to be taught and what is expected of those who take the course.
2. If there is time before the program begins, invite participants to comment on their knowledge of and experiences with the topic so they can compare them later with what they heard in the program.
3. Listen to or watch the program.

After the Program

1. Turn off the radio or TV.
2. Ask if anyone would like to open the discussion with comments on what they have heard. If open discussion begins freely, it might not be necessary to use the questions that follow.

3. Be sure participants listen carefully and respectfully to one another, and that everyone is given the chance to speak.
4. If it is necessary to prompt discussion, you can use some or all of the following questions:

(Here would follow a list of questions relevant to the lesson given in today's program.)

Final Notes on Today's Meeting:
How many participants were there in today's meeting?
Female_____Male _____Total_____

Comments from Facilitator

What were some interesting points or questions raised in today's meeting? (Write your notes here, then fold the page, stick it shut, and mail it or deliver it to the address on the other side of this page.)

On the other side of the back-to-back page will be the address to which these pages, complete with learner comments could be sent. The same page layout will be included in the Guide for each program in the series.

SUPPORT BOOKLETS FOR DISTANCE EDUCATION LEARNERS

Distance education projects designed to update the skills of community-helpers, be they professionals or semi-professionals, usually supply some type of a support booklet, to which learners can refer during and after the program. These booklets can be used to

1. register learners in the course,
2. provide a pre-test,
3. provide a calendar giving the dates and times of each lesson, as well as the radio or TV station through which the courses will be delivered,
4. reinforce the main points of each broadcast lesson,
5. provide illustrations where needed (particularly with radio programs), and tables (such as that shown with the lesson on malaria in the following sample)
6. give more specific knowledge on topics that cannot be openly discussed on public media, such as issues related to sexual health,
7. provide assignments which the learners are required to complete to enhance their learning and as a way of monitoring the program success and student progress. (*Assignments should be required only where learners are literate, where it is possible for the learners to submit them to the program office, and where there are staff in the program office who can respond to the learners' assignments.*)
8. provide a post-test,
9. provide a means for learners to send in questions and comments related to the program topics, or to send in written assignments if these are required.

The Pre- and Post-Test Pages

As demonstrated in the following sample booklet, pre- and post-tests can be delivered without having to bring the learners to a common meeting place. This can be done by giving the test on radio or television. Learners have the page of the Support Booklet in front of them as they listen to or watch the test being given. The tester will read the question and then read three or four possible answers. Learners are required simply to circle the number of what they believe to be each correct answer. This type of testing makes it difficult for the learners to cheat on the answers for several reasons:

- they do not see the answers written down, so they cannot take the written questions and search out the answers
- the possible answers are read fairly quickly so there is no time to write them down in the hope of checking the answers later
- the test is given only once and respondents must hand in or mail in their answers immediately, so there is little or no time for them to check their answers.

Another advantage of this type of testing is that it is suitable for low-literate students who might not be able to read written questions or give written responses.

Designing the Support Booklet

The support booklet should be designed specifically for each course, depending on such things as the existence of other support materials; the ease of distribution and collection of registration forms and assignments; the literacy level of the participants. The following is a sample of how a Support Booklet might be designed. Obviously, there will be differences depending on the topic, the audience, and the intentions and details of the project. This booklet was designed for a radio series, but can be easily adapted for a television project.

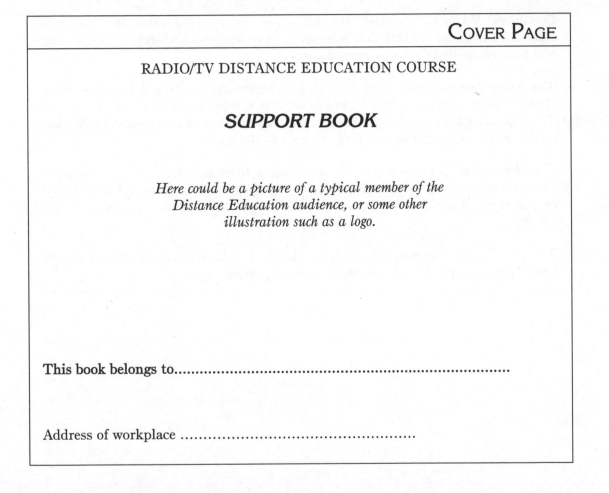

COVER PAGE

RADIO/TV DISTANCE EDUCATION COURSE

SUPPORT BOOK

Here could be a picture of a typical member of the Distance Education audience, or some other illustration such as a logo.

This book belongs to..

Address of workplace ....

RADIO DISTANCE EDUCATION COURSE: REGISTRATION AND ENTRY TEST

Page 1

Dear .... (The gap should be filled with the appropriate professional title: Teacher, Community Health Nurse, counselor, and so on.)

We are so happy that you are interested in taking our Training Course. We are sure that you will enjoy it and that the lessons will help you to be happier and more successful in your job.

When you have registered for this course, we will send you your course materials. These will be a Support Book, a pen, a calendar giving broadcast times, and a T-shirt (*or whatever incentive the project will be offering—if anything*).

Certificate: When you complete the full course and pass the Final Test, you will receive a *Certificate of Merit* that you can hang on your wall to show everyone that you have completed this important course.

The Entry Questionnaire: The first step in registration is completing the Entry Questionnaire. This is *NOT* a test to find out how much you know or do not know. These questions are to help the Distance Education Program developers decide what topics are of most interest and greatest need to the learners.

Completing the Questionnaire: You must listen to your radio or TV to complete the questionnaire on the next page. Have this questionnaire page and your pencil or pen ready. Tune to station ...... on ....(day and date) at.........time. Listen carefully.

Your host (name) will read the questions one by one. All you have to do is circle the letter that gives the *RIGHT* answer to each question.

Questionnaire page					Page 2

1	a	b	b	d	e
2	a	b	c	d	e
3	a	b	c	d	e
4	a	b	c	d	e
5	a	b	c	d	e
6	a	b	c	d	e
7	a	b	c	d	e
8	a	b	c	d	e
9	a	b	c	d	e
10	a	b	c	d	e
11	a	b	c	d	e
12	a	b	c	d	e
13	a	b	c	d	e
14	a	b	c	d	e
15	a	b	c	d	e
16	a	b	c	d	e
17	a	b	c	d	e
18	a	b	c	d	e
19	a	b	c	d	e
20	a	b	c	d	e (more lines can be added as needed)

Page 3

Mail in the Entry Questionnaire: When you have completed the questionnaire, please fold the page and mail it or take it to the address of the back of the page. Be sure to write your name and address in the space provided at the bottom of this same page. When we receive your questionnaire, we will send you your Registration Package. Then, all you have to do is join us every week at the times marked on the calendar in your registration package, and learn with us.

My name is..

I work at...

My address is (or I can be reached at) ....

....

....

Page 3 (back)

Mail this page to ....

....

....

The address to which the test should be mailed will be written here, or the address to which the test should be delivered, such as a local school or health center, or the radio or television station through which the lessons are being delivered.

INTRODUCTION TO THE DISTANCE EDUCATION COURSE

Page 4

This page will give a general overview of the course, stating how many lessons there will be; how the learners should listen to or watch (in groups, or separately; in a quiet undisturbed place), and how to use the Support Book.

This page will also remind learners of the certificate they can be granted at the end of the course (if there is to be one).

It will list the names of other resource materials that they can use and that might be referred to from time to time in their Support Book.

It will list the name and contacts address, telephone numbers, and other necessary information of the organization in charge of the project in case learners or others have questions about the course.

Lesson Notes

Page 5

From here on, each page will give a brief overview of one lesson, together with any necessary charts, or added information that might be needed to support or enrich the lesson. The following page was designed for the Ghana Radio Distance Education Course: 'The Front Liner':

Lesson #1: Knowing the Community

In this first lesson, you will meet Ayesha, who is your teacher for this course. She will be with you in every lesson.

You will also meet Abena who is a Community Health Nurse working in the community of Nyama Bekyere. We will be following Abena's life throughout this course. I am sure you will find that many of the difficulties and happy times she has are like the ones you also have.

Lesson 1 reminds us all of the important things we can do to get to know our community, and to let the people of the community get to know us.

Listen carefully. You can **write some notes** on the bottom of this page about things you want to remember.

When today's lesson is over, you should use what you have learned as you work with your own community.

MY NOTES on today's lesson:
(about ¼ page is left open on which the learners can make their own notes)

REMEMBER—if you would like to write to us, we would love to hear from you.
Write to us at:
(GIVE ADDRESS)
This reminder can be added from time to time on the bottom of the pages.

<u>Lesson #2: Malaria</u>   **Page 6**

These following sample pages demonstrate how the Support Booklet can be used to provide information that would be difficult to supply on radio or even television—and difficult for learners to recall unless they see it written down (as they could with an Internet lesson).

TOPIC: Malaria: Causes, Signs and Symptoms, Complications and Referrals
In this lesson, you will learn about:

- the different forms of malaria
- the treatments for different forms of malaria
- the importance of teaching community members how to prevent and treat malaria

Treatments

Uncomplicated Malaria: Treatment for a child
When a child has uncomplicated malaria, the CHN should do the following:

- Sponge child with tepid, lukewarm water
- Give Paracetamol according to the child's age to reduce the fever (See Table 11.1)
- Give oral anti-malarial according to age (See Table 11.2)
- If child has not been given any anti-malarial drugs at all, then give chloroquine as first line drug, for three days
- If child has been given chloroquine at home (full and correct dose) then give Sulfadoxine Pyrimethamine (Fansidar) as second line drug (See Table 11.3)—Give single dose in clinic.

Possible side effects: Chloroquine—Explain to the mother that

- she should watch her child carefully for 30 minutes after giving a dose of chloroquine. If the child vomits within 30 minutes, she should repeat the dose and return to the clinic for additional tablets.
- itching is a possible side effect of the drug but is not dangerous.

Uncomplicated Malaria: Treatment of an adult

1. Find out if s/he has taken any anti-malarials before reporting to you.
   a. If s/he has taken chloroquine—full and correct dose (see Table 11.2) then give Fansidar (see Table 11.3)
   b. If s/he has taken chloroquine but incomplete, give full and chloroquine treatment (again) (Table 11.1)
   c. If s/he has not taken any anti-malarial at all, start with chloroquine (Table 11.2)
   d. If s/he has taken both chloroquine and Fansidar, and is still not well, refer to the nearest hospital.

TABLE 11.1
PARACETAMOL

AGE	Syrup (120 mg/5 ml)	Tablet (500 mg)
Under 3 years	5 ml	¼ tablet
3–5 years	10 ml	½ tablet
5–12 years	–	1 tablet
12–15 years	–	1 ½ tablets
After 15 years	–	2 tablets

TABLE 11.2
CHLOROQUINE

Age	First Day	Second Day	Third Day
Under 12 months	½ tablet (5 ml syrup)	½ tablet (5 ml syrup)	¼ tablet (2.5 ml syrup)
1–4 years	1 tablet (10 ml syrup)	1 tablet (10 ml syrup)	½ tablet (5 ml syrup)
5–9 years	2 tablets	2 tablets	1 tablet
10–14 years	3 tablets	3 tablets	1 ½ tablets

TABLE 11.3
SULFADOXINE (500 mg) PYRIMETHAMINE (25 mg) [FANSIDAR]

Age	Dose
Under 12 months	½ tablet
1–4 years	1 tablet
5–9 years	1 ½ tablets
10–14 years	2 tablets
15 years or older	3 tablets

There should a page like this in the Support Booklet for each lesson in the series. Each page will begin in the same way with the
Title
Topic
In this lesson, you will learn about...

At the end of the book, there can be a closing test (like that shown on the next page)

The Closing Test

Now that you have completed all the lessons and have had a chance to share your new knowledge with your community in the most appropriate manner, you are ready to take the closing test.

When you complete the Closing Test correctly, you will be awarded your *CERTIFICATE of MERIT*. The names of all those who gain the certificate will be read over the air, and published in (name the newspaper).

Taking the Closing Test

This test will be broadcast at our regular time. Listen carefully to learn the date and the time at which the test will be given. Be ready with your pencil or pen to take the test on the test day.

Then listen as Ayesha reads the questions to you. Circle the letter of the correct answer for each question. That's all you have to do.

Then *MAIL* your test paper to...

(Or *BRING* your test paper to...)

On the day that we give the test, we will also announce the date on which we will be reading the names of all those of you who have been awarded the *CERTIFICATE of MERIT*.

GOOD LUCK with your test!

Closing Test Questions

Listen carefully, as Ayesha reads each question. Circle the letter of the correct answer for each question.

1	a	b	b	d	e
2	a	b	c	d	e
3	a	b	c	d	e
4	a	b	c	d	e
5	a	b	c	d	e
6	a	b	c	d	e
7	a	b	c	d	e
8	a	b	c	d	e
9	a	b	c	d	e
10	a	b	c	d	e
11	a	b	c	d	e
12	a	b	c	d	e
13	a	b	c	d	e
14	a	b	c	d	e
15	a	b	c	d	e
16	a	b	c	d	c
17	a	b	c	d	e
18	a	b	c	d	e
19	a	b	c	d	e
20	a	b	c	d	e

More questions can be added if needed.

Mail this page to ....

....

....

This will be the address to which the test should be mailed or the address to which the test should be delivered.

PROGRAM RESPONSE TECHNIQUES FOR LOW-LITERACY LEARNERS

In situations where distance learners have low-literacy levels, it is sometimes difficult to find effective ways of collecting responses from them to find out if the programs are appropriate and enjoyable to them. One answer to this problem is the use of Comment Cards and/or Quiz Cards. These cards can be made available at appropriate centers, such as the Health Post, Community Center, Government Office, School or the local Post Office, and the program hosts can remind the learners each week about the cards, where they can be obtained and the importance of sending responses to the program producers.

Comment Cards

The comment card, which can be printed on a simple file card, is designed with one side having the address to which comments should be sent and the other side left blank for the learner's comments. The card should be pre-stamped as an extra incentive for sending a comment. The program host can encourage learners to have someone write their comments for them if they are not confident that they can write their comments themselves. Often, a child in the family, who is attending school, can assist with writing down the comments. A sample Comment Card might look like this:

SAMPLE COMMENT/QUESTION CARD (FRONT)

```
From:                                          STAMPED

(Write your name &
address here):.....................................

.................................................

.................................................   To: (address—already printed)
```

SAMPLE COMMENT/QUESTION CARD (BACK)

Dear Listener,
We are happy that you are listening to our program (name) Please write your comments
or questions here, and then send the card to us:

Quiz Cards

Another useful tool for helping to determine how many people are listening to or watching the programs is the Quiz Card. The printed instruction on the card can be read aloud on the program each week so that even those who cannot read will know how to use the card. One card can be used to cover *ALL* programs, or several cards can be used, covering perhaps only 5 or 10 programs at a time. The number of responses received to the quizzes and the number of respondents who have all correct answers helps the program producers gauge the success of the program.

"Program Name......" QUIZ CARD
Tune in to (Program name) every week on (station) at (time). Use this card to answer the quiz question you will hear at the end of the program each week. Put a circle around the letter that is the RIGHT answer to the question. Do NOT mail the card until you have answered ALL the quizzes.

QUIZ 1: a b c d	*QUIZ 2:* a b c d	*QUIZ 3:* a b c d
QUIZ 4: a b c d	*QUIZ 5:* a b c d	*QUIZ 6:* a b c d
QUIZ 7: a b c d	*QUIZ 8:* a b c d	*QUIZ 9:* a b c d
QUIZ 10: a b c d	*QUIZ 11:* a b c d	*QUIZ 12:* a b c d
QUIZ 13: a b c d	*QUIZ 14:* a b c d	*QUIZ 15:* a b c d
QUIZ 16: a b c d	*QUIZ 17:* a b c d	*QUIZ 18:* a b c d

From: STAMPED

(Write your name &
address here):

Address to which cards
should be sent

The Internet and Distance Education
by Michael Bailey

PART 4

12

THE INTERNET AND DISTANCE EDUCATION
BY MICHAEL BAILEY

The Internet is growing in importance as a medium for Distance Education.

THE INTERNET: THE FUTURE OF DISTANCE EDUCATION

There is little doubt that the Internet is the road to the future for Distance Education. These days, it is widely used in countries that have advanced Internet Technology (IT) already in place. To date, Internet instruction is not commonly used by elementary school children. In some technologically advanced countries, however, home-bound students who are not healthy enough or not physically able to attend school, or whose parents opt for home-based education, can acquire a good deal of their instruction online. Many adolescent or adult students are already completing most, if not all, of their necessary college or university courses via the Internet. Even in countries where IT is not universally available, the Internet is gradually being introduced as a way of delivering course outlines and materials to institutions that can then use them for local students.

Just as with the other media discussed in this book, appropriate use of the Internet for Distance Education must begin with an understanding of how to use it effectively. Similarly, it is important to recognize the importance of interactivity for students acquiring instruction from the Internet as it is for all other forms of Distance Education.

E-LEARNING AND EDU-TAINMENT

'Edu-tainment'—the combination of education and entertainment—in distance education programs lends itself well to the Internet. Edu-tainment seeks to engage the students as actively as possible in order to bring about a more effective learning experience. Certainly, there is no disputing the fact that various combinations of animation, video, gaming and simulations can capture the attention of learners of all ages, but to date, that combination has not been regularly used with the intention of imparting or reinforcing knowledge. With proper planning, however, it is possible to employ the pedagogical principles (outlined on page 57 [under Lesson Design]) to deliver educational programs over the Internet in an effective as well as engaging and entertaining way.

Traditionally, when e-learning content was developed, it reflected hard-copy versions of previously existing courses that were input to a computer and electronically delivered in software applications such as PowerPoint or Hypertext Mark Up Language (HTML) files. This approach to distance teaching involves minimal cost and can be easily published to the Internet. However, it ignores the fact that students of all ages are more motivated to learn and remember their learning experience if they are truly personally engaged in it.

Learner Involvement

Edu-tainment, while still putting the primary emphasis on instruction, acknowledges the importance of learner involvement with the subject matter. This involvement often is achieved by the use of stories that engage both the mind and the heart of the learners. For example, in teaching army recruits how to navigate complex situations, some modern IT training packages are built around the oldest form of emotional experience: story-telling. 'Instead of moving the classroom into the field, we're moving the field into the classroom*', says Randy Hill, the Deputy Technology Director of the Institute for Creative Technologies (ICT) at the University of Southern California, USA. An ICT software package for desktop PCs called *Think Like a Commander* engages captains-in-training in conflict scenarios derived from interviews with senior officers who served in Bosnia or Afghanistan.

In one storyline, for example, warlords descend on a food-distribution out-post, and the trainee must quickly determine whom to trust and how to build alliances with the locals. This US Army training program provides a glimpse into the future of distance education. For many institutions, whether it is training for war or training for public health interventions, bringing the 'field' into the classroom will become more and more common. Categorizing the many forms of information delivery over the Internet can be difficult because new methods are introduced all the time. These tools represent new, innovative and accessible methods for transferring messages and conveying ideas. It is very important to consider all of the possible ways in which the Internet can provide a medium for teaching; for despite the presence of these new technologies, many practitioners involved in this field still rely upon traditional, static websites that fail to engage the user. While it is not possible to list all the possible combinations of software and hardware technologies that make up the Internet, the following is a brief introduction to some of the principal applications that can be used to support the development of distance education programs.

---

*Wired Issue 12 September 2004. The War Room, Steve Silberman.

Brief Overview of Internet Communication Interactivity

As with other forms of Distance Education, interactivity plays an important role in internet learning. Many forms of communication offer supporting roles in the overall experience of the Internet. Instant Messaging or IM, for example, can support other forms of communication such as e-mail or online gaming so that while someone is using the computer and waiting to log on to a game or e-mail—IM just happens. It is instantaneous and easy to use, and allows users to exchange information in real-time, any time. In a distance education setting, for example, IM allows teachers and students to communicate, not only during a lesson, but at any other time they are both on a computer.

Blogging

Perhaps the most popular new form of web interactivity is blogging. The word 'blog' is short for 'web log' and the word 'log' originally meant 'a journal' or a book in which records of events are kept, so a 'blog' is a way of using the web to record thoughts, ideas, and questions. The blog can provide people who do not have a technical background with immediate access to a web application for explanations, ideas, pictures, and links to other web logs. As explained by David Winer of Weblogs.Com News, 'Web logs are often-updated sites that point to articles elsewhere on the web, often with comments, and to on-site articles. A web log is kind of a continual tour, with a human guide whom you get to know. There are many guides to choose from, each develops an audience, and there's also camaraderie and politics between the people who run web logs, they point to each other, in all kinds of structures, graphs, loops, and so on'.

Advisor Blog

In terms of education, recognized experts in particular fields (or unrecognized experts who have risen to prominence through their blogging) have created a new category of bloggers known as the AdvisorBlog. Rather than write a book or speak at a conference, AdvisorBloggers submit their wit and wisdom to their blog, which records all their past entries, so that users can access everything they have written. With the proper links established to other AdvisorBlogs, the AdvisorBlogger can create entire networks of experts on subjects that range from computer technology (for example, http://advisor.com/adv/AdvisorBlogs) to politics and the media. Armed with a high-speed connection and a digital video camera some bloggers have used their sites as personal broadcast networks publishing news and personal events at a regularly scheduled time in order to accommodate their own growing audience and sidestepping the need for traditional broadcast and cable outlets. This use of the camera can be used in educational situations where students want to share personal experiences, related to their learning, with one another.

Virtual Communities

In such cases, where bloggers share a common interest, they can form a sense of community—a virtual community which is not unlike an actual community where everyone lives in the same area. A virtual community is a group of people utilizing technology to bring them together, but rather than relying on physical proximity to create a joint sense of belonging, they rely on a shared interest in a particular subject. What is most fascinating about virtual communities is their ability to spontaneously appear (and disappear) over ideas and only the Internet can provide the means for those communities to span the globe.

Other ways of allowing interactivity among Internet users include e-mail lists (or Listserves), bulletin boards, and chat rooms. The strength of community formation using these technologies depends less on the technology and more on the power of the idea that is under discussion. One of the first (and certainly the most famous) online communities originated with the *WELL* or Whole Earth 'Electronic Link Launched in 1985, the *WELL* presently has 4,000 members. It was, and still is, basically an e-mail account (although now web pages and other electronic amenities are provided to *WELL* members). Katie Hafner described the power of this early online community in her article 'The Epic Saga of the Well'*: 'AIDS or carpal tunnel syndrome or the Iran-contra scandal—whatever your interest was, there was perhaps no better place on earth than The Well for seeing what other people had to say about it. Maybe the debates did grow quarrelsome or repetitive, but at least you were guaranteed to see every possible point made, every conceivable solecism pointed out'.

Online Gaming

Another form of interaction on the Internet—in dramatic contrast to e-mail and blogging—is online gaming. Online gaming allows users to communicate with other users with text as well as sound and movement. A complete artificial world provides the backdrop where animated characters follow the user's commands. There are many types of online games that can keep users engaged for hours. Users have a wide variety of choices, from two player games, such as chess, to the most recent form of gaming known as massively multiplayer online games (*MMOG*), which allows thousands of users at a time to play in artificial worlds that seem never-ending.

Unlike the *WELL* where ideas expressed in e-mails brought people together; in *MMOG* the technology is often the principal driver behind virtual communities. City of Heroes, an online game that allows users to create heroes based on a selection of literally thousands of combinations of characteristics, is one of many examples of gaming environments that

---

*Wired Issue 5 May 1997. The Epic Saga of the Well Katie Hafner.

allows users to assume alternative virtual images with characteristics that match whatever physical and mental capabilities they desire. In this way, the character, not the user, provides the first impression to the community of users along a computer-generated cityscape. As with the *WELL*, users are able to chat with one another, but the 'chatter' tends to revolve around the capabilities of their own and other characters, as well as the steps necessary to graduate from one level of the game to the next.

Networks

Software that allows the creation of social networks has spawned yet another forum for interaction and the accelerated spread of ideas and messages. Websites such as Friendster.com provide working examples of how one person can create a virtual community of 'friends' by simply inviting a small number of personal friends to join the network; those friends in turn invite a number of their friends and so on. In this way, users gain the feeling that they are communicating within a network of trusted individuals. These networks can be organized around a number of concepts beyond the notion of increasing the circle of personal friends; networks on educational topics and on business, music, art and language.

None of these exciting interactive trends in software development, however, changes the fact that most websites are run using the language of the Internet: HTML is intended to enable users to create web pages and have those pages published to a web browser (such as Internet Explorer). These web pages can be as boring or engaging as the developer wants them to be, particularly with so many forms of multimedia available for use.

THE INTERNET AND CELLPHONES AND THE DEVELOPING WORLD

Despite significant inroads toward increasing Internet access among developing countries, many countries, particularly those in Africa, do not have the communication infrastructure to provide large groups of potential students of online learning with the means to access digital forms of educational content. The Western perspective often fails to consider the use of cellphones as a crucial alternative means for delivering this content. Cell phones—with a little ingenuity, can have nearly the same impact as the Internet while providing access to potentially millions of additional students. Cellphone usage has grown more than any other technology in the developing world and remains an unexploited means for educational delivery of digital educational material. Some statistics for 2006 make this abundantly clear:

- Worldwide, there are more than 2.4 billion cellphone users, with more than 1,000 new customers added every minute

- Fifty-nine percent of these 2.4 billion people live in developing countries, making cell phones the first telecommunications technology in history to have more users there than in the developed world
- Mobile phone shipments grew 19 percent to 810 million units in 2005, and grew 15 percent to 930 million units in 2006
- Cellphone usage in Africa is growing almost twice as fast as any other region and jumped from 63 million users two years ago to 152 million today
- A recent survey reported that 97 percent of Tanzanians now have access to a mobile phone thanks to the community payphone model (payphones are owned and operated by entrepreneurs who buy airtime from the network), despite the lack of electrical infrastructure for much of the country

Source: http://web.mit.edu/eprom/whyafrica.html

How can cellphones be used in an effective manner so that many of those left out of the Internet revolution can access some of its educational benefits? It is not always practical to take courses designed for the personal computer and try to broadcast them to mobile phones that have the ability to access the Internet. It is also costly to develop a course for the personal computer and then re-develop it for use on a mobile telephone. Because of the differences in screen dimensions it would be better to re-develop the application from the beginning.

THE PODCAST

There is an alternative, however, through the recent development and expansion in the use of *podcasts*. A Podcast is a method for distributing digital audio or visual material over the Internet and then loading it onto one's cellphone or other mobile device. A Podcast generally has an overall theme and is made up of more or less regular episodes which can be subscribed to for regular downloads as they become available. Podcasting consists of parts of two words 'iPod' and 'broadcasting' joined together. The iPod MP3 player, from the Apple computer company, is not required for podcasting since any kind of MP3-capable mobile device (such as an iPod) or cellphone can be used to listen to or view (depending on what type of file is used and what device it is played on) a podcast. What sets podcasting apart from other forms of distribution is the idea of being able to subscribe to a program that uses podcasts. But unlike traditional subscription services such as the morning newspaper, there is software that makes sure subscribers do not miss a delivery and can always save their individual podcasts on a mobile phone or computer to review any time. Podcasts can contain any file types that are available over the Internet such as audio or video but also image files, text, and other types.

Using Podcasts for Education

To use a podcast for educational purposes, the instructor begins by making a file available on the Internet. This file may be an audio file such as an MP3 file. This audio file can be a simple recording of a course being conducted live during a workshop or of an Edu-tainment program being presented to a live audience. The file is then posted on a publicly available webserver. This completed file would operate as a single episode or lesson of a podcast. It may be that would be the only lesson, but often courses will involve several presentations with each new lesson being posted as it becomes available.

The instructor then acknowledges the existence of that file by referencing it in another file known as a 'feed'. The feed is a list of the *URLs* (or web addresses) by which episodes (or lessons) of the podcast may be accessed. The feed may contain entries for all episodes in the series, but is typically limited to a short list of the most recent episodes, as is the case with many news feeds. Standard podcasts consist of a feed from one author. More recently, multiple authors have been able to contribute episodes to a single podcast feed using concepts such as public podcasting and social podcasting.

Subscribers (that is, the students) use a type of software known as an aggregator, sometimes called a podcatcher or podcast receiver, to subscribe to and manage the feeds. In this case they would have access to the Internet through their cellphone. Alternatively, they could go to a community-based computer with an Internet connection and then upload their desired podcasts to their cellphone to review at a later date.

Duke University in North Carolina, USA, took the use of podcastng as an e-learning method seriously in 2004 by distributing iPods to 1,500 first-year students. Additionally, there is a multi-year 'Duke Digital Initiative' (DDI) underway to examine new ways to integrate technology into learning. Despite these advances, research still needs to be conducted to determine the best ways to integrate these tools into existing e-learning programs for prospective students or gain a better understanding of how prospective students use their cell phones in order to design e-learning programs that are useful on mobile devices. E-learning development along these lines will be particularly valuable in developing countries.

HARNESSING ONLINE TOOLS FOR EDUCATION

The previous paragraphs explain some of the tools of communication available through the Internet. One challenge for the instructor is to bring these tools together in some coherent fashion that facilitates the online learning experience. If there were some existing framework or repository for learning that integrated all of these elements into a functional program, then it might be possible to harness their power for the delivery of online instruction through a central location to a wide array of destinations. Fortunately there are a number of systems—known as Learning Management Systems—that bring all of these elements (and more) together in one place.

Learning Management Systems include proprietary solutions developed by private companies such as Blackboard that have products that cost thousands of dollars a year to use and maintain. Fortunately there is Moodle, an open source alternative that can be freely downloaded from Moodle.org. With support from a large user community and some basic knowledge regarding program installation on a server, it is possible to set up an entire distance education site that contains many of the tools of communication discussed earlier in this section.

MOODLE

Moodle has the following features and more:

- Forums
- Content managing (resources)
- Quizzes with different kinds of questions
- Podcast support
- Blogs
- Wikis
- Database activities
- Surveys
- Chat
- Glossaries
- Peer assessment (allows fellow students to assess inputs from other students)
- Multi-language support (over 60 languages are supported for the interface)

The pedagogical approach of Moodle includes a constructivist and social constructionist approach to education, which emphasizes the contributions of the community of students as well as the educators. This is reflected in the tools that Moodle has designed into its application. Tools such as a forum for every course offered online—thereby allowing teachers and students to pass along e-mails to one another in a forum that ensures, with each new posting, that all students receive a copy automatically through their e-mail address. Other tools, like the chat function and podcast support, provide a variety of ways for students and teachers to interact with each other. At the same time, Moodle can also serve as a simple one-way delivery mechanism for educational content—where the educator limits access to these communication tools and simply uses the testing functions and online postings of educational content to determine if a student successfully absorbs the material or not. A screenshot of an educational site using Moodle is presented on the next page. The development of this sample site is discussed in more detail later in the book.

Sample Educational Site Using the Moodle Learning Management System

As can be seen in this screenshot, the user not only has access to the educational material offered in the upper right column (in this case, courses entitled 'Maternal Health' and 'Reproductive Health'), but also a calendar of events which details such activities as scheduling of quizzes, new postings by teachers, and so on. The support for languages other than English is also clear with this screenshot, as much of the course is presented in Arabic. Log-in functions for participant verification, a Chat function for students to text each other online, and many other features which are not pictured in this rather small screenshot illustrate the importance of an educational site having a Learning Management System as its primary framework, in order to deliver an educational experience that directly involves the user community.

13

Barriers to the Internet and Overcoming the Barriers
by Michael Bailey

Limited access to modern computer equipment is a major barrier in many developing countries.

BARRIERS TO USING THE INTERNET

In any form of instruction, the educator has three primary considerations: the learners to be reached, the instruction to be given, and the resources available to provide the instruction. When using the Internet for Distance Education, there is a fourth consideration: Does the intended audience of learners have access to the Internet? If so, are there any limitations to that access?

There are regions of the world that would benefit greatly from Internet access; but because of region-specific limitations, students are unable to access courses available on the web. These limitations include:

- access charges for telephone service
- usage charges for Internet service
- available income
- the telecommunications reform process that a country is undergoing which can delay the creation and availability of an accessible network
- the cost and the prices charged by the transmission network to Internet Service Providers (ISPs), Internet cafes, telecenters, and others that provide Internet services to the public
- the capacity of the transmission network in a country to supply Internet Service Providers (ISPs) and others
- the effectiveness of telecom regulation in providing a framework conducive to the development and growth of Internet services*

These physical barriers to access are often made worse by governments that enact policies restricting access to the average user. When the government remains the sole

---

*Fair Access to Internet Report (FAIR) Prepared by the LINK Centre and Mike Jensen and Research ICT Africa, February 2004, p. 5.

provider for Internet access or when there are only one or two private providers to the Internet, the lack of competition results in costs to the user that can be much higher than in countries where there are multiple providers.

Access points to Internet use can be placed into the following basic categories:

- Dial-up users
- Cybercafé users
- Organizational users with permanent leased lines (not including cybercafés).
- Community Access Points (which include subsidized points of access to the Internet such as telecenters, and community kiosks).

An educator concerned with providing information to an audience of learners has to contend with the fact that each one of these access points must deal with the limitations imposed locally, by any of the barriers mentioned earlier. Each type of user deals with these barriers in different ways. For example, cybercafés users will pay more for access on an individual basis. While the government of a country often subsidizes costs associated with Community Access Points, this usually results in fewer computers available per person. As a comparison, putting aside the fact that different users use different types of access, in South Africa, an attempt to offer educational material to all potential users could reach up to 680 users per 10,000 inhabitants—the largest number for the African continent. On the other hand, in Algeria, the reach would be only 160 users out of 10,000 inhabitants.

This suggests that it may be more appropriate to consider the notion of 'indirect access' when measuring a potential learning audience. 'Indirect access' can mean including people who gather around a single computer as a group or who do not pay for their access but are able to gain limited time through a CAP. 'Indirect access' also refers to people who never actually view the material on a computer screen, but are told about the information by someone who does view it. The educator's goal may still be accomplished, therefore, in spite of access limitations. Acknowledging these limitations, however, does mean that instructional material should promote a 'buzz'; that is, it has to become the subject of intense discussion in a community of users and non-users of the Internet in order to overcome limitations and contend with all the other websites competing for the learners' attention.

Finding the Balance between Access and Impact

It can be argued that, in some ways, the Internet offers too many options and too many temptations. With the technology available today, an instructor could develop an online course that requires the use of everything that can be found in a television studio, from video equipment to audio technicians and animators.

On the other hand, it is perfectly possible to build an entire course requiring nothing but exclusive use of e-mail. Online educators can deliver material on a one-to-one basis or to an entire group. They can attach reports, graphics, and other relevant material to the e-mail, which can be downloaded by a student for later review. If a student needs individual assistance, the educator can provide it privately without including the other members of the course. In a technological sense, the student would not require a sophisticated desktop computer; e-mail access alone with a dial-up connection would satisfy the basic access requirements. In this way an online developer of educational material could ensure the largest possible audience for a course. The question remains, however, would such a course have the desired impact on the user?

E-mail alone might be a very effective medium for a truly motivated user and one who is comfortable with a text-driven approach to learning, enjoys typing and is highly literate in the language used for instruction. The educator would also have to be highly motivated as each student's response to a question or forwarded comment would require an individual response. Given the reliance on text in such a one-to-one system, the instructor might as well deliver the majority of the material using the traditional postal system and use e-mail in a supporting role for unanticipated questions and comments.

Figure 13.1 illustrates the fact that if an educator desires to provide instruction that has the greatest impact per user, it is likely that the number of users will be limited, because of the technological limitations of the average user. At the same time, as Figure 13.2

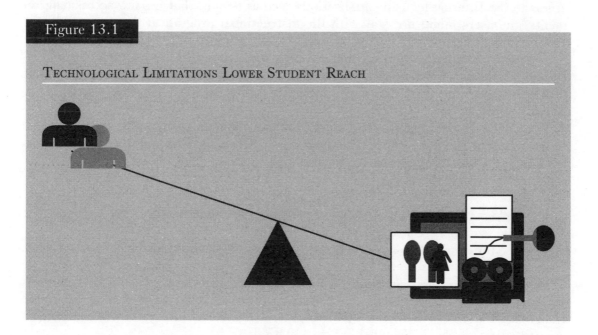

Figure 13.1

TECHNOLOGICAL LIMITATIONS LOWER STUDENT REACH

Figure 13.2

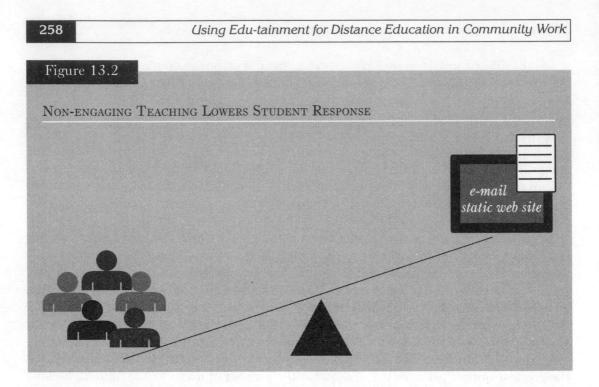

NON-ENGAGING TEACHING LOWERS STUDENT RESPONSE

illustrates, while it might be possible to accommodate more users who have limited access to the Internet by using applications such as e-mail, that has few access requirements, the users might not stay with the instructional program if the material is not truly engaging.

This is not to say that there are not well-designed courses that rely completely on text-based materials delivered in an asynchronous fashion (that is, delivery of material is not dependent upon the student and educator being online at the same time), but they are the exception.

The trade-off between access and impact arises when the instructor attempts to create course material that integrates all the forms of instructional media and then tries to implement on to a website all of these elements:

- Text
- Graphics (including pictures, photos, animations, diagrams)
- Audio (sound effects, voice, music)
- Video (on-demand or asynchronous video, live or synchronous video)

Slow connection speeds and limited user experience with these technologies combined with the barriers listed previously can make this educational experience even less satisfying than text-based instruction. The challenge, therefore, is to present valuable knowledge in an attractive, usable, and compelling presentation.

WHAT IS THE BEST APPROACH FOR USING INTERNET FOR DISTANCE EDUCATION?

The best approach will be to use instructional material that meets the needs of the users and the pedagogical requirements of the instruction delivered through a combination of technologies that provide a balance between access and impact.

User Needs

When considering the use of the Internet for distance education, one way to categorize user needs is in terms of support and type of instruction required. The given chart can be useful in summarizing this relationship in terms of timely support.

Relationship between Internet Delivery and User Support Requirements

	Asynchronous Delivery	*Synchronous Delivery*
Needs facilitation	*time constraints limit effectiveness*	*Examples include:* *chat programs* *online gaming* *teleconferencing* *discussion boards* *dynamic web sites*
Self-paced instruction	*Examples include:* *e-mail* *list-servs* *static web sites* *forums* *file sharing* *blogs*	*immediate delivery in real time prevents self-paced instruction*

With synchronous delivery, users can be supported in real-time: that is, if they have a question at the time they are reviewing material, they can contact the instructor and feedback will be immediate. With asynchronous delivery, the user may have to wait overnight for a response to an inquiry or question. Indeed, in some cases, there may be no availability of support.

This chart can look quite different, however, if user needs are approached in terms of experience with using and navigating the Internet and the software applications that are a part of it. For example, almost everyone who has used a computer understands how to compose and send e-mail, but a brand new online gaming application might require training prior to actual use, even for relatively experienced users. When looked at from the perspective of the type of instruction required, user needs take on a different dimension (Static Delivery and Dynamic Delivery are explained in the following diagram).

Relationship between Material Delivery and User Training Requirements

	Static Delivery	Dynamic Delivery
Cognitive	Examples include: e-mail, static web sites, diagrams, forums, file sharing, blogs	Dynamic delivery unnecessary for much conceptual material
Skills-based	Static Delivery inappropriate for skills training	Examples include: simulations, online gaming, training videos, testing and quizzes, scenario-based

Static Delivery

Generally, instruction involving a cognitive understanding of the material like the periodic table of the elements, for example, would not require a wide variety of instructional media in the delivery of the information. To meet the minimum requirements for providing instruction for the periodic table of the elements, the developer could prepare a structured course that can be placed on a static (unchanging) website with a single diagram and text explaining each element.

Dynamic Delivery

Instruction involving the transfer of skills for a process, such as that involved in IUD insertion, would necessitate the use of images as well as text (Dynamic Delivery). Ideally, these images would be animated through the use of video or animated drawings and synchronized with audio instruction. This is not to suggest that animation could not be used for the periodic table example or that IUD insertion could not be explained exclusively through text; but these examples demonstrate how knowledge delivery can be adjusted to suit the learning that must take place.

COMBINING THE INTERNET WITH OTHER DISTANCE EDUCATION MEDIA

There is no reason for developers of Distance Education programs to restrict themselves to the Internet even when that technology is a realistic option. Most educational programs cannot be divided neatly into cognitive and skill-based areas. It is important, therefore, to consider combining several delivery approaches to the educational material. Combining other Distance Education approaches with the use of the Internet has proved to be quite effective in making use of existing distance resources (such as radio) and filling gaps in the delivery of educational material. Some advantages to this combined approach include:

- **Advance Delivery:** In cases where there is a need to conduct a workshop or to provide technical assistance in a remote location, it might be possible to provide some of the learning materials in advance through the Internet (or on CD-ROM) before a trainer actually conducts the workshop. In this way, the participants can prepare themselves in advance for the instruction.
- **Long-Term Reference:** With the use of such aides as CD-ROM or pre-recorded audio, the user has reference material to review long after the actual workshop or training is completed. This is particularly important in behavior change maintenance, when the material covers specific steps in a procedure or the development of a particular skill. For example, a recent study was made of a curriculum that described specific steps health officials could take to implement a new HIV prevention strategy. The study showed that those who had access to CD-ROM curriculum support were twice as likely to apply their learning to modify existing approaches or implement completely new programs as those who had the educational programs without CD-ROM support (Kelly et al.).
- **Increased Access with Mobile Devices:** Innovative approaches to delivering educational messages include the use of mobile devices such as cellphones. Websites are now able to send and receive text messages from cellphones using the

cellphone provider's wireless network. It is becoming increasingly common for people in Africa and Asia to have access to a cellphone rather than a computer or a landline telephone. It is valuable, therefore, to consider integrating this technology, even in a supporting role, into the overall delivery of distance educational material.

- **Background Material for Radio and Television:** With the use of radio and television for Distance Education in the form Edu-tainment programming, audiences can be directed, following the broadcast, to websites for more detailed information. The Internet also can provide a resource (particularly for radio) that allows users to listen to archived episodes of a particular program well after the initial broadcast.

It is always challenging to determine the best medium or combination of media to use for a given Distance Education situation. When using the Internet, there is the added challenge of deciding which technology or combination of technologies is best suited to particular educational requirements. Final determination can be made only after the full curriculum for instruction is created. In the next chapter, the issues surrounding curriculum development for the Internet will be examined as a guide to the decision-making process.

14

Curriculum Development for Internet-Based Distance Education
by Michael Bailey

Preparing the 'programs' for Internet Edu-tainment programs requires a variety of skills and knowledge.

THE 5 PHASES OF CURRICULUM DEVELOPMENT

Many instructional models of curriculum development which are used when developing Information Technology (IT) programs were originally designed for face-to-face (classroom) instruction. The primary components of a Curriculum Guide have already been explained in Chapter 3, but it is necessary to make some adaptation of this process when working on curriculum development for Internet-based teaching. The table below segments the elements for curriculum development over the stages of instructional development, from Analysis to Evaluation, and augments the process with considerations specific to instruction delivery by Internet.

In the table, the term 'authoring tools' refers to various software applications that developers can use when creating websites. These tools allow developers to integrate various forms of media (video, audio, animation) into web pages. There are many brands of 'authoring tools'; currently, two of the most popular being Flash and Dreamweaver, both created by Macxromedia Inc. It is possible to develop websites without these tools by coding in programming languages such as Java or HTML, but these approaches take longer and require greater expertise.

Phases for Instructional Development	Curriculum Development for Distance Education	Considerations for Internet Use
Analysis	Information about the chosen audience	Audience acceptance of Internet as instructional medium
	Justification and availability of the chosen medium	Internet Access

(Contd.)

Phases for Instructional Development	Curriculum Development for Distance Education	Considerations for Internet Use
	The overall Objectives and Purposes of the course Overall Learning Style(s)	Authoring tools available to meet learning style
Design	The number of lessons; the length of each lesson; frequency of presentation, etc. The detailed scope and sequence of the curriculum Instructional Strategy	Prototyping: User-Interface Design Navigation Flowcharting for sequence Mix of applications/media to deliver instruction
Development	Content Development for each lesson Measurable Objectives for and purposes of each lesson Lesson Assignments	Storyboarding Media Development Technical development to determine how feedback/ data are collected Programming assignments
Implementation	Proposed support materials Methods of assignment collection/delivery Pre- and Post-tests Registration and Promotional activities Timelines	Technical Support Facilitator training Beta-Testing/User Testing
Evaluation	Formative Evaluation	User Feedback Error reporting

ANALYSIS PHASE

The Audience

For Internet lesson delivery, it is necessary to go beyond the personal audience characteristics usually required for curriculum development and determine to what extent the intended audience is willing—and able—to accept the Internet as an instructional medium.

If few members of the intended audience have had experience with the Internet for learning purposes, it might be necessary to set up an orientation course or tutorial explaining the basics of accessing, navigating and using the Internet. Ideally, the tutorial, which would be held in advance of the commencement of the teaching course, would include sample screens and events that relate specifically to the type of applications that will be in use during the online instruction.

The Medium

During the analysis phase, as discussed earlier, it is important to strike a balance between access to the Internet and the desired impact of the instructional material, based on the types of applications available. As well as pre-existing technologies, such as e-mail, there is a vast array of authoring tools that can be used to develop specific instructional applications. The actual role of an Internet-based application must be determined in relation to other media such as radio or television. Will the Internet play a central role or a supplementary one? Will the user simply access—from a website or via e-mail—materials that are supplementary to the course, or will actual instruction take place online? If it is likely that the intended audience will have some difficulty accessing the Internet, then its role in instructional delivery may have to be reduced.

The Learning Style

In addition to considering user access to the Internet, it is important to ensure that the program design is understandable and usable by the intended learners, in light of their overall previous learning style and habits. Therefore, after the audience analysis phase is complete, it is helpful to develop immediately a prototype of the software; that is, a model of the final version of the program that will be used. Focus groups representing a sample of the intended users should try out the prototype so that feedback can be immediate, and necessary changes made before final course development takes place.

The prototype should:

- consist of functional or non-functional screens that represent what the actual program will look like
- have a variety of user-interface designs in order to test which are more acceptable to the learners
- be linked to a variety of other applications that will be used during instruction such as bulletin boards, blogs or e-mail
- be developed within an authoring environment that will be used for the final version of the application, or developed using simpler tools such as PowerPoint.

DESIGN PHASE

Once the detailed scope and sequence of the curriculum have been decided, it is necessary to determine such matters as the style of instruction, the sequence of user access to the material, the rate at which material is absorbed and understood, and so on. In order to ensure that these things are appropriate, it is helpful for the program designer to sit with some typical users and go through the process of accessing the Internet and working through a sequence of instructional material. During this trial run, special attention should be paid to

- how the user interacts with the interface design
- level of tolerance for the amount of text offered per screen
- use of and reaction to different types of media (sound, video, animation) during a session
- other important user approaches to the material that may be valuable in the evaluation of the design.

DEVELOPMENT PHASE

Following the overall design stage, the instructional content can be put into the framework. In an ideal situation, a recognized content or subject expert works closely with the instructional designer to prepare the lessons for the online environment. However, access to such expertise on a regular basis might be beyond the budget of the project; so there are less expensive options to consider when developing a unique or specialized curriculum content:

- There might be already a substantial amount of material available on the subject (in books, for example) that has not been adapted for use on the Internet. If that is the case, an instructional designer, with the help of someone who actually teaches the topic, could act as an editor and re-engineer the material for use online. Needless to say, it is necessary to gain written permission from the author(s) of the print material to adapt it to the Internet course.
- Courses that have been delivered through other media (such as radio or television) might be available in which the actual lesson content is already spelled out. Here again, the instructional designer can develop ways in which this content can be delivered successfully via Internet. As with print material, it is usually necessary to gain written permission to adapt existing materials.
- In both cases, the 'recognized expert' can then be called upon to review the final material, even if the expert was not available for the complete design process.

Feedback

With an online course, the student and teacher are not in constant contact as they are in the classroom, and this makes it difficult, if not impossible, to use traditional feedback mechanisms to determine if the users have satisfied their own (and the instructor's) objectives, or completed necessary assignments. E-mail offers an obvious, easy way to ensure that connections and feedback can be provided, but answering e-mail can take up a lot of the instructor's or facilitator's time. The need to respond to individual e-mails can become particularly burdensome when the lesson material is somewhat unstructured (for example, writing courses), allowing for a large number of possible questions arising from the material and the assignments.

Structured material obviously makes it easier to anticipate possible responses. Users can make a selection in the form of a 'yes' or 'no' response or from a multiple-choice question. These structured responses can then be stored online for easy assessment, review, or even for grading and certification.

Feedback Mechanisms

Online instruction almost always requires some method by which students can provide feedback to questions. In addition to creating standard feedback mechanisms such as radio buttons for true/false or yes/no responses (radio buttons are the little circular buttons normally offered in pairs that allow the user only one choice), a developer of online instructional material should have templates available for standard types of instructional situations. Templates are a crucial time-saving device when developing online educational material for multiple audiences. A template can allow a developer to create a web page, for example, that can be changed by anyone who wants to add new content, even without having full knowledge of the entire program. Some examples of templates used in instructional programs include:

- Templates for the presentation of procedural material (for example, Step 1, then Step 2...)
- Columns for material that may show an opposing view or before and after segment
- Screen templates that provide components necessary for a case study, such as an introduction, a placeholder for an image, a conclusion, and so on
- Worksheet templates that provide space for feedback and/or storage of responses
- Lists or list boxes when appropriate.

Needless to say, templates do not provide the answer to every instructional need. Frequently, the instructor will have to create a unique or specially customized screen for instructional material, and this can lead to extra cost. The use of XML (eXtensible Markup Language) is already gaining favor as a way to cut costs on future developments of this sort. The intention of XML is to ease the transfer of text from one type of document into another type of document (although it should be noted that XML can also be applied to images and other forms of expression such as mathematics). For example, an online catalogue or database or chart might have available a considerable amount of information on commonly used drugs and their effectiveness for a range of diseases. If all that data is structured or tagged using XML, it can be more easily transported to a structure that is appropriate for e-learning. Moreover, it can be done without extensive cost or effort.

For example, take the basic information about this book:

P###.2006
Communication for Behavior Change: Volume 3
Using Edu-tainment for Distance Education in Community Work
Esta de Fossard
SAGE Publications India Pvt Ltd.

Under typical circumstances, this information could not be recognized by applications that store (such as a database) or represent (such as a web browser) data. Through the use of XML, however, it becomes possible to tag that data once and then apply those tags to all data of the same type allowing this transfer among different applications to take place automatically. This is how that same information would look when tagged for future use:

```
<book>
<call_number>P###.2006</call_number>
<title> Communication for Behavior Change: Volume 3</title>
<subtitle> Using Edu-tainment for Distance Education in Community Work </subtitle>
<author>de Fossard, Esta<author>
<publisher>SAGE Publications India Pvt. Ltd. </publisher>
</book>
```

This is not necessarily appropriate for all instructional applications, but where there is a need for the use of a lot of text and information over time, XML can provide the answer. The application of XML on the material and media intended for use in online instruction will be dealt with in the next chapter when discussing the type of personnel required to put together an instructional program.

Although use of XML for instructional content may be something for the future, it is possible to categorize and store the information (assets) needed for production during the development phase. The developer can then access this information as needed when creating the lesson. This information includes audio files, online reports, links to relevant websites, and so on. There are many ways of categorizing this content including:

- by file type (WAV, SWF, PDF, MP3 and so on)
- by instructional application (testing, presentation, and so on)
- by creator
- by file size
- by date of creation

It is important to create these information libraries, so that material that might have been developed weeks, months, and even years earlier can be reused often and in completely different circumstances.

IMPLEMENTATION PHASE

By now, most of the hard work is done—the framework for the instructional material is in place, the sequence of activities for the user is clear, the range of applications that will play a part in the instruction, from e-mail to dynamic websites, is in place—so, the next step is to integrate all the pieces into a coherent instructional program that can be used effectively by the selected learners.

Support Materials

One important part of the Implementation plan is the determination of supplementary or support materials that are needed but not placed on the Internet. As discussed earlier, an instructional program should consider a variety of media in combination in order to provide an overall learning experience. Although the Internet provides a unique opportunity for interactive learning, other materials should be provided, where necessary, through more traditional means (such as the postal service). Readings or text books that can accompany a course should be available and ready for delivery at this stage. If the main instructional piece is actually to be given through television or radio broadcasts, then the development of accompanying web-based resources should already be prepared and synchronized with each broadcast. This means that following the instructional radio or television broadcast, the announcer will refer learners to a website for access to more in-depth material. An archiving and conversion process should also be in place when radio programs are used, so that the recordings can be made accessible on the accompanying website for users who may have missed the original broadcast.

At this point, facilitators should be appointed to provide support for content or for general questions about access and navigation. Despite all the new technologies available, most of the support required for course content and technical issues will be addressed through e-mail. This has the advantage of being available to the user all the time, even when the facilitator sets aside only a limited period of time each day to reply to comments and requests. Normally, response to an inquiry over e-mail is given within 24 hours and many of the questions (whether they are concerned with content or are technical in nature) will be anticipated and repeated, making the facilitator's job easier. Nevertheless, it is wise to have experts available for assistance when facilitators run into questions that they cannot resolve concerning content or technical problems.

Beta-Testers

Facilitation and general course progression will be greatly improved through the use of beta-testers. 'Beta'* in this sense refers to the instructional program just prior to completion, to be sure that all aspects of the program function well together. The testers themselves may consist of the actual users, or be a part of a testing team. In either case, they will be aware of the fact that the program is not complete and that they are expected to provide feedback regarding performance. Unlike the testing that took place in the Design Phase, the beta-testers are testing a fully functional portion of the program (probably the first section). With feedback provided from actual users during this session, the developers of the course material can refine the remaining sections of the instructional program and the facilitators have a better chance of anticipating the nature of the questions they will be receiving.

EVALUATION PHASE

While the evaluation phase is often the easiest to create, it is sometimes quite difficult to generate useful results from it because feedback desired by the developer is totally dependent on the users' motivation to provide it. Essentially, the developer of any instructional material would like to have feedback from the users regarding how the course met or did not meet their educational objectives. With distance education, it is harder than it is in the traditional classroom to gain a complete picture of what worked and what did not. Normally, there are no opportunities for face-to-face meetings; so the feedback has to be provided online, through e-mail or through online surveys. The easiest way to ensure some feedback following a course is to use surveys with a basic scoring

---

*The Greek word 'beta' is the second letter in the Greek alphabet, and therefore stands for 'the second in a series or system of classification'. In this case, it is the second test to be undertaken.

structure (1 through 10, low to high, and so on). However, while these are the most likely to be completed, they offer little by way of recommendations on how to improve a section that receives a 'low' rating. Motivated students might go beyond a structured survey and offer their comments on the pros and cons of the instructional program, but often they have their own interests at heart and are not looking at the course with evaluation in mind. Their evaluation can still prove quite valuable on specific topics, however, and when combined with structured surveys, it can help the developer gain insight into why a particular section is receiving low ratings.

It is important to request an evaluation—whether structured or unstructured or a combination of both—following each module or section of a course rather than a single evaluation at the end. One of the advantages of online instruction is that it is possible to prevent access to a following module until evaluation of the current one is completed. At the same time, it is important not to force an evaluation on a student, who might be tempted to complete it, however inaccurately, merely to gain access to the next section. The intention of the evaluation should be to gain honest responses that assist in future improvement of the course.

15

THE PRODUCTION TEAM FOR INTERNET-BASED DISTANCE EDUCATION MATERIAL
BY MICHAEL BAILEY

Effective preparation of an Internet-based Distance Education program requires the cooperation of many skilled professionals.

THE IMPORTANCE OF THE TEAM

The key to any successful distance education project delivered by Internet is a competent and reliable **development team**. The mix of capabilities and commitment can determine the extent to which deadlines are met and users come away with a successful learning experience. The capabilities required to achieve the task of putting an entire curriculum onto the web do not exist in one particular person or even two. A range of experience is required to develop the content and then place that content into a medium that is still relatively new. The table on the next page summarizes the team roles that are typically required to develop and implement an online educational curriculum.

The roles for each activity can overlap, particularly if the development team is small. For example, often the Project Leader will be involved in content selection or in the development and design of the website in addition to the overall management of the program. Subject Matter Specialists (whether or not they have instructional design experience) might also perform the duties of Instructional Designer by adapting for the Internet materials previously designed for another medium. Similarly, if a Subject Matter Specialist (for example, a specialist in HIV/AIDS counseling) is not readily available, the Instructional Designer can adapt existing materials for use in the program. The accuracy of the interpretation and adaptation of the material to the Internet and its suitability for the intended learners can then be reviewed by specialists. In terms of technology development, a particularly talented programmer might be able to develop the user-interface as well as integrating any database used for storing test results or managing a registry of users.

Role	Primary Phase of Development Process	Activities
Project Leader (alias: Project Manager or Technical Leader)	All Phases	• Make sure all involved feel part of process • Work with client and subject experts • General Management duties for each phase
Instructional Design	Analysis, Design, and Development	• Apply pedagogical principles to course design • Consider content and how it can be fashioned and presented to meet user needs
Content Matter Specialist or Subject Matter Specialist	Analysis, Design and Development	Content Development for each lesson
Program Developers	Design, Development and Implementation	Range of skills required: • Development of user-interface • Graphic Design and Layout • Sound and Video Production • Software Development
Maintenance and Support	Deployment	Includes: • Maintenance support of software • Help Desk support for content • Help Desk support for technical difficulties
Facilitator/Instructor	Deployment	Includes: • Encourages discussion between students on subject matter • Responds to feedback from students • Leads online discussion of material (if subject matter expert)

CASE STUDY: EGYPT'S 'ASK CONSULT' DISTANCE EDUCATION TRAINING FOR PHARMACISTS

In Egypt, the USAID-supported 'Communication for Healthy Living' (CHL) Project was created to promote better health for the general population in Egypt through integrated communication approaches designed to motivate positive behavior change in the areas of family planning and reproductive health, maternal and child health, infectious disease control and to encourage healthy lifestyles and practices. In support of the CHL Project, the 'Ask, Consult' (AC) distance education program was set up to assist pharmacists to be able to respond correctly and adequately to family health needs.

Program Goals

The 'Ask, Consult' program had two main goals:

1. To improve the health status of Egyptians across all areas of Family Health including Family Planning and Reproductive Health, Maternal and Child Health; reduction of infectious diseases, including HIV/AIDS; increase in the number of those with healthy lifestyles (including reduction of tobacco use).
2. To strengthen sustainability of the pharmacist in the marketplace without ongoing donor assistance.

The Need for Education for Pharmacists

In Egypt, the pharmacist is a key player in the health system. As in many developing countries, the pharmacist in Egypt is often the first responder to individuals seeking medical advice and assistance. This happens in Egypt largely because:

- There are over 33,000 private pharmacists throughout the country.
- The population can access their services for free through the day and night.
- Much of the population visits the pharmacist before seeing a doctor.
- Sixty-one percent of pharmacists reported that they offered medical advice to customers.

Because the population depends so heavily on the pharmacists, it is vitally important for them to be up to date in their medical and service knowledge. Thus a key training goal of the 'Ask, Consult' program was to improve the pharmacist's knowledge of family health topics so they could provide adequate counsel to families unable or unwilling to see a doctor. Additionally, the program was designed with the cooperation of the Egyptian Pharmacist Syndicate and other USAID sponsored projects, to nurture and sustain the growth of this network of pharmacists so they continue to work together. The 'Ask, Consult' project created a web-based educational program that provided pharmacists with the knowledge and support they need to respond to client inquiries regarding their health. This program included a complete Learning Management System to deliver realistic scenario-based educational content.

WHY DISTANCE EDUCATION FOR THIS PROJECT?

Distance Education was chosen as the most efficient and effective way to provide necessary knowledge to the pharmacists because of:

1. Convenience: The number of pharmacists in Egypt is too great to provide face-to-face training with the available resources. Participants can review the material whenever it fits their schedule, thus avoiding any loss of business and additional travel costs that would be associated with face-to-face training.
2. Accessibility: Everyone with access to the Internet will be able to benefit from the information.
3. Cost Effectiveness: Because the material is placed on a single computer server, content can be changed in one place for everybody at the same time.
4. Sustainability: The website content was designed so that ultimately it could be managed and maintained entirely through the 'Ask, Consult' Network/ Association. Moreover, the software framework was designed so that it could accommodate future training needs, which means that as a central source for continuing education, the program will nurture future growth of the Network/ Association.

ACHIEVING THE TRAINING GOALS

In order to improve the pharmacist's knowledge of family health and nurture the continued growth of the network, it was agreed that an effective web-based, distance education program should:

1. Expand possibilities: Distance education is able to provide information that was not previously available in traditional forms of training and could enable pharmacists from everywhere in Egypt to communicate over and learn more about specific health issues.
2. Provide realistic training: The programs were designed, using what is called a 'Scenario-based Approach' that demonstrates situations that pharmacists could encounter in real-life/work situations.

3. Create a reusable resource: The program can be used not only as a training tool but also as a dynamic reference which can change as the needs of the users change.

4. Create a memorable experience: The use of the Scenario-based Approach to training makes for a much more engaging (entertaining) educational experience and thus the knowledge is more likely to be retained.

Why a Learning Management System?

A Learning Management System (LMS) provides a means of delivering and managing a course for thousands of participants. The LMS includes the following 'tools' that allow instructors to use the online environment for content delivery and then focus on discussion, questions, and problem-solving. The 'Ask, Consult' LMS is designed to support:

- Pre- and Post-Tests that measure the pharmacists' understanding of the content before and after they read over the material.
- A resource section that provides learners with access to websites, articles, and readings for reference.
- Assignments, that allow learners' performance and understanding to be tracked with results graded and listed online.

Other Support Programs

- A Chat function that allows users to 'talk' to one another in real-time.
- Instant polls that can collect learners' opinions on a topic.
- Forums that allow learners to explore topics in greater depth with teachers and other students.

Why the Edu-tainment Approach?

1. Realistic: The 'scenario-based' educational approach allows learners to practice their knowledge and skills in a relevant and appropriate situation, which is, at the same time, free of risk. The 'Ask, Consult' program was based around a family in which each family member has a medical history that relates directly to the educational objectives of the training program. Each family member had his or her own story (or scenario) to tell—thereby introducing the pharmacist learners to a particular health challenge.

2. Authentic: Selected scenarios used for instruction were based on actual stories provided by the pharmacists themselves, and all the scenarios were carefully reviewed for accuracy by a core group of pharmacists involved with the development of the program. In this way, it was possible to ensure that the issues most important and relevant to the learners were addressed.

STEPS IN PREPARING THE DISTANCE EDUCATION PROGRAM FOR INTERNET

The Egyptian Case Study is an excellent example of how a distance education series can be created for Internet users. More than 10,000 pharmacists and 3,000 physicians voluntarily participated in the 'Ask, Consult' health network activity, that provides consultation services to the public. The Egyptian government promoted this network with the aim of improving the credibility of its membership through program education. Most participating providers previously received only short 'Continuing Medical Education' (CME) courses, which were developed into Evidence-based Medicine (EBM) courses with learning supplements. The Egyptian government chose to expand the expertise and the network of providers through the adaptation of an Internet distance education program based on the Edu-tainment approach.

The development of the project required working with the Egyptian government to establish a set of criteria or requirements to set the foundation for the entire process of developing the education program. These requirements included a program that:

- is adaptable to the busy schedules of the intended audience of physicians and pharmacists
- is both instructional and entertaining (it is recognized that users acquire more knowledge more quickly when the material is presented in an entertaining fashion)
- expands the user's knowledge of treatment alternatives for health problems that are important to Egyptian families, such as child survival, maternal and child health, and infectious diseases (such as Tuberculosis)
- is available in both Arabic and English
- not only instructs, but also assesses the user's knowledge and understanding of each issue both before and after using the program
- enables the users to recognize symptoms of diseases in order to enhance their diagnosis of problems and their competence in considering treatment alternatives
- is interactive and can provide feedback to the user if there are questions about or problems with the material presented and
- that establishes a recognized process to award certificates after the completion of the education program

The developers had to meet these requirements as they worked through the entire process to complete the production of the distance education package. The main phases of the process were:

- Analysis
- Design
- Development
- Implementation
- Evaluation

At each phase of the process, the following points had to be considered:

- **Activities** for each phase
- **Responsibilities** for each Team Member
- **Outputs** from each phase

Analysis Phase

Activities

Determine most appropriate media mix to use to suit the audience based on access and impact. While both radio and television are available to the intended Egyptian audience, both have limitations for this project in terms of scheduling and providing opportunities for interactivity. Similarly, while text books and hard copy may be the least expensive options, they also present problems in terms of interactivity. A carefully organized survey determined that an IT-based program could be most effective because most of the pharmacists and nearly half of the physicians have access to the Internet and over 90 percent of both groups have a computer that can read CD-ROMs.

Include an analysis of the audience's learning style and needs. Pharmacists are well educated and welcome intellectual challenges, but they are busy people and will not take the time for additional instruction without cause. While they are comfortable with the technology, they have little patience with technical difficulties or new forms of web interaction that do not have an immediate payoff. At the same time, the material requirements call for both a cognitive (for example, the proper diagnosis of patients with multiple symptoms) and skill based (for example, understanding how to properly administer pharmaceutical regimen for TB) educational approach.

Responsibilities

The **Project Manager** acted as the liaison to the medical association (which is the point of contact for the pharmacists and doctors) and the client (the Egyptian government).

The **Project Manager** formed a focus group with members of the intended audience, and together with a web developer from the **Developer** group, tested some sample screens of the proposed approach. **Subject Matter Experts** (SMEs) provided direction with regard to the certification requirements and the typical educational needs of the target audience and reviewed existing material to determine, in conjunction with the **Instructional Designers**, how it could be adapted for the Internet and CD-ROM delivery. From the Developer group someone familiar with computer hardware and network or Internet access evaluated the results of the computing and Internet environment survey, and determined what the audience's average access rates are for the Internet and the typical computer capabilities for the audience such as monitor size and resolution, hard drive capacity, memory size, and so on.

INTERNET ACCESS AND COMPUTER CAPABILITIES

The results of the computer environment survey for the intended audience found that on average the system capabilities for the pharmacists were:

- Computers with a 500 MHz Pentium processor
  This is a measure of the speed of the computer's Central Processing Unit (CPU) measured in terms of the processor's clock speed. Older processors are measured at a rate of 'mega' or million hertz (MHz) where hertz simply means an event that occurs one time per second. Therefore, 500 MHz means that the clock speed of the CPU runs at a frequency of 500,000,000 hertz per second. 'Pentium' is simply the brand name of the processor.

- 128 MB of random access memory (RAM)
  This is a measure of the amount of short-term memory available to applications that are running on the computer. 128 megabytes of RAM means that it is possible to run multiple programs at the same time until that capacity is exceeded. For the e-learning package this figure is more important when using a CD-ROM version, where the application is drawing directly from the computer's RAM to run, while the package available over the Internet would require much less RAM to operate.

- 40 GB hard disk space
  The hard disk stores the user's files and programs. Unlike RAM, it keeps data even if the computer is turned off, and has a large capacity (in this case 40,000,000,000 or 40 gigabytes of information). As is the case with the RAM, the hard disk space is important with regard to the CD-ROM version of the application where the user may have to store the program directly onto the hard drive.

- Microsoft Windows XP
  This is the operating system of the computer. Microsoft Windows is by far the most common operating system and will run all the applications related to the e-learning program. In terms of the Arabic language version, however, it was important to determine that the computers were running a version of Windows that supports Arabic script which is read and written from right to left. Many earlier versions of Windows did not support Arabic requiring a separate operating system to function correctly.

- A Computer Monitor Display at 800 × 600 resolution
  The resolution represents the number of pixels that can be displayed horizontally (800) and vertically (600) across the screen of the computer's monitor. The **Developers** needed to know this number in order to design the graphics for the application and to optimize the fit of those graphics onto the computer screen. Most computer screens that access the Internet now have an 800 × 600 resolution but that is changing as newer computers come with a 1024 × 768 resolution, which means that developers can design their applications for resolutions that can represent images with greater detail.

Other points that were considered in the computer environment survey were that the majority of users have access to a mouse or pointing device, a CD-ROM drive, a 15- or 17-inch monitor, sound speakers, a printer, and the other software applications such as a word processor.

In terms of access to the Internet, the survey found that almost all members of the intended audience used Microsoft's Internet Explorer as the web browser of choice. Other browsers such as the Mozilla Firefox browser made up a small percentage of the target population. Access speeds to the Internet varied tremendously, so the design of the e-learning program could not consider speeds that were too slow to access the information over the Internet within a reasonable wait time. Determining what was reasonable could be done only after testing representatives of the target audience. Knowing that there would be a CD-ROM version of the product for those without access or with slow access to the Internet enabled the developers to create a package that could bring lots of media into play to help meet the requirement that the program must be engaging.

Preliminary User Test Results from Focus Group Testing

Sample screens produced by the developer group and tested in front of a sample of the intended audience led to a report that defined the appropriate navigation scheme and user-interface design for the target audience.

Design Phase

Activities/Responsibilities

The development team adapted the outputs from the Analysis Phase and used that information to guide them during design. The results from the survey determined the computing environment, and the **Developer** group defined the capabilities of the target audience in terms of computer hardware and Internet access. This allowed the **Developer** group to understand what the media mix could be for the program. It was also important for them to combine their understanding of the target computing environment with the results of the Preliminary User Test. For example, although the **Developers** knew they were producing a CD-ROM version of the package, allowing them to use video and other graphics, the User Test determined that the target audience does not always have patience for videos of 'talking heads' on computer screens. They prefer to have visuals only when they apply directly to the information that needs to be conveyed. This was the biggest challenge for the team: to design for optimal balance between meeting the educational goals of the client (that is, the Egyptian Government) and the habits and tendencies of the audience. Some guidelines that the **Developers** kept in mind as they undertook the design of the application included:

The educational goals
Despite the users' tendencies to be impatient with the technology, the Egyptian Government has a goal of user certification in specific health areas to achieve.

The users' needs
Although the client wants to certify the users for additional health activities, the users will not be fully engaged, and therefore will not fully learn, unless they are comfortable with the application.

The need for navigation through the site and CD-ROM application to be logical
The Developer group knew that the target users do not have patience for unnecessary text or visual images; so each section had to have a logical point of entry and exit.

The need to design the interface for a consistent look
The users should recognize where they are in the application and know what each button or graphic means without a lot of instruction. This means the screens had to be designed to be consistent in terms of the information they were trying to convey, without being boring.

At this point, the **Subject Matter Expert** and the **Instructional Designer** worked closely with the **Developer** group to design screens that logically held the information to be presented based on the computer environment requirements. Multimedia elements were adapted specifically to achieve educational goals and the **Instructional Designer** prepared the various scenarios based on the materials provided and the health issues that needed to be addressed. For example, within the educational module for Child Survival there is a section requiring coverage of Oral Rehydration Therapy (ORT). The **Instructional Designer** had come up with a scenario where a young, inexperienced mother was rushing her child, who had diarrhea, to the doctor's office. The sample, based on material provided by the **Subject Matter Expert**, from standardized medical text books, had to contain: photos of a child (provided by the **Graphics Designer** who is part of the **Developer** group); text describing the condition; specific directions on next steps for the doctor to take.

Meanwhile the **Project Manager** provided a detailed schedule of activities for the remaining phases of program development and refined the budgetary requirements that were presented in the original contract based on the outputs from the Analysis Phase. The **programmers** determined what additional supporting applications should be provided for users who would be able to access the Internet. This additional support included collaborative applications such as a chat function built within the e-learning application (so users could collaborate on specific health issues within the instructional material) and e-mail access (so users could send questions via e-mail to those providing technical support). As the design process moved into development, the **Developers** determined what free media players (such as the Flash Player which supports the use of animation or Adobe Acrobat which support specific types of text files) would be required for the variety of media that would be used in the application.

Outputs

- A report providing an outline of how the e-learning application would be designed to meet user needs and the educational goals of the client.
- Initial screen designs illustrating the basic look and feel of the application along with an illustration of how a user would navigate from screen to screen. This process is also known as prototyping.
- A list and description of the instructional material that would be adapted from existing material for use within the application.
- A list and description of the multimedia assets (video, graphics, sound) that would be used and for what purpose.

Development Phase

Activities/Responsibilities

Work then became more focused as the direction was clear and the material needs had been determined. At this point the **Project Manager** spent more time coordinating the

Developer group than making contact with the client or target audience. The **Developer** group had **programmers** creating functions that would test the users' understanding of each module and developing databases to store the users' scores and their user profiles. **Graphics designers** began incorporating forms of media that would meet the **Instructional Designer's** requirements regarding the creation of all the proposed scenarios for each of the health education modules. The **Subject Matter Expert** adapted the material for each of the sections from existing medical literature. The requirement to provide both an English and Arabic version of the material meant that there had to be translation from one version to the other. Rather than develop two entirely new versions, the Developer group decided to create a single version in English first and then simply flip the text fields and graphic objects to the other side of the screen and provide the Arabic text. This meant that the original English version had to be designed to contain Arabic script as well as English. This requirement, in turn, mandated the testing of each type of software that would be used in the development of the program to see if it could support the use of Arabic.

Support systems had to be established, for the technical operation of the e-learning application and for help on the specific content. Because of the high cost associated with round-the-clock support, it was determined that the initial support would be provided through e-mail with a 'guaranteed' response within a 24-hour period. During working hours, however, telephone support also would be available.

Module testing or testing each of the program's educational sections went on throughout the development phase as programmers and graphics designers completed sections and then tested them over the Internet. The Subject Matter Experts also used the application to determine if the presentation of the material was sufficient to achieve the certification requirements and whether the tests designed by the Instructional Designers reflected the material presented.

Outputs

The outputs by this stage of development were:

- A complete prototype representing all the sections of the program and suitable for user testing. (This is also known as the beta version) At this stage, the focus was on testing functionality, rather than design. The test aim here was to ensure that everything 'works' harmoniously together
- A listing of all assignments and tests related to those assignments
- A plan for providing user support
- A listing of all known problems that had yet to be solved
- A listing of support materials
- A deployment plan

Implementation Phase

Activities/Responsibilities

At this point only the **Project Leader** and part of the **Developer** group were actively involved with the implementation of the e-learning program. A small number of applications were burned onto CD-ROMs and delivered to a number of users, representative of the audience, in order to conduct user testing. At the same time another set of selected users, again representative of the audience, were notified of a website that contained the application along with a password to gain entry so that they could test the application over the Internet. In both cases, the users were provided with a small survey to record their impressions regarding usability and the effectiveness of the content. All other unstructured feedback was welcome, particularly any 'bugs' in the program that needed correcting. After a designated period, all feedback was collected and changes were made to the program to address reported problems. It was important, as it typically is, not to overreact to these problems, since many are often subjective and can represent a single user's bias toward a particular color or even the use of a particular word. Following the completion of all corrections, actual deployment of the program could begin. The established number of CD-ROMs were burned and mailed out to those who required them, while others were notified by e-mail of the web address or URL of the e-learning package. All were notified of the course requirements and where they could obtain help, scheduling requirements for completing each section, and so on.

Outputs at this Stage

- A completed program ready for use
- Packaging and CD-ROM versions completed and sent out for delivery
- Trained facilitators prepared for e-mail and chat support
- An evaluation plan prepared

Evaluation

Activities/Responsibilities

Ideally, formative evaluation is conducted by an organization unrelated to the one that created the original e-learning package. In that way, a more objective assessment can be made of whether or not the original requirements have been met by the completed program. The users should be provided with an online survey that can be completed following each section. This allows the **Subject Matter Experts** and the **Instructional Designers** to specify changes in content by section and allows the **Developer** group to isolate problems in navigation and software that reappear in each section.

Outputs

- An evaluation report

Deployment

Activities/Responsibilities

No matter how well designed an online instructional program may be, its success may still depend on the ability of a facilitator or online instructor to generate interest in the material. It is easy for any educational course, live or online, to be viewed as a gruelling requirement by the prospective student rather than an enlightening experience. Attempts to shorten the time required in front of a computer screen may involve bypassing educational material and making reasonable guesses at online questionnaires. Rather then policing the course and attempting to identify when users try to 'cheat' the system, it is much better for all involved to find ways to ensure that all the users understand and appreciate the importance of the material they are trying to absorb.

Obviously, there will be some questions on the material which should be answered promptly and in an open forum (rather than a private e-mail) to ensure that all participants have an opportunity to see if a question relates to their own experience. Aside from these obvious responsibilities, the facilitator also needs to encourage interest and discussion in the material, and there are a number of ways to do this.

User Response

The best way is to solicit material from the users themselves. For the 'Ask, Consult' scenario-based program, stories were requested from the pharmacists themselves so that they could be adapted for use in the instructional material. Increasingly, the Internet has become a place where people can present their ideas to a larger audience for consideration and discussion. Collaborative workspaces and filtering technologies help ensure that the intelligence of the collective minds has an opportunity to be heard. The notion of a single expert on a subject is giving way to the idea of mediated input from a variety of sources. This is a good thing as long as the instructor or facilitator can accept the fact that the tools used in a virtual education environment (such as blogs, forums, chat rooms, Wikis, and the like) can lead to online discussions that question the very assumptions upon which a course may be based. This type of wide response calls for very judicious management of online input from users and, more importantly, the setting of an example on the structure and content of any inputs provided.

Online Discussion

There is a wide variety of rules and principles relating to how to start a discussion of a subject on a forum or other online text-based communication tools. The basic rules, however, apply in all cases whether it is a software developer providing input on an open-source development project or a facilitator for an online health communication course. Karl Fogel, in his book *Producing Open Source Software: How to Run a Successful Free Software Project*, explains some of the basic principles a facilitator should apply when trying to set an example for online communication:

'Make things easy for your readers. There's a ton of information floating around in any [project], and readers cannot be expected to be familiar with most of it—indeed, they cannot always be expected to know how to become familiar. Wherever possible, your posts should provide information in the form most convenient for readers. If you have to spend an extra two minutes to dig up the URL to a particular thread in the mailing list archives, in order to save your readers the trouble of doing so, it's worth it. If you have to spend an extra 5 or 10 minutes summarizing the conclusions so far of a complex thread, in order to give people context in which to understand your post, then do so. Think of it this way: the more successful a project, the higher the reader-to-writer ratio in any given forum. If every post you make is seen by n people, then as n rises, the worthwhileness [sic] of expending extra effort to save those people time rises with it. And as people see you imposing this standard on yourself, they will work to match it in their own communications'.

Accuracy and Review

The most important point contained in the given quotation, regarding these online operating principles, is that fellow participants will measure their own submissions against those of a facilitator to determine their own level of effort in a submission. Furthermore, other users will respond to even a single user's attempt to match wits with a sharp facilitator. All of this effort will hopefully lead to well-developed contributions from a variety of users during the deployment period of an online course—allowing developers to reduce their own efforts at keeping the dialogue lively. Liveliness, however, is not the most important component of an online submission—accuracy is. There is nothing more distressing then a casually written piece that gets the facts wrong. Karl Fogel has more advice on this very subject—as follows:

'Edit twice. For any message longer than a medium-sized paragraph, re-read it from top to bottom before sending it, but after you think it's done the first time. This is familiar advice to anyone who's taken a Communications composition class, but it's especially important in online discussion. Because the process of online composition tends to be highly discontinuous (in the course of writing a message, you may need to go back and check other mails, visit certain web pages,... and so on), it's especially easy to lose your sense of narrative place. Messages that were composed discontinuously and not checked before being sent are often recognizable as such, much to the chagrin (or so one would hope) of their authors. Take the time to review what you send. The more your posts hold together structurally, the more they will be read'.

Wikis

Establishing these high standards from the start is important, particularly if program planners want to go beyond the delivery of online educational content and into the establishment of a community of users. A number of Learning Management Systems, such as Moodle, have developed tools that accommodate the development of user communities around a particular subject. One of the most applicable tools is known as the 'Wiki'. Wikis are web pages that can be changed by anyone. A person can make an initial entry on a subject, but from that point on anyone else can come and edit that content as they see fit. Wiki is based on the Hawaiian word for 'quick', but also stands for 'what I know is…'. Wikis then provide an opportunity for collective intelligence to be expressed and, depending on the level of trust among the users, this input can be mediated or not. Although Wikis for education tend to be designed for small groups of people, there are large Wikis that have captured the attention of the entire community of Internet users.

Wikipedia is by far the most famous example of a large-scale successful Wiki. This site gets more visitors than CNN or the *New York Times* sites and has become an indispensable source of information for writers and researchers alike. How can one trust Wikipedia as a major source of information if it can be edited by anyone? The journal *Nature* put this idea to the test by commissioning a study that compared the accuracy of a sample of submissions taken from Wikipedia with sample articles taken from the Encyclopaedia Britannica. *Nature*'s experts found 162 errors in Wikipedia's articles and 123 errors in Britannica's. Although Wikipedia had a third more errors, the fact that Britannica had nearly as many suggests that the Wikipedia model can work and that the collective intelligence of a committed user community can function as a worthwhile resource. The implications of these developments are fairly obvious for online instruction and the relationship these courses can have with their students. A facilitator who has the right temperament for the job and can use the tools within a Learning Management System can begin to harness effectively a lot of the experience that users have, and feed that experience right back into the educational material and into the discussions surrounding that material.

The world of Distance Education via the Internet will grow rapidly in the coming years. While currently it might not be widely accessible in many developing countries, there is no doubt that specialists in training programs for community workers should begin to prepare for the time when online learning will be universal.

Sample Curriculum Guide

This Curriculum Guide sample was prepared in India for a synergistic radio series proposed by The State Innovations in Family Planning Services Agency (SIFPSA). The synergistic series was designed to use a Distance Education Edu-tainment series—*Darpan* (a sample script of which is shown in Chapter 7)—and a drama serial for the general public, entitled *Bright Dreams, Brighter Ways*.

The Curriculum Guide for the Distance Education series *Darpan* began with a Table of Contents and a full list of all those who attended the Curriculum Guide Design Workshop. These two sections have been omitted from this sample. The main body of the Curriculum Guide was as follows:

PART 1: BACKGROUND AND OVERALL DESCRIPTION

1. Justification for the Project

The State Innovations in Family Planning Services Agency (**SIFPSA**) in India formulated a communication strategy for Health and Family Planning in Uttar Pradesh. An over-arching campaign was developed with the aim of bringing the hitherto taboo subject of family planning out into the open and triggering dialogue across audience groups: between spouse(s), between policy-makers and implementers, and between the service provider and client.

Overall Objectives of the Campaign

- Increase in number of community members who recognize and respect the work of Health Service Providers (HSPs), and seek advice from HSPs on all aspects of child spacing, family planning, and family life.

- Increase in adoption and continuation of spacing methods by couples.
- Increase in number of couples who make appropriate and timely use of HSPs for information and counseling on family planning.
- Increase in adoption of permanent methods by couples who choose to have no more children.
- Increase in number of women and family influentials aware of and adopting appropriate maternal and child health practices.
- Increase in the number of men and women who recognize that the male is entirely responsible for the sex of the child; the woman cannot be blamed or held responsible for the sex of the child.

Synergistic Radio Programs

In order to achieve these goals, it is planned to create two radio projects, each of 26 episodes. One series will be a Distance Education series, designed for Auxiliary Nurse Midwives (ANMs) and other Health Service Providers (HSPs); the other 26 programs will be in the form of a drama serial for the general public. It is hoped that broadcasting these synergistic programs will increase the adoption of spacing methods and permanent methods of family planning with support from HSPs.

The Distance Education Series: Training for Health Service Providers

Grassroots level HSPs in Uttar Pradesh are trained in technical skills but display a low self-image and perceive a lack of appreciation for their role by both the community they operate in as well as their seniors in the hierarchy. The need to build community and systemic sensitivity toward the service providers and then to move to a situation where quality health services are perceived as a right by the community remains one of the key challenges of communication.

2. Information About the Chosen Audience

In examining the various HSP audiences for which the Distance Education program will be created, the following information was noted:

What We Know

The majority of health service providers are:

- Overburdened with multiple roles, multiple reporting.
- Perceive a lack of appreciation and recognition.
- Conscious that they have no ladder of growth.
- Lacking training and infrastructure.

Motivators for Change

- Pride in achievements
- Positive community response
- The provision of a window for community interaction beyond his/her area of operation
- The creation of a substantial and responsible role toward him/her by the society

3. Justification and Availability of the Chosen Medium

Radio is an important component of mass media with a reach of 27 percent across rural Uttar Pradesh, thus offering an important media edge both in terms of cost effectiveness and reach. This is more so in the context of rural audiences that are the largest and most critical segment of our program's target groups. HSPs typically have access to radio. So this justifies the use of radio for this Distance Education project.

Advantages of Radio for this Audience (Health Service Providers)

1. It is portable
2. One can listen and work at the same time
3. It is cheap
4. No electricity is needed
5. Cost per message is low
6. Cost per listener is low
7. Radio is the medium of imagination
8. Wider access to radio possible because it is cheap
9. There is often better recall of message from radio. No distractions (unlike TV and its constantly moving images)
10. No channel clutter
11. Easy to reproduce and replicate on audio tapes. NGOs/others can play back the cassettes or distribute them
12. More people listen to the radio than watch TV

Limitations

1. Radio is an audio-only medium; it is not suitable for some things that are better understood when seen
2. Everything depends on dialogue and sound effects. Silent scenes are not possible
3. Need for support materials and supplementary materials to illustrate various points
4. Channel reception difficulties in some parts of Uttar Pradesh
5. People do not always know the schedule of programs
6. Radio is a one-way medium. But radio can be made interactive by including interactive questions, open-ended questions, requests for letters, listener forum, quiz questions, and so on.

4. Overall Measurable Objective(s) of the Distance Education Course as a Whole

There will be a measurable increase in the number of Auxiliary Nurse Midwives (ANMs) along with Anganwadi Works (AWW) Community-Based Distribution workers (CBD), and Traditional Birth Attendants (TBA) who demonstrate:

1. Increase in knowledge about Family Planning, Maternal Child Health, Reproductive Tract Infections/Sexually Transmitted Infections, and increase in sharing of this knowledge with community members
2. Improvement in knowledge and use of Interpersonal Communication skills
3. Increase in self-esteem
4. Improvement and increase in interaction with an appropriate counseling of clients.

5. The Overall Purpose(s)

The overall purposes of this Distance Education Course are:

1. To reinforce and upgrade the knowledge of all health providers, especially ANMs.
2. To demonstrate to them how to interact with clients, and to motivate health service providers to follow these guidelines for both counseling and knowledge provision.
3. To encourage HSPs to be proud of the work they do and to develop an improved level of self-respect.

6. The Attitude to be Encouraged in Learners

The main **attitude** or emotional focus to be encouraged by the series will be **confidence** in their ability to provide quality healthcare services, as well as **pride**, derived from improved self-image and appreciation from the community. Service providers will be encouraged throughout the series to be **proud** of the work they do, to do it as well as they can, and to acquire a better level of **self-esteem**.

7. The Number of Programs; Length of Each Program and Frequency of Presentation

- 26 programs
- 27 minutes in length (to fit into a 30-minute broadcast slot)
- broadcast once a week for 6 months

8. The Detailed Scope and Sequence of the Curriculum

The messages to be included in the programs will cover the following topics in this order:

Family Planning

1. Interpersonal Communication—develop a rapport with clients, informed choice, need to decide what is best suited with clients, importance of regular follow up.
2. Importance of Family Planning (FP), consequence of not using FP methods, Child Spacing, benefits of small family. Spacing can result in more resources for each child, and can result in improved quality of life and health for mother and child.
3. Benefits of a small family regardless of the sex of the children. Biologically, the father determines the sex of the child, not the mother.
4. Establish links with elders, gatekeepers, and influential people in the society.
5. Contraceptives: Oral Contraceptive Pill.
6. Contraceptives: Condoms.
7. Contraceptives: Copper Ts.
8. Contraceptives: Female Sterilization.
9. Contraceptives: Non-Scalpel Vasectomy.
10. Knowledge on RTIs/STIs—transmission/avoidance.
11. Knowledge of HIV/AIDS—transmission/avoidance.
12. RCH camp—various types of services available, trained providers, free services, accessible, and so on.
13. Listener's Program or Summary program.
14. Age at marriage—awareness/impacts/consequences/delay in age at marriage/benefits.

Maternal and Child Health

15. Care during pregnancy—good nutrition, husband, in-laws, other family members caring for the pregnant woman, sharing her work load, and so on.
16. Importance of Ante-Natal care—3 check-ups, 2 TT shots, 100 IFA tablets.
17. How to prepare for safe delivery—transport planning, skilled attendant at delivery (5 cleans), seek institutional delivery services in case of high risk/emergency case.
18. Emergency Obstetric Care—prevention from risks during delivery, danger signs during delivery, and emergency management.
19. Post-Natal care—its importance and benefits.
20. Immunization schedule, its importance and dangers of not immunizing.
21. Breast-feeding—Colostrum benefits, duration and how to deal with the lactation problems.
22. Child nutrition—introducing other foods—when, what.
23. Malnutrition and weighing.
24. Diarrhea—what it is, cause, prevention, ORS.
25. Other childhood diseases—Vitamin A deficiency, pneumonia, worms, and others.
26. Final Summary or Listener's Program.

Runner Themes

The following themes will be reflected throughout ALL programs of the series:

- Family Planning—Male involvement and role in Family Planning
- Maternal Child health—Father actively involved in caring for wife and children
- Supervisor Skills—Positive role modeling, enhance performance, motivate health workers
- Health workers—Professional pride
- Importance of good counseling and training

PART 2: INDIVIDUAL LESSONS: THE LESSON PLAN FOR EACH PROGRAM

Lesson plans for each lesson in the series are contained in the following pages of this document. Each lesson plan will contain the following information as explained in the Curriculum Guide Contents on page 67:

9. Measurable Objectives
10. Purposes
11. Precise Lesson Content
12. Glossary Entries

PART 3: IMPLEMENTATION PLANS

The details for these parts of the Curriculum Guide will be determined as the program design moves forward.

13. Proposed support materials other than assignment materials.

14. Pilot Testing. Three sample scripts from both the Distance Education series and the General Public serial drama will be tested with several focus groups to ensure their suitability before ongoing scripting gets under way.

15. Timelines for writing, production, pilot testing, evaluation, and so on will be finalized within the next few weeks and shared with all who need them. The producer and the broadcast outlet will be consulted as to the number of scripts for production, or ready-to-air program they require at one time.

16. Evaluation Plans. SIFPSA's evaluation department will be called upon to determine how ongoing and after-program evaluation will be done.

17. Promotional Activities—yet to be determined.

18. Writers' Support Team members will be determined, and writers and support team members will be notified.

19. Script Review team members will be determined and notified.

20. Format description. The programs will be presented in a series format, with specific parts of each program providing clear teaching, other parts providing demonstration of how learners can transform what they have learned into interaction with their own clients. There will be testing in the form of Interactive Questions in the middle and at the end of each program to help learners ensure that they have absorbed the important points of the lessons. There will be attractive 'characters' who present the lessons and a humorous character to provide entertainment and 'learning relief' for the audience. Each program will end with an invitation to learners to carry out an assignment or task for the coming week, and with an indication of the lesson topic for the following week.

Lesson Plan Presentation

The following samples from Part 2 of the Curriculum Guide demonstrate how the lesson plan for each program was laid out.

DISTANCE EDUCATION RADIO PROGRAMS

Curriculum Content

Episode #: __14__
Topic: *Family Planning*
Sub-Topic: *Age at marriage*

Measurable Objectives: After listening to this episode, the audience will:

KNOW:
- The legal age of marriage in Uttar Pradesh
- The benefits of avoiding marriage before the legal age
- Negative consequences of early marriage
- How to educate and guide clients in planning parenthood

DO:
- Gain understanding of and appreciate the need to guide the client about the benefits and opportunities of delaying marriage until the legal age
- Create awareness in the community about the legal age of marriage and encourage delayed marriage

- Educate clients about the dangers for young girls of marrying and becoming pregnant too young.

ATTITUDE:

- Be convinced and confident about the need for delayed marriage.
- Feel responsible for imparting the correct knowledge and encouraging correct action; confident in their ability to do this.

PURPOSE:

The purposes of this program are:

- To ensure that HSPs have complete knowledge on the health impact of early marriage on the woman and the child.
- To encourage the HSPs to initiate discussion with clients regarding the consequences of early marriage.
- To equip HSPs with the information with which to guide, support, and motivate clients on topics related to early marriage.

CONTENTS:

One of the most important contributions that HSPs can make to their community is to encourage families to delay the marriage of their children until they reach the correct legal age.

The legally right age of marriage is 18 years for females and 21 years for males.

The benefits of delaying marriage until the legal age are compelling and every family in the community should know and understand them. The HSP should encourage community members to understand:

- Girls and boys are not truly physically and mentally ready for marriage before the legal age
- Girls particularly need to be properly physically mature enough to handle motherhood without risk; such maturity requires the girl to be at least 18 years of age
- The child has a better chance of being healthy when the mother is physically and mentally mature
- There is greater opportunity for higher education when marriage is delayed; this is important for girls as well as boys. There is strong evidence to show that educated women make better mothers
- Delayed marriage provides better opportunity for economic independence for the man to be able to provide for the needs of the growing family.

The disadvantages of an early marriage are:

- Physical immaturity and danger for the woman. Before the legal age, the girl is not physically developed enough and early pregnancy may result in physical weakness, leading to miscarriage and in some cases even death of the child or mother. The mother is more likely to suffer from poor health and anemia when she is physically immature.

- The couple begins life with fewer economic resources which will affect the quality of nutrition, amenities, and life in general.

The HSP can help to encourage couples to delay the marriage of their children by talking to them about the importance of obeying the law; about the serious health dangers there are for girls who marry too young; and about the increased chances of happiness and health a family has if the parents are sufficiently mature at the time of marriage and childbirth.

Episode #: __15__
Topic: *Maternal and Child Health*
Sub-Topic: *Care during Pregnancy*

Measurable Objectives: After listening to this episode, the audience will:

KNOW:
- The importance of all family members helping to correctly care for a pregnant woman in the family.
- How to educate community members more effectively about correct care of a pregnant woman.

DO:
- Educate families about proper care for pregnant women and help them understand the importance of caring for pregnant women properly.
- Encourage everyone in the community to help ensure that pregnant women are always given proper care.

HAVE AN ATTITUDE OF:
- Confidence in her ability to communicate effectively with community members in this matter.
- Responsibility for ensuring that all pregnant women in her community are correctly cared for.

PURPOSE:
The purposes of this episode are:

- To upgrade HSPs' knowledge about appropriate care for pregnant women.
- To upgrade and reinforce the knowledge and skills of HSPs about educating families on care of pregnant women.
- To motivate HSPs to take on, more seriously, this responsibility of educating families about the care of pregnant women.

CONTENT:
- Pregnancy is an important and precious event in every family. It is the beginning of the gift of a new life, and it is up to everyone in the family to ensure that the pregnant woman is properly cared for.

- It is the responsibility of the whole family to ensure that the pregnant woman remains healthy, and they should all feel personal pride when the mother and baby come through delivery well.
- The family also needs to be taught that problems can arise in any pregnancy, even those that look perfectly normal.
- Once the community health worker knows there is a pregnancy in the community, she should educate the woman, her husband, and family members about how they can all support her health. She should meet with all members of the family together and explain to them the special needs of the pregnant woman.
- To begin with, she should explain to them that a new life is being developed and that they all need to take on the responsibility of ensuring that this new precious life is kept safe, which means taking special care of the mother.
- To motivate the families of the pregnant women, the health workers should explain the following facts to the pregnant woman and her family:

Pregnant women:

- need more food than usual.
- need more rest than usual, so as well as the usual 8 hours at night, she should have 2 hours of rest during the day.
- should not lift or carry heavy objects, as this can cause a miscarriage.

The HSP should inform all members of the family that if a pregnant woman has one of the following symptoms, she should be taken to the hospital immediately:

- Bleeding from vagina
- Dirty discharge from vagina
- Severe pain in abdomen
- High fever
- Excessive vomiting
- Severe swelling in hands/feet
- Convulsions
- Baby stops moving in the mother's body
- Blurring of vision/fainting

While it might not be possible for all family members to recall all these symptoms, they should know that if anything seems to be wrong with the pregnant woman, they should immediately take her to the hospital for care.

So, HSPs should encourage all family members to know that it is the responsibility of the entire family to take care of the pregnant woman so that she remains healthy and gives birth to a healthy 'bundle of joy'.

Curriculum Content

Episode #: __16__
Topic: *MCH*
Sub-Topic: *Ante-natal Care*

Measurable Objectives: After listening to this episode, the audience will:

KNOW:
- Importance of enrolling all pregnant women in the community.
- How to motivate pregnant women to have adequate ante-natal services.
- How to motivate their family members to ensure that the woman has ante-natal care.
- How to provide ante-natal services in line with standard protocols.

DO:
- Enroll pregnant women in her community.
- Motivate all pregnant women to have adequate ante-natal services.
- Motivate family members to ensure that the pregnant women have ante-natal care.
- Provide ante-natal services, following standard protocols.

HAVE AN ATTITUDE OF:
- Will feel confident, responsible and motivated to perform their duties toward pregnant women.

PURPOSE:
The purposes of this episode are:

- To upgrade and reinforce HSP knowledge and skills regarding importance of enrolling all pregnant women.
- To remind HSPs how to motivate women to attend ante-natal services, and how to motivate family members to ensure that she has these services.
- To reinforce knowledge of the standard protocols for ante-natal care.

CONTENT:
- All HSPs should know it is extremely important to identify and enroll all pregnant women in the community that they serve, and to provide advice, guidance, and ante-natal services to them as well as safeguarding them from grave health risks.
- All health providers have a vital role to play in the identification of all pregnant women within the first three months of pregnancy. During home visits to the families, they should identify pregnant women by asking them simple questions.
- Once they identify the women their names should be given to the ANM so that she can register them and provide Ante-natal Care (ANC) services to them.
- All health workers should work toward motivating all women to avail themselves of these services by telling them the importance of ante-natal services.

The following facts should be explained in a simple manner:

The Government of India's standard protocol (being followed in Uttar Pradesh) basically covers the following: check-ups, tetanus injections, and iron tablets.

The protocol recommends:

- Three ANC check-ups (the first at 20 weeks of pregnancy or upon first detection of pregnancy, the second at 32 weeks, and the third at 36 weeks). In these visits, the ANM must check on weight, height, abdomen, and check for anemia (eyes, tongue check) and swelling in the body.
- Iron and Folic Acid tablets (IFA): a total of 100 tablets will be given (one daily) for routine use; however, if the woman is anemic, she must be given 2 tablets, instead of 1, daily for the same period.
- Two Tetanus Toxoid (TT) injections to be given—one, as soon as the pregnancy is known and the second, one month later. If the woman's previous pregnancy was less than two years back, and she had been given two TT injections then, only one TT needs to be given at this time. If not, then both doses are a must, since only one dose will not give any protection.

The primary responsibility for ante-natal care is that of the ANM.

(All lessons in the series were detailed this way so that the writer would be perfectly clear about what had to be taught and demonstrated in each program.)

GLOSSARY:

The Curriculum Guide was written in English, and so it was necessary to provide a fairly extensive glossary giving the meaning of technical or special terms in Hindi, so that the writer could be sure to describe everything correctly and exactly. The type of words, initials and acronyms in the Glossary were numerous and included the following:

ANM, AWW, AIDS, CBD, IFA, ORS, STI, and other acronyms and initials.
Colostrum,
Contraceptive,
Counseling,
Diarrhea,
Miscarriage,
Night Blindness,
Safe Delivery,
Sexual Intercourse,
Vitamin A.

References

de Fossard, Esta. 2005. *Communication for Behavior Change, Vol. 1: Writing and Producing Radio Dramas*. India: Sage Publications.

de Fossard, Esta and Riber John. 2005. *Communication for Behavior Change, Vol. 2: Writing and Producing for Television and Film*. India: Sage Publications.

Fair Access to Internet Report (FAIR). Prepared by the LINK Centre and Mike Jensen and Research ICT Africa, February 2004, p. 5.

Gustafson, D.H., R. Hawkins, E.W. Boberg, S. Pingree, F. Serlin, F. Graziano and Chen Lung Chen. 1999. 'Impact of Patient-Centered Computer-Based Health Information and Support Systems'. *American Journal of Preventive Medicine*, 16: 1–9.

Hafner, Katie. 1997. 'The Epic Saga of the Well', *Wired Issue*, 5.5 (May).

Jenkins, J. and A.S. Sadiman. 2000. 'Open Schooling at Basic Level' in Chapter 12 of *Basic Education at a Distance* edited by Chris Yates and J. Bradley. Routledge Falmer.

Kelly, Jeffrey A., Anton M. Somlai, Eric G. Benotsch, Timothy L. McAuliffe, Yuri A. Amirkhanian, Kevin D. Brown, L. Yvonne Stevenson, M. Isa Fernandez, Cheryl Sitzler, Cherly Gore-Felton, Steven D. Pinkerton, Lance S. Weinhardt and Karen M. Opgenorth. 2004. 'Distance Communication Transfer of HIV Prevention Interventions to Service Providers'. *Science*, 24 September, 305(5692): 1953–55.

Pridmore, P. and S. Nduba. 2000. 'The Power of Open and Distance Learning in Basic Education for Health and the Environment' in Chapter 11 of *Basic Education at a Distance, World Review of Distance Education and Open Learning, Vol. 2*, p. 192. Routledge Farmer.

Silberman, Steve. 2004. 'The War Room', *Wired Issue*, 12.9 (September).

Storey, D., M. Boulay, Y. Karki, K. Heckert and D.M. Karmacharya. 1999. 'Impact of the Integrated Radio Communication Project in Nepal, 1994–97'. *Journal of Health Communication*, 4: 271–94. Copyright 1999 Taylor and Francis.

Werner, D. and D. Bower. 1982. 'Helping Health Workers Learn'. The Hesperian Foundation.

All scripts used in this book were created in projects supported by Johns Hopkins University Bloomberg School of Public Health, Center for Communication Programs.

INDEX

About the Author

Esta de Fossard was Senior Technical Advisor, at Johns Hopkins University Center for Communication Programs (JHU/CCP) for more than 10 years. She has over 20 years of experience as Independent Consultant in Behavior Change Communication, Distance Education and Interactive Radio Instruction. de Fossard is the author of more than 50 books, including children's books, school and college text books, and books on Behavior Change Communication, published in the US and in Australia. She has won an Honourable Mention in the Australian Children's Book Awards.

Michael Bailey (the contributor) has worked in the development and management of multimedia software applications for distance education and decision-making support for over 15 years. He has directed teams of consultants and development staff in over 25 individual and distinct versions of CD-ROM and Web-based training applications in over seven languages. As a member of Johns Hopkins University staff, he is presently developing the Community-Based Intervention System (CBIS), a health intervention planning application in conjunction with the JHU School of Medicine, which will assist in health surveillance in Baltimore City. Mr Bailey is also responsible for creating a distance-learning program that targets up to 10,000 pharmacists for additional medical training in Egypt.